On
Strategy for
Healthcare

HBR's 10 Must Reads series is the definitive collection of ideas and best practices for aspiring and experienced leaders alike. These books offer essential reading selected from the pages of *Harvard Business Review* on topics critical to the success of every manager.

Titles include:

On
Strategy
for
Healthcare

HARVARD BUSINESS REVIEW PRESS
Boston, Massachusetts

Copyright 2018 Harvard Business School Publishing Corporation
All rights reserved
Printed in the United States of America
10 9 8 7 6 5 4 3 2 1

The web addresses referenced in this book were live and correct at the time of the book's publication but may be subject to change.

Library of Congress Cataloging-in-Publication Data

Title: HBR's 10 must reads on strategy for healthcare.
Other titles: Harvard Business Review's ten must reads | HBR's 10 must reads (Series)
Description: Boston, Massachusetts : Harvard Business Review Press, [2018] | Series: HBR's 10 must reads
Identifiers: LCCN 2017058068 | ISBN 9781633694309 (pbk. : alk. paper)
Subjects: LCSH: Health planning. | Health services administration.
Classification: LCC RA394.9 .H37 2018 | DDC 362.1068—dc23 LC record available at https://lccn.loc.gov/2017058068

Contents

Rediscovering Strategy

by Thomas H. Lee, MD

Health care leaders are facing pressures for performance that demand departures from business as usual. In the United States, patients and their employers are becoming more sensitive to service costs and quality. Meanwhile, reimbursements are decreasing, yielding flat or declining revenues for health care providers. As Michael E. Porter and I argued in our 2015 *New England Journal of Medicine* article "Why Strategy Matters Now," these factors mean that health care organizations need to start making more and smarter choices about how to differentiate themselves. These kinds of decisions lie at the heart of classic business strategy, and it is incumbent on health care leaders to approach strategy development and execution with the same ferocity as do their counterparts in other sectors.

Until recently, the U.S. health care marketplace frequently allowed leaders of health care organizations to get by without a real strategy as it is understood in most other business sectors. The amount of money pouring into health care was growing rapidly. Commercial insurance payment increases made up for shortfalls for Medicare, Medicaid, and uninsured patients, so that, overall, fee-for-service contracts usually covered the provider's costs plus a modest margin. Meanwhile, quality was considered difficult or impossible to measure, so competition was based on organizations' brands. Patients could go to almost any provider, so as long as provider brands brought patients in the door; organizations could thrive by focusing on operational effectiveness—disciplined adoption of best practices, hiring good people, and working hard.

Operational effectiveness remains critical to health care providers' success; indeed, the most brilliant strategy cannot save an organization with poor management. However, the changes in the health care marketplace over the last decade made operational effectiveness table stakes, requiring providers to find other sources of differentiation.

The most conspicuous of these changes are economic. Arguments about how much of the economy can be devoted to health care now seem moot; the practical reality is that taxpayers and employers are simply unable and unwilling to support payment rates that rise faster than general inflation. In the past, health care providers could argue that their costs should be covered as long as their work was noble and good, and some still do. Today, however, no one is really listening, as company and personal budgets are stretched to their limits. For example, 43% of Americans with health insurance report having difficulty affording their deductible expenses, and one-third report difficulty affording their premiums—and both of these rates increased from 2015 to 2017.

A less obvious change—but one that, in the long run, may prove more compelling—is that quality of care is no longer considered unmeasurable. The 1999 and 2001 reports from the Institute of Medicine *To Err Is Human* and *Crossing the Quality Chasm* made explicit that health care had serious problems in safety, technical quality, access, and patient experience. Those reports created a true sense of urgency about improving quality in health care, and efforts to develop and use measures of quality moved into a new, higher gear. Government and private payers first provided modest financial incentives for organizations to collect and report these data, then reporting became mandatory, and then financial consequences emerged, either in direct incentives or through threats to market share.

As a result of these changes, the meaning of "performance" for health care organizations is being redefined: Measures of quality are being considered in that evaluation as well as traditional financial outcomes. And the particular quality measures used are shifting from those that gauge process (for example, how reliably did providers perform an action that was supported by guidelines, such as screening patients for various types of cancer) to those that assess outcomes that matter most to patients. Forward-looking providers like the Cleveland Clinic are collecting a wide array of outcomes data and publishing it online. For example, patients considering radiation therapy for prostate cancer can see data on not only survival rates at this institution, but also what proportion of patients had urinary incontinence, fatigue, and diarrhea.

Combine this with patients' and their employers' pressure for higher-quality care and lower prices, and the pieces are now in place for a health care marketplace driven by competition on value for patients. The prospect of such a marketplace may not immediately seem good news to all health care stakeholders, since competition is always less comfortable than no competition. But the alternative to such a marketplace is one in which purchasers focus on price, and price alone, and provide no direct reward for improvement in safety, outcomes, or the disutility of care. Such a marketplace will not be good for patients or the rest of health care's stakeholders.

But to achieve differentiation, health care leaders must make choices about their unique approach to creating value for patients. Each health care provider cannot be all things to all patients: A hospital must choose to be a trauma center or a cancer specialist, to serve a local population or a full region. Indeed, in our *New England Journal of Medicine* article, we suggested six strategic questions that health care leaders should ask themselves:

1. What is our fundamental goal?

2. What businesses are we in?

3. What scope of businesses should we compete in?

4. How will we be different in each business?

5. What synergies can we create across business units and sites?

6. What should be our geographic density and scope?

Another common challenge in today's health care world is change management: As new policies and directions are instituted, there are sure to be many upset constituents. If they perceive decisions as dictated by internal or external politics, the risks rise for unending discussions about which stakeholders are winning or losing, and paralyzing internal negotiations. But the good news is that if decisions are clearly based on the two issues at the core of strategy—how to create value for the organization's customers and how the organization is going to differentiate itself from competitors—then consensus can be easier to achieve.

———————

The *Harvard Business Review* articles in this collection prepare health care leaders to address these questions and execute upon the decisions that flow from them. Three of these articles have a clear health care focus, but the more general, classic articles that form the bulk of this volume are those that have shaped thinking about strategy across all business sectors.

The first two articles define at a high level what we have to do and why we have to do it. Michael Porter's landmark 1996 article "What Is Strategy?" opens with the distinction between operational effectiveness and strategy, and then describes the concept of strategic positioning to achieve sustainable competitive advantage. The second piece, also by Porter, is his 2008 synthesis of how strategy can serve as the antidote to the threats posed by competitive forces and the way to identify the opportunities. I am sure that I am not the only reader who felt, after absorbing these two articles, that a switch had been flipped, a dark room was illuminated, and the work to be done became visible with a new clarity.

We have chosen the other articles because they, too, provide frameworks that change the way leaders view their work and can help health care leaders decide how to move forward. We have included landmark articles on building an organization's vision (Collins and Porras), reinventing business models (Johnson, Christensen, and Kagerman), and perceiving opportunities in new markets (Kim and Mauborgne). Health care–specific articles describe the nature of competition in this sector and the role that various stakeholders can and should play (Dafny and Lee); and the health care threats and opportunities presented by disruptive innovation (Christensen et al.).

In a marketplace driven by competition on value, leaders have to identify the levels of their organization at which they can measure and create value. That means segmenting customers (that is, patients) into groups tailored to strategic decisions (Yankelovich and Meer), and then connecting strategies to execution (Kaplan and Norton). The final article, by Michael Porter and me, offers a six-component framework for health care leaders to integrate these insights from strategy and create a path forward for their organizations.

This path must be one that leads to better value for patients. Clarity on this goal leads to strategies that are inherently good for patients and the professional satisfaction of health care organizational personnel. Lack of clarity and lack of strategy set the stage for organizations that will never feel that they are thriving and leaders who do not lead. Our hope is that these must-read articles will help health care leaders set their goals, make choices that serve their patients, and ensure that their organizations succeed.

On
Strategy for
Healthcare

What Is Strategy?

by Michael E. Porter

I. Operational Effectiveness Is Not Strategy

For almost two decades, managers have been learning to play by a new set of rules. Companies must be flexible to respond rapidly to competitive and market changes. They must benchmark continuously to achieve best practice. They must outsource aggressively to gain efficiencies. And they must nurture a few core competencies in race to stay ahead of rivals.

Positioning—once the heart of strategy—is rejected as too static for today's dynamic markets and changing technologies. According to the new dogma, rivals can quickly copy any market position, and competitive advantage is, at best, temporary.

But those beliefs are dangerous half-truths, and they are leading more and more companies down the path of mutually destructive competition. True, some barriers to competition are falling as regulation eases and markets become global. True, companies have properly invested energy in becoming leaner and more nimble. In many industries, however, what some call *hypercompetition* is a self-inflicted wound, not the inevitable outcome of a changing paradigm of competition.

The root of the problem is the failure to distinguish between operational effectiveness and strategy. The quest for productivity, quality, and speed has spawned a remarkable number of management tools and techniques: total quality management, benchmarking, time-based competition, outsourcing, partnering, reengineering,

A Bit of Context

For many leaders of health care organizations, this article and the next may be the equivalent of looking in the mirror under harsh, unforgiving light. These articles force leaders to confront the questions of (1) whether they have a real strategy, and (2) whether they are using onetime tactics to get through every year, as opposed to creating sustainable competitive differentiation. Leaders may find it deeply uncomfortable to honestly assess where they stand on these issues, but having a clear picture of their strategic position is essential for health care organizations if they mean to survive in an increasingly competitive environment.

When Michael Porter discusses with health care leaders the ideas at the core of these articles, he often begins by emphasizing what is *not* strategy. He argues that the term has been used loosely in health care, a holdover from the days when funding was expanding rapidly, and it was a generally accepted notion that the more services that were being delivered, the better. However, those conditions have lapsed, and organizations must confront the reality that their strategy cannot be simply "growth." Nor can it be achieving a specific financial margin target or merging with other organizations to deflect competitive pressures.

Instead, as Porter argues, defining a real competitive strategy requires clarity on what the organization is trying to do for whom, and in health care, as we've seen, that means how it is creating value for patients. The more effectively that organizations design their work around meeting the needs of patients, the more successfully they will compete for market

change management. Although the resulting operational improvements have often been dramatic, many companies have been frustrated by their inability to translate those gains into sustainable profitability. And bit by bit, almost imperceptibly, management tools have taken the place of strategy. As managers push to improve on all fronts, they move farther away from viable competitive positions.

Operational effectiveness: necessary but not sufficient
Operational effectiveness and strategy are both essential to superior performance, which, after all, is the primary goal of any enterprise. But they work in very different ways.

share. This article helps leaders identify where and how they need to make difficult choices about this design: what activities the hospital or health care system or other provider will or will not do.

For example, many hospitals are facing the worrisome combination of flat revenues, rising costs, and full occupancy. Their reflex response is to try to move even more patients through the same old system and to replace higher-paid employees with lower-paid personnel. Both of these moves are important for survival, but their competitors are doing the same thing. To thrive, to have a sustainable competitive advantage, the hospital must make choices. For example, should academic medical centers try to compete for market share on the basis of providing primary care? Or should they try to make their high-end specialty services as high value as possible? Should hospitals concede that their volumes for some services (for example, cancer surgeries) are too low for excellence or efficiency, and work with other institutions to consolidate some aspects of the care (for example, the operations themselves)?

As in any sector, these choices frequently cause discontent among constituents, and health care organizations, in particular, have a hard time working well with disgruntled personnel. But they can mitigate this discontent by reminding stakeholders that their organization's focus is on meeting the needs of patients and doing so with increasing effectiveness and efficiency. Strategy in the pursuit of this goal is inherently good. These articles help leaders articulate this message and bring their organizations' strategy to life.

—Thomas H. Lee

A company can outperform rivals only if it can establish a difference that it can preserve. It must deliver greater value to customers or create comparable value at a lower cost, or do both. The arithmetic of superior profitability then follows: delivering greater value allows a company to charge higher average unit prices; greater efficiency results in lower average unit costs.

Ultimately, all differences between companies in cost or price derive from the hundreds of activities required to create, produce, sell, and deliver their products or services, such as calling on customers, assembling final products, and training employees. Cost is generated by performing activities, and cost advantage arises from performing particular activities more efficiently than competitors. Similarly, differentiation arises from both the choice of activities and how they are performed. Activities, then, are the basic units of competitive advantage. Overall advantage or disadvantage results from all a company's activities, not only a few.[1]

Operational effectiveness (OE) means performing similar activities *better* than rivals perform them. Operational effectiveness includes but is not limited to efficiency. It refers to any number of practices that allow a company to better utilize its inputs by, for example, reducing defects in products or developing better products faster. In contrast, strategic positioning means performing *different* activities from rivals' or performing similar activities in *different* ways.

Differences in operational effectiveness among companies are pervasive. Some companies are able to get more out of their inputs than others because they eliminate wasted effort, employ more advanced technology, motivate employees better, or have greater insight into managing particular activities or sets of activities. Such differences in operational effectiveness are an important source of differences in profitability among competitors because they directly affect relative cost positions and levels of differentiation.

Differences in operational effectiveness were at the heart of the Japanese challenge to Western companies in the 1980s. The Japanese were so far ahead of rivals in operational effectiveness that they could offer lower cost and superior quality at the same time. It is worth dwelling on this point, because so much recent thinking about competition depends on it. Imagine for a moment a *productivity frontier* that constitutes the sum of all existing best practices at any given time. Think of it as the maximum value that a company delivering a particular product or service can create at a given cost, using the best available technologies, skills, management techniques, and purchased inputs. The productivity frontier can apply to individual activities, to groups of linked activities such as order processing and manufacturing, and to an entire company's activities. When a company improves its operational effectiveness, it moves toward the frontier. Doing so may require capital investment, different personnel, or simply new ways of managing.

Idea in Brief

The myriad activities that go into creating, producing, selling, and delivering a product or service are the basic units of competitive advantage. **Operational effectiveness** means performing these activities better—that is, faster, or with fewer inputs and defects—than rivals. Companies can reap enormous advantages from operational effectiveness, as Japanese firms demonstrated in the 1970s and 1980s with such practices as total quality management and continuous improvement. But from a competitive standpoint, the problem with operational effectiveness is that best practices are easily emulated. As all competitors in an industry adopt them, the **productivity frontier**—the maximum value a company can deliver at a given cost, given the best available technology, skills, and management techniques—shifts outward, lowering costs and improving value at the same time. Such competition produces absolute improvement in operational effectiveness, but relative improvement for no one. And the more benchmarking that companies do, the more **competitive convergence** you have—that is, the more indistinguishable companies are from one another.

Strategic positioning attempts to achieve sustainable competitive advantage by preserving what is distinctive about a company. It means performing *different* activities from rivals, or performing *similar* activities in different ways.

The productivity frontier is constantly shifting outward as new technologies and management approaches are developed and as new inputs become available. Laptop computers, mobile communications, the Internet, and software such as Lotus Notes, for example, have redefined the productivity frontier for sales-force operations and created rich possibilities for linking sales with such activities as order processing and after-sales support. Similarly, lean production, which involves a family of activities, has allowed substantial improvements in manufacturing productivity and asset utilization.

For at least the past decade, managers have been preoccupied with improving operational effectiveness. Through programs such as TQM, time-based competition, and benchmarking, they have changed how they perform activities in order to eliminate inefficiencies, improve customer satisfaction, and achieve best practice.

Idea in Practice

Three key principles underlie strategic positioning.

1. **Strategy is the creation of a unique and valuable position, involving a different set of activities.** Strategic position emerges from three distinct sources:

   - serving few needs of many customers (Jiffy Lube provides only auto lubricants)

   - serving broad needs of few customers (Bessemer Trust targets only very highwealth clients)

   - serving broad needs of many customers in a narrow market (Carmike Cinemas operates only in cities with a population under 200,000)

2. **Strategy requires you to make trade-offs in competing—to choose what *not* to do.** Some competitive activities are incompatible; thus, gains in one area can be achieved only at the expense of another area. For example, Neutrogena soap is positioned more as a medicinal product than as a cleansing agent. The company says "no" to sales based on deodorizing, gives up large volume, and sacrifices manufacturing efficiencies. By contrast, Maytag's decision to extend its product line and acquire other brands represented a failure to make difficult trade-offs: the boost in revenues came at the expense of return on sales.

3. **Strategy involves creating "fit" among a company's activities.** Fit has to do with the ways a company's activities interact and reinforce one another. For example, Vanguard Group aligns all of its activities with a low-cost strategy; it distributes funds directly to consumers and minimizes portfolio turnover. Fit drives both competitive advantage and sustainability: when activities mutually reinforce each other, competitors can't easily imitate them. When Continental Lite tried to match a few of Southwest Airlines' activities, but not the whole interlocking system, the results were disastrous.

Employees need guidance about how to deepen a strategic position rather than broaden or compromise it. About how to extend the company's uniqueness while strengthening the fit among its activities. This work of deciding which target group of customers and needs to serve requires discipline, the ability to set limits, and forthright communication. Clearly, strategy and leadership are inextricably linked.

Operational effectiveness versus strategic positioning

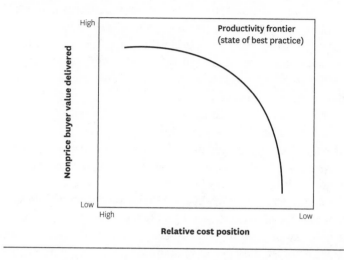

Hoping to keep up with shifts in the productivity frontier, managers have embraced continuous improvement, empowerment, change management, and the so-called learning organization. The popularity of outsourcing and the virtual corporation reflect the growing recognition that it is difficult to perform all activities as productively as specialists.

As companies move to the frontier, they can often improve on multiple dimensions of performance at the same time. For example, manufacturers that adopted the Japanese practice of rapid change-overs in the 1980s were able to lower cost and improve differentiation simultaneously. What were once believed to be real trade-offs— between defects and costs, for example—turned out to be illusions created by poor operational effectiveness. Managers have learned to reject such false trade-offs.

Constant improvement in operational effectiveness is necessary to achieve superior profitability. However, it is not usually sufficient. Few companies have competed successfully on the basis of operational effectiveness over an extended period, and staying ahead of rivals gets harder every day. The most obvious reason for that is the rapid diffusion of best practices. Competitors can quickly imitate management techniques, new technologies, input improvements, and superior ways of meeting customers' needs. The most generic solutions—those that can be used in multiple settings—diffuse the fastest. Witness the proliferation of OE techniques accelerated by support from consultants.

OE competition shifts the productivity frontier outward, effectively raising the bar for everyone. But although such competition produces absolute improvement in operational effectiveness, it leads to relative improvement for no one. Consider the $5 billion-plus U.S. commercial-printing industry. The major players—R.R. Donnelley & Sons Company, Quebecor, World Color Press, and Big Flower Press—are competing head to head, serving all types of customers, offering the same array of printing technologies (gravure and web offset), investing heavily in the same new equipment, running their presses faster, and reducing crew sizes. But the resulting major productivity gains are being captured by customers and equipment suppliers, not retained in superior profitability. Even industry-leader Donnelley's profit margin, consistently higher than 7% in the 1980s, fell to less than 4.6% in 1995. This pattern is playing itself out in industry after industry. Even the Japanese, pioneers of the new competition, suffer from persistently low profits. (See the sidebar "Japanese Companies Rarely Have Strategies.")

The second reason that improved operational effectiveness is insufficient—competitive convergence—is more subtle and insidious. The more benchmarking companies do, the more they look alike. The more that rivals outsource activities to efficient third parties, often the same ones, the more generic those activities become. As rivals imitate one another's improvements in quality, cycle times, or supplier partnerships, strategies converge and competition becomes a series of races down identical paths that no one can win. Competition based on operational effectiveness alone is mutually destructive, leading to wars of attrition that can be arrested only by limiting competition.

Japanese Companies Rarely Have Strategies

THE JAPANESE TRIGGERED A GLOBAL revolution in operational effectiveness in the 1970s and 1980s, pioneering practices such as total quality management and continuous improvement. As a result, Japanese manufacturers enjoyed substantial cost and quality advantages for many years.

But Japanese companies rarely developed distinct strategic positions of the kind discussed in this article. Those that did—Sony, Canon, and Sega, for example—were the exception rather than the rule. Most Japanese companies imitate and emulate one another. All rivals offer most if not all product varieties, features, and services; they employ all channels and match one anothers' plant configurations.

The dangers of Japanese-style competition are now becoming easier to recognize. In the 1980s, with rivals operating far from the productivity frontier, it seemed possible to win on both cost and quality indefinitely. Japanese companies were all able to grow in an expanding domestic economy and by penetrating global markets. They appeared unstoppable. But as the gap in operational effectiveness narrows, Japanese companies are increasingly caught in a trap of their own making. If they are to escape the mutually destructive battles now ravaging their performance, Japanese companies will have to learn strategy.

To do so, they may have to overcome strong cultural barriers. Japan is notoriously consensus oriented, and companies have a strong tendency to mediate differences among individuals rather than accentuate them. Strategy, on the other hand, requires hard choices. The Japanese also have a deeply ingrained service tradition that predisposes them to go to great lengths to satisfy any need a customer expresses. Companies that compete in that way end up blurring their distinct positioning, becoming all things to all customers.

This discussion of Japan is drawn from the author's research with Hirotaka Takeuchi, with help from Mariko Sakakibara.

The recent wave of industry consolidation through mergers makes sense in the context of OE competition. Driven by performance pressures but lacking strategic vision, company after company has had no better idea than to buy up its rivals. The competitors left standing are often those that outlasted others, not companies with real advantage.

After a decade of impressive gains in operational effectiveness, many companies are facing diminishing returns. Continuous improvement has been etched on managers' brains. But its tools unwittingly draw companies toward imitation and homogeneity. Gradually, managers have let operational effectiveness supplant strategy. The result is zero-sum competition, static or declining prices, and pressures on costs that compromise companies' ability to invest in the business for the long term.

II. Strategy Rests on Unique Activities

Competitive strategy is about being different. It means deliberately choosing a different set of activities to deliver a unique mix of value.

Southwest Airlines Company, for example, offers short-haul, low-cost, point-to-point service between midsize cities and secondary airports in large cities. Southwest avoids large airports and does not fly great distances. Its customers include business travelers, families, and students. Southwest's frequent departures and low fares attract price-sensitive customers who otherwise would travel by bus or car, and convenience-oriented travelers who would choose a full-service airline on other routes.

Most managers describe strategic positioning in terms of their customers: "Southwest Airlines serves price- and convenience-sensitive travelers," for example. But the essence of strategy is in the activities—choosing to perform activities differently or to perform different activities than rivals. Otherwise, a strategy is nothing more than a marketing slogan that will not withstand competition.

A full-service airline is configured to get passengers from almost any point A to any point B. To reach a large number of destinations and serve passengers with connecting flights, full-service airlines employ a hub-and-spoke system centered on major airports. To attract passengers who desire more comfort, they offer first-class or business-class service. To accommodate passengers who must change planes, they coordinate schedules and check and transfer baggage. Because some passengers will be traveling for many hours, full-service airlines serve meals.

Southwest, in contrast, tailors all its activities to deliver low-cost, convenient service on its particular type of route. Through fast turnarounds at the gate of only 15 minutes, Southwest is able to keep planes flying longer hours than rivals and provide frequent departures with fewer aircraft. Southwest does not offer meals, assigned seats, interline baggage checking, or premium classes of service. Automated ticketing at the gate encourages customers to bypass travel agents, allowing Southwest to avoid their commissions. A standardized fleet of 737 aircraft boosts the efficiency of maintenance.

Southwest has staked out a unique and valuable strategic position based on a tailored set of activities. On the routes served by Southwest, a full-service airline could never be as convenient or as low cost.

Ikea, the global furniture retailer based in Sweden, also has a clear strategic positioning. Ikea targets young furniture buyers who want style at low cost. What turns this marketing concept into a strategic positioning is the tailored set of activities that make it work. Like Southwest, Ikea has chosen to perform activities differently from its rivals.

Consider the typical furniture store. Showrooms display samples of the merchandise. One area might contain 25 sofas; another will display five dining tables. But those items represent only a fraction of the choices available to customers. Dozens of books displaying fabric swatches or wood samples or alternate styles offer customers thousands of product varieties to choose from. Salespeople often escort customers through the store, answering questions and helping them navigate this maze of choices. Once a customer makes a selection, the order is relayed to a third-party manufacturer. With luck, the furniture will be delivered to the customer's home within six to eight weeks. This is a value chain that maximizes customization and service but does so at high cost.

In contrast, Ikea serves customers who are happy to trade off service for cost. Instead of having a sales associate trail customers around the store, Ikea uses a self-service model based on clear, in-store displays. Rather than rely solely on third-party manufacturers,

Finding New Positions: The Entrepreneurial Edge

STRATEGIC COMPETITION CAN BE THOUGHT of as the process of perceiving new positions that woo customers from established positions or draw new customers into the market. For example, superstores offering depth of merchandise in a single product category take market share from broadline department stores offering a more limited selection in many categories. Mail-order catalogs pick off customers who crave convenience. In principle, incumbents and entrepreneurs face the same challenges in finding new strategic positions. In practice, new entrants often have the edge.

Strategic positionings are often not obvious, and finding them requires creativity and insight. New entrants often discover unique positions that have been available but simply overlooked by established competitors. Ikea, for example, recognized a customer group that had been ignored or served poorly. Circuit City Stores' entry into used cars, CarMax, is based on a new way of performing activities—extensive refurbishing of cars, product guarantees, no-haggle pricing, sophisticated use of in-house customer financing—that has long been open to incumbents.

New entrants can prosper by occupying a position that a competitor once held but has ceded through years of imitation and straddling. And entrants coming from other industries can create new positions because of distinctive activities drawn from their other businesses. CarMax borrows heavily from Circuit City's expertise in inventory management, credit, and other activities in consumer electronics retailing.

Most commonly, however, new positions open up because of change. New customer groups or purchase occasions arise; new needs emerge as societies evolve; new distribution channels appear; new technologies are developed; new machinery or information systems become available. When such changes happen, new entrants, unencumbered by a long history in the industry, can often more easily perceive the potential for a new way of competing. Unlike incumbents, newcomers can be more flexible because they face no trade-offs with their existing activities.

Ikea designs its own low-cost, modular, ready-to-assemble furniture to fit its positioning. In huge stores, Ikea displays every product it sells in room-like settings, so customers don't need a decorator to help them imagine how to put the pieces together. Adjacent to the furnished showrooms is a warehouse section with the products in boxes on pallets. Customers are expected to do their own pickup and delivery, and Ikea will even sell you a roof rack for your car that you can return for a refund on your next visit.

Although much of its low-cost position comes from having customers "do it themselves," Ikea offers a number of extra services that its competitors do not. In-store child care is one. Extended hours are another. Those services are uniquely aligned with the needs of its customers, who are young, not wealthy, likely to have children (but no nanny), and, because they work for a living, have a need to shop at odd hours.

The origins of strategic positions

Strategic positions emerge from three distinct sources, which are not mutually exclusive and often overlap. First, positioning can be based on producing a subset of an industry's products or services. I call this *variety-based positioning* because it is based on the choice of product or service varieties rather than customer segments. Variety-based positioning makes economic sense when a company can best produce particular products or services using distinctive sets of activities.

Jiffy Lube International, for instance, specializes in automotive lubricants and does not offer other car repair or maintenance services. Its value chain produces faster service at a lower cost than broader line repair shops, a combination so attractive that many customers subdivide their purchases, buying oil changes from the focused competitor, Jiffy Lube, and going to rivals for other services.

The Vanguard Group, a leader in the mutual fund industry, is another example of variety-based positioning. Vanguard provides an array of common stock, bond, and money market funds that offer predictable performance and rock-bottom expenses. The company's investment approach deliberately sacrifices the possibility of extraordinary performance in any one year for good relative performance in every year. Vanguard is known, for example, for its index funds. It avoids making bets on interest rates and steers clear of narrow stock groups. Fund managers keep trading levels low, which holds expenses down; in addition, the company discourages

The Connection with Generic Strategies

IN *COMPETITIVE STRATEGY* (The Free Press, 1985), I introduced the concept of generic strategies—cost leadership, differentiation, and focus—to represent the alternative strategic positions in an industry. The generic strategies remain useful to characterize strategic positions at the simplest and broadest level. Vanguard, for instance, is an example of a cost leadership strategy, whereas Ikea, with its narrow customer group, is an example of cost-based focus. Neutrogena is a focused differentiator. The bases for positioning—varieties, needs, and access—carry the understanding of those generic strategies to a greater level of specificity. Ikea and Southwest are both cost-based focusers, for example, but Ikea's focus is based on the needs of a customer group, and Southwest's is based on offering a particular service variety.

The generic strategies framework introduced the need to choose in order to avoid becoming caught between what I then described as the inherent contradictions of different strategies. Trade-offs between the activities of incompatible positions explain those contradictions. Witness Continental Lite, which tried and failed to compete in two ways at once.

customers from rapid buying and selling because doing so drives up costs and can force a fund manager to trade in order to deploy new capital and raise cash for redemptions. Vanguard also takes a consistent low-cost approach to managing distribution, customer service, and marketing. Many investors include one or more Vanguard funds in their portfolio, while buying aggressively managed or specialized funds from competitors.

The people who use Vanguard or Jiffy Lube are responding to a superior value chain for a particular type of service. A variety-based positioning can serve a wide array of customers, but for most it will meet only a subset of their needs.

A second basis for positioning is that of serving most or all the needs of a particular group of customers. I call this *needs-based positioning,* which comes closer to traditional thinking about targeting a segment of customers. It arises when there are groups of customers with differing needs, and when a tailored set of activities can serve those needs best. Some groups of customers are more price sensitive than others, demand different product features, and need varying amounts of information, support, and services. Ikea's customers are a good example of such a group. Ikea seeks to meet all the home furnishing needs of its target customers, not just a subset of them.

A variant of needs-based positioning arises when the same customer has different needs on different occasions or for different types of transactions. The same person, for example, may have different needs when traveling on business than when traveling for pleasure with the family. Buyers of cans—beverage companies, for example—will likely have different needs from their primary supplier than from their secondary source.

It is intuitive for most managers to conceive of their business in terms of the customers' needs they are meeting. But a critical element of needs-based positioning is not at all intuitive and is often overlooked. Differences in needs will not translate into meaningful positions unless the best set of activities to satisfy them *also* differs. If that were not the case, every competitor could meet those same needs, and there would be nothing unique or valuable about the positioning.

In private banking, for example, Bessemer Trust Company targets families with a minimum of $5 million in investable assets who want capital preservation combined with wealth accumulation. By assigning one sophisticated account officer for every 14 families, Bessemer has configured its activities for personalized service. Meetings, for example, are more likely to be held at a client's ranch or yacht than in the office. Bessemer offers a wide array of customized services, including investment management and estate administration, oversight of oil and gas investments, and accounting for racehorses and aircraft. Loans, a staple of most private banks, are rarely needed by Bessemer's clients and make up a tiny fraction of its client balances and income. Despite the most generous compensation of account officers and the highest personnel cost as a percentage of operating expenses, Bessemer's differentiation with its target families produces a return on equity estimated to be the highest of any private banking competitor.

Citibank's private bank, on the other hand, serves clients with minimum assets of about $250,000 who, in contrast to Bessemer's clients, want convenient access to loans—from jumbo mortgages to deal financing. Citibank's account managers are primarily lenders. When clients need other services, their account manager refers them to other Citibank specialists, each of whom handles prepackaged products. Citibank's system is less customized than Bessemer's and allows it to have a lower manager-to-client ratio of 1:125. Biannual office meetings are offered only for the largest clients. Both Bessemer and Citibank have tailored their activities to meet the needs of a different group of private banking customers. The same value chain cannot profitably meet the needs of both groups.

The third basis for positioning is that of segmenting customers who are accessible in different ways. Although their needs are similar to those of other customers, the best configuration of activities to reach them is different. I call this *access-based positioning*. Access can be a function of customer geography or customer scale—or of anything that requires a different set of activities to reach customers in the best way.

Segmenting by access is less common and less well understood than the other two bases. Carmike Cinemas, for example, operates movie theaters exclusively in cities and towns with populations under 200,000. How does Carmike make money in markets that are not only small but also won't support big-city ticket prices? It does so through a set of activities that result in a lean cost structure. Carmike's small-town customers can be served through standardized, low-cost theater complexes requiring fewer screens and less sophisticated projection technology than big-city theaters. The company's proprietary information system and management process eliminate the need for local administrative staff beyond a single theater manager. Carmike also reaps advantages from centralized purchasing, lower rent and payroll costs (because of its locations), and rock-bottom corporate overhead of 2% (the industry average is 5%). Operating in small communities also allows Carmike to practice a highly personal form of marketing in which the theater manager knows patrons and promotes attendance through personal contacts. By being the dominant if not the only theater in its markets—the main competition is often the high school football team—Carmike is also able to get its pick of films and negotiate better terms with distributors.

Rural versus urban-based customers are one example of access driving differences in activities. Serving small rather than large customers or densely rather than sparsely situated customers are other examples in which the best way to configure marketing, order processing, logistics, and after-sale service activities to meet the similar needs of distinct groups will often differ.

Positioning is not only about carving out a niche. A position emerging from any of the sources can be broad or narrow. A focused competitor, such as Ikea, targets the special needs of a subset of customers and designs its activities accordingly. Focused competitors thrive on groups of customers who are overserved (and hence overpriced) by more broadly targeted competitors, or underserved (and hence underpriced). A broadly targeted competitor—for example, Vanguard or Delta Air Lines—serves a wide array of customers, performing a set of activities designed to meet their common needs. It ignores or meets only partially the more idiosyncratic needs of particular customer customer groups.

Whatever the basis—variety, needs, access, or some combination of the three—positioning requires a tailored set of activities because it is always a function of differences on the supply side; that is, of differences in activities. However, positioning is not always a function of differences on the demand, or customer, side. Variety and access positionings, in particular, do not rely on *any* customer differences. In practice, however, variety or access differences often accompany needs differences. The tastes—that is, the needs—of Carmike's small-town customers, for instance, run more toward comedies, Westerns, action films, and family entertainment. Carmike does not run any films rated NC-17.

Having defined positioning, we can now begin to answer the question, "What is strategy?" Strategy is the creation of a unique and valuable position, involving a different set of activities. If there were only one ideal position, there would be no need for strategy. Companies would face a simple imperative—win the race to discover and preempt it. The essence of strategic positioning is to choose activities that are different from rivals'. If the same set of activities were best to produce all varieties, meet all needs, and access all customers, companies could easily shift among them and operational effectiveness would determine performance.

III. A Sustainable Strategic Position Requires Trade-Offs

Choosing a unique position, however, is not enough to guarantee a sustainable advantage. A valuable position will attract imitation by incumbents, who are likely to copy it in one of two ways.

First, a competitor can reposition itself to match the superior performer. J.C. Penney, for instance, has been repositioning itself from a Sears clone to a more upscale, fashion-oriented, soft-goods retailer. A second and far more common type of imitation is straddling. The straddler seeks to match the benefits of a successful position while maintaining its existing position. It grafts new features, services, or technologies onto the activities it already performs.

For those who argue that competitors can copy any market position, the airline industry is a perfect test case. It would seem that nearly any competitor could imitate any other airline's activities. Any airline can buy the same planes, lease the gates, and match the menus and ticketing and baggage handling services offered by other airlines.

Continental Airlines saw how well Southwest was doing and decided to straddle. While maintaining its position as a full-service airline, Continental also set out to match Southwest on a number of point-to-point routes. The airline dubbed the new service Continental Lite. It eliminated meals and first-class service, increased departure frequency, lowered fares, and shortened turnaround time at the gate. Because Continental remained a full-service airline on other routes, it continued to use travel agents and its mixed fleet of planes and to provide baggage checking and seat assignments.

But a strategic position is not sustainable unless there are trade-offs with other positions. Trade-offs occur when activities are incompatible. Simply put, a trade-off means that more of one thing necessitates less of another. An airline can choose to serve meals—adding cost and slowing turnaround time at the gate—or it can choose not to, but it cannot do both without bearing major inefficiencies.

Trade-offs create the need for choice and protect against repositioners and straddlers. Consider Neutrogena soap. Neutrogena Corporation's variety-based positioning is built on a "kind to the skin," residue-free soap formulated for pH balance. With a large detail force calling on dermatologists, Neutrogena's marketing strategy looks more like a drug company's than a soap maker's. It advertises in medical journals, sends direct mail to doctors, attends medical conferences, and performs research at its own Skincare Institute. To reinforce its positioning, Neutrogena originally focused its distribution on drugstores and avoided price promotions. Neutrogena uses a slow, more expensive manufacturing process to mold its fragile soap.

In choosing this position, Neutrogena said no to the deodorants and skin softeners that many customers desire in their soap. It gave up the large-volume potential of selling through supermarkets and using price promotions. It sacrificed manufacturing efficiencies to achieve the soap's desired attributes. In its original positioning, Neutrogena made a whole raft of trade-offs like those, trade-offs that protected the company from imitators.

Trade-offs arise for three reasons. The first is inconsistencies in image or reputation. A company known for delivering one kind of value may lack credibility and confuse customers—or even undermine its reputation—if it delivers another kind of value or attempts to deliver two inconsistent things at the same time. For example, Ivory soap, with its position as a basic, inexpensive everyday soap, would have a hard time reshaping its image to match Neutrogena's premium "medical" reputation. Efforts to create a new image typically cost tens or even hundreds of millions of dollars in a major industry—a powerful barrier to imitation.

Second, and more important, trade-offs arise from activities themselves. Different positions (with their tailored activities) require different product configurations, different equipment, different employee behavior, different skills, and different management systems. Many trade-offs reflect inflexibilities in machinery, people, or systems. The more Ikea has configured its activities to lower costs by having its customers do their own assembly and delivery, the less able it is to satisfy customers who require higher levels of service.

However, trade-offs can be even more basic. In general, value is destroyed if an activity is overdesigned or underdesigned for its use. For example, even if a given salesperson were capable of providing a high level of assistance to one customer and none to another, the salesperson's talent (and some of his or her cost) would be wasted on the second customer. Moreover, productivity can improve when variation of an activity is limited. By providing a high level of assistance all the time, the salesperson and the entire sales activity can often achieve efficiencies of learning and scale.

Finally, trade-offs arise from limits on internal coordination and control. By clearly choosing to compete in one way and not another, senior management makes organizational priorities clear. Companies that try to be all things to all customers, in contrast, risk confusion in the trenches as employees attempt to make day-to-day operating decisions without a clear framework.

Positioning trade-offs are pervasive in competition and essential to strategy. They create the need for choice and purposefully limit what a company offers. They deter straddling or repositioning, because competitors that engage in those approaches undermine their strategies and degrade the value of their existing activities.

Trade-offs ultimately grounded Continental Lite. The airline lost hundreds of millions of dollars, and the CEO lost his job. Its planes were delayed leaving congested hub cities or slowed at the gate by baggage transfers. Late flights and cancellations generated a thousand complaints a day. Continental Lite could not afford to compete on price and still pay standard travel-agent commissions, but neither could it do without agents for its full-service business. The airline compromised by cutting commissions for all Continental flights across the board. Similarly, it could not afford to offer the same frequent-flier benefits to travelers paying the much lower ticket prices for Lite service. It compromised again by lowering the rewards of Continental's entire frequent-flier program. The results: angry travel agents and full-service customers.

Continental tried to compete in two ways at once. In trying to be low cost on some routes and full service on others, Continental paid an enormous straddling penalty. If there were no trade-offs between the two positions, Continental could have succeeded. But the absence of trade-offs is a dangerous half-truth that managers must unlearn. Quality is not always free. Southwest's convenience, one kind of high quality, happens to be consistent with low costs because its frequent departures are facilitated by a number of low-cost practices—fast gate turnarounds and automated ticketing, for example. However, other dimensions of airline quality—an assigned seat, a meal, or baggage transfer—require costs to provide.

In general, false trade-offs between cost and quality occur primarily when there is redundant or wasted effort, poor control or accuracy, or weak coordination. Simultaneous improvement of cost and differentiation is possible only when a company begins far behind the productivity frontier or when the frontier shifts outward. At the frontier, where companies have achieved current best practice, the trade-off between cost and differentiation is very real indeed.

After a decade of enjoying productivity advantages, Honda Motor Company and Toyota Motor Corporation recently bumped up against the frontier. In 1995, faced with increasing customer resistance to higher automobile prices, Honda found that the only way to produce a less-expensive car was to skimp on features. In the United States, it replaced the rear disk brakes on the Civic with lower-cost drum brakes and used cheaper fabric for the back seat, hoping customers would not notice. Toyota tried to sell a version of its best-selling Corolla in Japan with unpainted bumpers and cheaper seats. In Toyota's case, customers rebelled, and the company quickly dropped the new model.

For the past decade, as managers have improved operational effectiveness greatly, they have internalized the idea that eliminating trade-offs is a good thing. But if there are no trade-offs companies will never achieve a sustainable advantage. They will have to run faster and faster just to stay in place.

As we return to the question, What is strategy? we see that tradeoffs add a new dimension to the answer. Strategy is making tradeoffs in competing. The essence of strategy is choosing what *not* to do. Without trade-offs, there would be no need for choice and thus no need for strategy. Any good idea could and would be quickly imitated. Again, performance would once again depend wholly on operational effectiveness.

IV. Fit Drives Both Competitive Advantage and Sustainability

Positioning choices determine not only which activities a company will perform and how it will configure individual activities but also how activities relate to one another. While operational effectiveness is about achieving excellence in individual activities, or functions, strategy is about *combining* activities.

Southwest's rapid gate turnaround, which allows frequent departures and greater use of aircraft, is essential to its high-convenience, low-cost positioning. But how does Southwest achieve it? Part of the answer lies in the company's well-paid gate and ground crews, whose productivity in turnarounds is enhanced by flexible union rules. But the bigger part of the answer lies in how Southwest performs other activities. With no meals, no seat assignment, and no interline baggage transfers, Southwest avoids having to perform activities that slow down other airlines. It selects airports and routes to avoid congestion that introduces delays. Southwest's strict limits on the type and length of routes make standardized aircraft possible: every aircraft Southwest turns is a Boeing 737.

What is Southwest's core competence? Its key success factors? The correct answer is that everything matters. Southwest's strategy involves a whole system of activities, not a collection of parts. Its competitive advantage comes from the way its activities fit and reinforce one another.

Fit locks out imitators by creating a chain that is as strong as its *strongest* link. As in most companies with good strategies, Southwest's activities complement one another in ways that create real economic value. One activity's cost, for example, is lowered because of the way other activities are performed. Similarly, one activity's value to customers can be enhanced by a company's other activities. That is the way strategic fit creates competitive advantage and superior profitability.

Types of fit

The importance of fit among functional policies is one of the oldest ideas in strategy. Gradually, however, it has been supplanted on the management agenda. Rather than seeing the company as a whole, managers have turned to "core" competencies, "critical" resources, and "key" success factors. In fact, fit is a far more central component of competitive advantage than most realize.

Fit is important because discrete activities often affect one another. A sophisticated sales force, for example, confers a greater advantage when the company's product embodies premium technology and its marketing approach emphasizes customer assistance and support. A production line with high levels of model variety is more valuable when combined with an inventory and order processing system that minimizes the need for stocking finished goods, a sales process equipped to explain and encourage customization, and an advertising theme that stresses the benefits of product variations that meet a customer's special needs. Such complementarities are pervasive in strategy. Although some fit among activities is generic and applies to many companies, the most valuable fit is strategy-specific because it enhances a position's uniqueness and amplifies trade-offs.[2]

There are three types of fit, although they are not mutually exclusive. First-order fit is *simple consistency* between each activity (function) and the overall strategy. Vanguard, for example, aligns all activities with its low-cost strategy. It minimizes portfolio turnover and does not need highly compensated money managers. The company distributes its funds directly, avoiding commissions to brokers. It also limits advertising, relying instead on public relations and word-of-mouth recommendations. Vanguard ties its employees' bonuses to cost savings.

Consistency ensures that the competitive advantages of activities cumulate and do not erode or cancel themselves out. It makes the strategy easier to communicate to customers, employees, and shareholders, and improves implementation through single-mindedness in the corporation.

Second-order fit occurs when *activities are reinforcing*. Neutrogena, for example, markets to upscale hotels eager to offer their guests a soap recommended by dermatologists. Hotels grant Neutrogena the privilege of using its customary packaging while requiring other soaps to feature the hotel's name. Once guests have tried Neutrogena in a luxury hotel, they are more likely to purchase it at the drugstore or ask their doctor about it. Thus Neutrogena's medical and hotel marketing activities reinforce one another, lowering total marketing costs.

In another example, Bic Corporation sells a narrow line of standard, low-priced pens to virtually all major customer markets (retail, commercial, promotional, and giveaway) through virtually all available channels. As with any variety-based positioning serving a broad group of customers, Bic emphasizes a common need (low price for an acceptable pen) and uses marketing approaches with a broad reach (a large sales force and heavy television advertising). Bic gains the benefits of consistency across nearly all activities, including product design that emphasizes ease of manufacturing, plants configured for low cost, aggressive purchasing to minimize material costs, and in-house parts production whenever the economics dictate.

Yet Bic goes beyond simple consistency because its activities are reinforcing. For example, the company uses point-of-sale displays and frequent packaging changes to stimulate impulse buying. To handle point-of-sale tasks, a company needs a large sales force. Bic's is the largest in its industry, and it handles point-of-sale activities better than its rivals do. Moreover, the combination of point-of-sale activity, heavy television advertising, and packaging changes yields far more impulse buying than any activity in isolation could.

Third-order fit goes beyond activity reinforcement to what I call *optimization of effort*. The Gap, a retailer of casual clothes, considers product availability in its stores a critical element of its strategy. The Gap could keep products either by holding store inventory or by restocking from warehouses. The Gap has optimized its effort across these activities by restocking its selection of basic clothing almost daily out of three warehouses, thereby minimizing the need to carry

Mapping activity systems

Activity-system maps, such as this one for Ikea, show how a company's strategic position is contained in a set of tailored activities designed to deliver it. In companies with a clear strategic position, a number of higher-order strategic themes (in dark grey) can be identified and implemented through clusters of tightly linked activities (in light grey).

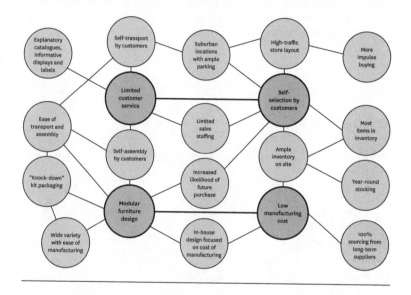

large in-store inventories. The emphasis is on restocking because the Gap's merchandising strategy sticks to basic items in relatively few colors. While comparable retailers achieve turns of three to four times per year, the Gap turns its inventory seven and a half times per year. Rapid restocking, moreover, reduces the cost of implementing the Gap's short model cycle, which is six to eight weeks long.[3]

Coordination and information exchange across activities to eliminate redundancy and minimize wasted effort are the most basic types of effort optimization. But there are higher levels as well. Product design choices, for example, can eliminate the need for after-sale service or make it possible for customers to perform

Vanguard's activity system

Activity-system maps can be useful for examining and strengthening strategic fit. A set of basic questions should guide the process. First, is each activity consistent with the overall positioning—the varieties produced, the needs served, and the type of customers accessed? Ask those responsible for each activity to identify how other activities within the company improve or detract from their performance. Second, are there ways to strengthen how activities and groups of activities reinforce one another? Finally, could changes in one activity eliminate the need to perform others?

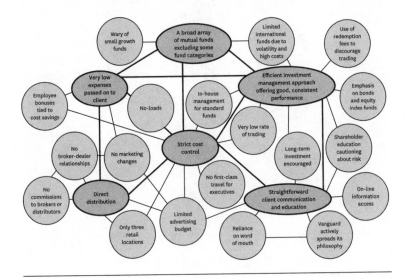

service activities themselves. Similarly, coordination with suppliers or distribution channels can eliminate the need for some in-house activities, such as end-user training.

In all three types of fit, the whole matters more than any individual part. Competitive advantage grows out of the *entire system* of activities. The fit among activities substantially reduces cost or increases differentiation. Beyond that, the competitive value of individual activities—or the associated skills, competencies, or resources—cannot be decoupled from the system or the strategy. Thus in competitive

Southwest Airlines' activity system

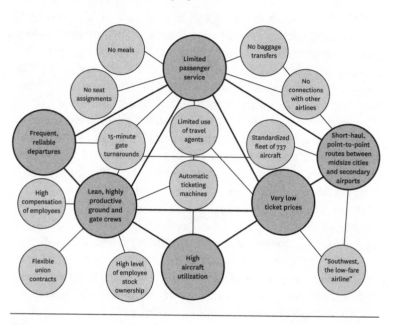

companies it can be misleading to explain success by specifying individual strengths, core competencies, or critical resources. The list of strengths cuts across many functions, and one strength blends into others. It is more useful to think in terms of themes that pervade many activities, such as low cost, a particular notion of customer service, or a particular conception of the value delivered. These themes are embodied in nests of tightly linked activities.

Fit and sustainability

Strategic fit among many activities is fundamental not only to competitive advantage but also to the sustainability of that advantage. It is harder for a rival to match an array of interlocked activities than it is merely to imitate a particular sales-force approach, match a process technology, or replicate a set of product features. Positions built on systems of activities are far more sustainable than those built on individual activities.

Consider this simple exercise. The probability that competitors can match any activity is often less than one. The probabilities then quickly compound to make matching the entire system highly unlikely (.9 x .9 = .81; .9 x .9 x .9 x .9 = .66, and so on). Existing companies that try to reposition or straddle will be forced to reconfigure many activities. And even new entrants, though they do not confront the trade-offs facing established rivals, still face formidable barriers to imitation.

The more a company's positioning rests on activity systems with second- and third-order fit, the more sustainable its advantage will be. Such systems, by their very nature, are usually difficult to untangle from outside the company and therefore hard to imitate. And even if rivals can identify the relevant interconnections, they will have difficulty replicating them. Achieving fit is difficult because it requires the integration of decisions and actions across many independent subunits.

A competitor seeking to match an activity system gains little by imitating only some activities and not matching the whole. Performance does not improve; it can decline. Recall Continental Lite's disastrous attempt to imitate Southwest.

Finally, fit among a company's activities creates pressures and incentives to improve operational effectiveness, which makes imitation even harder. Fit means that poor performance in one activity will degrade the performance in others, so that weaknesses are exposed and more prone to get attention. Conversely, improvements in one activity will pay dividends in others. Companies with strong fit among their activities are rarely inviting targets. Their superiority in strategy and in execution only compounds their advantages and raises the hurdle for imitators.

When activities complement one another, rivals will get little benefit from imitation unless they successfully match the whole system. Such situations tend to promote winner-take-all competition. The company that builds the best activity system—Toys R Us, for instance—wins, while rivals with similar strategies—Child World and Lionel Leisure—fall behind. Thus finding a new strategic position is often preferable to being the second or third imitator of an occupied position.

The most viable positions are those whose activity systems are incompatible because of tradeoffs. Strategic positioning sets the trade-off rules that define how individual activities will be configured and integrated. Seeing strategy in terms of activity systems only makes it clearer why organizational structure, systems, and processes need to be strategy-specific. Tailoring organization to strategy, in turn, makes complementarities more achievable and contributes to sustainability.

One implication is that strategic positions should have a horizon of a decade or more, not of a single planning cycle. Continuity fosters improvements in individual activities and the fit across activities, allowing an organization to build unique capabilities and skills tailored to its strategy. Continuity also reinforces a company's identity.

Conversely, frequent shifts in positioning are costly. Not only must a company reconfigure individual activities, but it must also realign entire systems. Some activities may never catch up to the vacillating strategy. The inevitable result of frequent shifts in strategy, or of failure to choose a distinct position in the first place, is "me-too" or hedged activity configurations, inconsistencies across functions, and organizational dissonance.

What is strategy? We can now complete the answer to this question. Strategy is creating fit among a company's activities. The success of a strategy depends on doing many things well—not just a few—and integrating among them. If there is no fit among activities, there is no distinctive strategy and little sustainability. Management reverts to the simpler task of overseeing independent functions, and operational effectiveness determines an organization's relative performance.

V. Rediscovering Strategy

The failure to choose

Why do so many companies fail to have a strategy? Why do managers avoid making strategic choices? Or, having made them in the past, why do managers so often let strategies decay and blur?

Commonly, the threats to strategy are seen to emanate from outside a company because of changes in technology or the behavior

Alternative Views of Strategy

The Implicit Strategy Model of the Past Decade

- One ideal competitive position in the industry
- Benchmarking of all activities and achieving best practice
- Aggressive outsourcing and partnering to gain efficiencies
- Advantages rest on a few key success factors, critical resources, core competencies
- Flexibility and rapid responses to all competitive and market changes

Sustainable Competitive Advantage

- Unique competitive position for the company
- Activities tailored to strategy
- Clear trade-offs and choices vis-à-vis competitors
- Competitive advantage arises from fit across activities
- Sustainability comes from the activity system, not the parts
- Operational effectiveness a given

of competitors. Although external changes can be the problem, the greater threat to strategy often comes from within. A sound strategy is undermined by a misguided view of competition, by organizational failures, and, especially, by the desire to grow.

Managers have become confused about the necessity of making choices. When many companies operate far from the productivity frontier, trade-offs appear unnecessary. It can seem that a well-run company should be able to beat its ineffective rivals on all dimensions simultaneously. Taught by popular management thinkers that they do not have to make trade-offs, managers have acquired a macho sense that to do so is a sign of weakness.

Unnerved by forecasts of hypercompetition, managers increase its likelihood by imitating everything about their competitors. Exhorted to think in terms of revolution, managers chase every new technology for its own sake.

The pursuit of operational effectiveness is seductive because it is concrete and actionable. Over the past decade, managers have been under increasing pressure to deliver tangible, measurable performance improvements. Programs in operational effectiveness produce reassuring progress, although superior profitability may remain elusive. Business publications and consultants flood the market with information about what other companies are doing, reinforcing the best-practice mentality. Caught up in the race for operational effectiveness, many managers simply do not understand the need to have a strategy.

Companies avoid or blur strategic choices for other reasons as well. Conventional wisdom within an industry is often strong, homogenizing competition. Some managers mistake "customer focus" to mean they must serve all customer needs or respond to every request from distribution channels. Others cite the desire to preserve flexibility.

Organizational realities also work against strategy. Trade-offs are frightening, and making no choice is sometimes preferred to risking blame for a bad choice. Companies imitate one another in a type of herd behavior, each assuming rivals know something they do not. Newly empowered employees, who are urged to seek every possible source of improvement, often lack a vision of the whole and the perspective to recognize trade-offs. The failure to choose sometimes comes down to the reluctance to disappoint valued managers or employees.

The growth trap

Among all other influences, the desire to grow has perhaps the most perverse effect on strategy. Trade-offs and limits appear to constrain growth. Serving one group of customers and excluding others, for instance, places a real or imagined limit on revenue growth. Broadly targeted strategies emphasizing low price result in lost sales with customers sensitive to features or service. Differentiators lose sales to price-sensitive customers.

Managers are constantly tempted to take incremental steps that surpass those limits but blur a company's strategic position. Eventually, pressures to grow or apparent saturation of the target market lead managers to broaden the position by extending product lines, adding

Reconnecting with Strategy

MOST COMPANIES OWE THEIR INITIAL success to a unique strategic position involving clear trade-offs. Activities once were aligned with that position. The passage of time and the pressures of growth, however, led to compromises that were, at first, almost imperceptible. Through a succession of incremental changes that each seemed sensible at the time, many established companies have compromised their way to homogeneity with their rivals.

The issue here is not with the companies whose historical position is no longer viable; their challenge is to start over, just as a new entrant would. At issue is a far more common phenomenon: the established company achieving mediocre returns and lacking a clear strategy. Through incremental additions of product varieties, incremental efforts to serve new customer groups, and emulation of rivals' activities, the existing company loses its clear competitive position. Typically, the company has matched many of its competitors' offerings and practices and attempts to sell to most customer groups.

A number of approaches can help a company reconnect with strategy. The first is a careful look at what it already does. Within most well-established companies is a core of uniqueness. It is identified by answering questions such as the following:

- Which of our product or service varieties are the most distinctive?
- Which of our product or service varieties are the most profitable?

new features, imitating competitors' popular services, matching processes, and even making acquisitions. For years, Maytag Corporation's success was based on its focus on reliable, durable washers and dryers, later extended to include dishwashers. However, conventional wisdom emerging within the industry supported the notion of selling a full line of products. Concerned with slow industry growth and competition from broad-line appliance makers, Maytag was pressured by dealers and encouraged by customers to extend its line. Maytag expanded into refrigerators and cooking products under the Maytag brand and acquired other brands—Jenn-Air, Hardwick Stove, Hoover, Admiral, and Magic Chef—with disparate positions. Maytag has grown substantially from $684 million in 1985 to a peak of $3.4 billion in 1994, but return on sales has declined from 8% to 12% in the 1970s and 1980s to an average of less than 1% between 1989 and 1995. Cost cutting will

- Which of our customers are the most satisfied?

- Which customers, channels, or purchase occasions are the most profitable?

- Which of the activities in our value chain are the most different and effective?

Around this core of uniqueness are encrustations added incrementally over time. Like barnacles, they must be removed to reveal the underlying strategic positioning. A small percentage of varieties or customers may well account for most of a company's sales and especially its profits. The challenge, then, is to refocus on the unique core and realign the company's activities with it. Customers and product varieties at the periphery can be sold or allowed through inattention or price increases to fade away.

A company's history can also be instructive. What was the vision of the founder? What were the products and customers that made the company? Looking backward, one can reexamine the original strategy to see if it is still valid. Can the historical positioning be implemented in a modern way, one consistent with today's technologies and practices? This sort of thinking may lead to a commitment to renew the strategy and may challenge the organization to recover its distinctiveness. Such a challenge can be galvanizing and can instill the confidence to make the needed trade-offs.

---

improve this performance, but laundry and dishwasher products still anchor Maytag's profitability.

Neutrogena may have fallen into the same trap. In the early 1990s, its U.S. distribution broadened to include mass merchandisers such as Wal-Mart Stores. Under the Neutrogena name, the company expanded into a wide variety of products—eye-makeup remover and shampoo, for example—in which it was not unique and which diluted its image, and it began turning to price promotions.

Compromises and inconsistencies in the pursuit of growth will erode the competitive advantage a company had with its original varieties or target customers. Attempts to compete in several ways at once create confusion and undermine organizational motivation and focus. Profits fall, but more revenue is seen as the answer. Managers are unable to make choices, so the company embarks on a new round of broadening and compromises. Often, rivals continue to match each other until desperation breaks the cycle, resulting in a merger or downsizing to the original positioning.

Profitable growth

Many companies, after a decade of restructuring and cost-cutting, are turning their attention to growth. Too often, efforts to grow blur uniqueness, create compromises, reduce fit, and ultimately undermine competitive advantage. In fact, the growth imperative is hazardous to strategy.

What approaches to growth preserve and reinforce strategy? Broadly, the prescription is to concentrate on deepening a strategic position rather than broadening and compromising it. One approach is to look for extensions of the strategy that leverage the existing activity system by offering features or services that rivals would find impossible or costly to match on a stand-alone basis. In other words, managers can ask themselves which activities, features, or forms of competition are feasible or less costly to them because of complementary activities that their company performs.

Deepening a position involves making the company's activities more distinctive, strengthening fit, and communicating the strategy better to those customers who should value it. But many companies succumb to the temptation to chase "easy" growth by adding hot features, products, or services without screening them or adapting them to their strategy. Or they target new customers or markets in which the company has little special to offer. A company can often grow faster—and far more profitably—by better penetrating needs and varieties where it is distinctive than by slugging it out in potentially higher growth arenas in which the company lacks uniqueness. Carmike, now the largest theater chain in the United States, owes its rapid growth to its disciplined concentration on small markets. The company quickly sells any big-city theaters that come to it as part of an acquisition.

Globalization often allows growth that is consistent with strategy, opening up larger markets for a focused strategy. Unlike broadening domestically, expanding globally is likely to leverage and reinforce a company's unique position and identity.

Emerging Industries and Technologies

DEVELOPING A STRATEGY IN A newly emerging industry or in a business undergoing revolutionary technological changes is a daunting proposition. In such cases, managers face a high level of uncertainty about the needs of customers, the products and services that will prove to be the most desired, and the best configuration of activities and technologies to deliver them. Because of all this uncertainty, imitation and hedging are rampant: unable to risk being wrong or left behind, companies match all features, offer all new services, and explore all technologies.

During such periods in an industry's development, its basic productivity frontier is being established or reestablished. Explosive growth can make such times profitable for many companies, but profits will be temporary because imitation and strategic convergence will ultimately destroy industry profitability. The companies that are enduringly successful will be those that begin as early as possible to define and embody in their activities a unique competitive position. A period of imitation may be inevitable in emerging industries, but that period reflects the level of uncertainty rather than a desired state of affairs.

In high-tech industries, this imitation phase often continues much longer than it should. Enraptured by technological change itself, companies pack more features—most of which are never used—into their products while slashing prices across the board. Rarely are trade-offs even considered. The drive for growth to satisfy market pressures leads companies into every product area. Although a few companies with fundamental advantages prosper, the majority are doomed to a rat race no one can win.

Ironically, the popular business press, focused on hot, emerging industries, is prone to presenting these special cases as proof that we have entered a new era of competition in which none of the old rules are valid. In fact, the opposite is true.

Companies seeking growth through broadening within their industry can best contain the risks to strategy by creating stand-alone units, each with its own brand name and tailored activities. Maytag has clearly struggled with this issue. On the one hand, it has organized its premium and value brands into separate units with different strategic positions. On the other, it has created an umbrella appliance company for all its brands to gain critical mass. With shared design, manufacturing, distribution, and customer service, it will be hard to avoid homogenization. If a given business unit attempts to compete with different positions for different products or customers, avoiding compromise is nearly impossible.

The role of leadership
The challenge of developing or reestablishing a clear strategy is often primarily an organizational one and depends on leadership. With so many forces at work against making choices and tradeoffs in organizations, a clear intellectual framework to guide strategy is a necessary counterweight. Moreover, strong leaders willing to make choices are essential.

In many companies, leadership has degenerated into orchestrating operational improvements and making deals. But the leader's role is broader and far more important. General management is more than the stewardship of individual functions. Its core is strategy: defining and communicating the company's unique position, making trade-offs, and forging fit among activities. The leader must provide the discipline to decide which industry changes and customer needs the company will respond to, while avoiding organizational distractions and maintaining the company's distinctiveness. Managers at lower levels lack the perspective and the confidence to maintain a strategy. There will be constant pressures to compromise, relax trade-offs, and emulate rivals. One of the leader's jobs is to teach others in the organization about strategy—and to say no.

Strategy renders choices about what not to do as important as choices about what to do. Indeed, setting limits is another function of leadership. Deciding which target group of customers, varieties, and needs the company should serve is fundamental to developing a strategy. But so is deciding not to serve other customers or needs and not to offer certain features or services. Thus strategy requires constant discipline and clear communication. Indeed, one of the most important functions of an explicit, communicated strategy is to guide employees in making choices that arise because of trade-offs in their individual activities and in day-to-day decisions.

Improving operational effectiveness is a necessary part of management, but it is *not* strategy. In confusing the two, managers have unintentionally backed into a way of thinking about competition that is driving many industries toward competitive convergence, which is in no one's best interest and is not inevitable.

Managers must clearly distinguish operational effectiveness from strategy. Both are essential, but the two agendas are different.

The operational agenda involves continual improvement everywhere there are no trade-offs. Failure to do this creates vulnerability even for companies with a good strategy. The operational agenda is the proper place for constant change, flexibility, and relentless efforts to achieve best practice. In contrast, the strategic agenda is the right place for defining a unique position, making clear trade-offs, and tightening fit. It involves the continual search for ways to reinforce and extend the company's position. The strategic agenda demands discipline and continuity; its enemies are distraction and compromise.

Strategic continuity does not imply a static view of competition. A company must continually improve its operational effectiveness and actively try to shift the productivity frontier; at the same time, there needs to be ongoing effort to extend its uniqueness while strengthening the fit among its activities. Strategic continuity, in fact, should make an organization's continual improvement more effective.

A company may have to change its strategy if there are major structural changes in its industry. In fact, new strategic positions often arise because of industry changes, and new entrants unencumbered by history often can exploit them more easily. However, a company's choice of a new position must be driven by the ability to find new trade-offs and leverage a new system of complementary activities into a sustainable advantage.

Originally published in November 1996. Reprint 96608

Notes

1. I first described the concept of activities and its use in understanding competitive advantage in *Competitive Advantage* (New York: The Free Press, 1985). The ideas in this article build on and extend that thinking.

2. Paul Milgrom and John Roberts have begun to explore the economics of systems of complementary functions, activities, and functions. Their focus is on the emergence of "modern manufacturing" as a new set of complementary activities, on the tendency of companies to react to external changes with coherent bundles

of internal responses, and on the need for central coordination—a strategy—to align functional managers. In the latter case, they model what has long been a bedrock principle of strategy. See Paul Milgrom and John Roberts, "The Economics of Modern Manufacturing: Technology, Strategy, and Organization," *American Economic Review* 80 (1990): 511–528; Paul Milgrom, Yingyi Qian, and John Roberts, "Complementarities, Momentum, and Evolution of Modern Manufacturing," *American Economic Review* 81 (1991) 84–88; and Paul Milgrom and John Roberts, "Complementarities and Fit: Strategy, Structure, and Organizational Changes in Manufacturing," *Journal of Accounting and Economics,* vol. 19 (March–May 1995): 179–208.

3. Material on retail strategies is drawn in part from Jan Rivkin, "The Rise of Retail Category Killers," unpublished working paper, January 1995. Nicolaj Siggelkow prepared the case study on the Gap.

The Five Competitive Forces That Shape Strategy

by Michael E. Porter

IN ESSENCE, THE JOB of the strategist is to understand and cope with competition. Often, however, managers define competition too narrowly, as if it occurred only among today's direct competitors. Yet competition for profits goes beyond established industry rivals to include four other competitive forces as well: customers, suppliers, potential entrants, and substitute products. The extended rivalry that results from all five forces defines an industry's structure and shapes the nature of competitive interaction within an industry.

As different from one another as industries might appear on the surface, the underlying drivers of profitability are the same. The global auto industry, for instance, appears to have nothing in common with the worldwide market for art masterpieces or the heavily regulated health-care delivery industry in Europe. But to understand industry competition and profitability in each of those three cases, one must analyze the industry's underlying structure in terms of the five forces. (See "The five forces that shape industry competition.")

If the forces are intense, as they are in such industries as airlines, textiles, and hotels, almost no company earns attractive returns on investment. If the forces are benign, as they are in industries such as software, soft drinks, and toiletries, many companies are profitable. Industry structure drives competition and profitability, not whether an industry produces a product or service, is emerging or mature, high tech or low tech, regulated or unregulated. While a myriad of factors can affect industry profitability in the short run—including the weather and the business cycle—industry structure, manifested in the competitive forces, sets industry profitability in the medium and long run. (See "Differences in Industry Profitability.")

Understanding the competitive forces, and their underlying causes, reveals the roots of an industry's current profitability while providing a framework for anticipating and influencing competition (and profitability) over time. A healthy industry structure should be as much a competitive concern to strategists as their company's own position. Understanding industry structure is also essential to effective strategic positioning. As we will see, defending against the competitive forces and shaping them in a company's favor are crucial to strategy.

Forces That Shape Competition

The configuration of the five forces differs by industry. In the market for commercial aircraft, fierce rivalry between dominant producers Airbus and Boeing and the bargaining power of the airlines that place huge orders for aircraft are strong, while the threat of entry, the threat of substitutes, and the power of suppliers are more benign. In the movie theater industry, the proliferation of substitute forms of entertainment and the power of the movie producers and distributors who supply movies, the critical input, are important.

The strongest competitive force or forces determine the profitability of an industry and become the most important to strategy formulation. The most salient force, however, is not always obvious.

For example, even though rivalry is often fierce in commodity industries, it may not be the factor limiting profitability. Low returns in the photographic film industry, for instance, are the result of a superior substitute product—as Kodak and Fuji, the world's leading producers of photographic film, learned with the advent of digital photography. In such a situation, coping with the substitute product becomes the number one strategic priority.

Idea in Brief

You know that to sustain long-term profitability you must respond strategically to competition. And you naturally keep tabs on your **established** rivals. But as you scan the competitive arena, are you also looking *beyond* your direct competitors? As Porter explains in this update of his revolutionary 1979 HBR article, four additional competitive forces can hurt your prospective profits:

- Savvy **customers** can force down prices by playing you and your rivals against one another.

- Powerful **suppliers** may constrain your profits if they charge higher prices.

- Aspiring **entrants,** armed with new capacity and hungry for market share, can ratchet up the investment required for you to stay in the game.

- **Substitute offerings** can lure customers away.

Consider commercial aviation: It's one of the least profitable industries because all five forces are strong. **Established rivals** compete intensely on price. **Customers** are fickle, searching for the best deal regardless of carrier. **Suppliers**— plane and engine manufacturers, along with unionized labor forces—bargain away the lion's share of airlines' profits. **New players** enter the industry in a constant stream. And **substitutes** are readily available—such as train or car travel.

By analyzing all five competitive forces, you gain a complete picture of what's influencing profitability in your industry. You identify game-changing trends early, so you can swiftly exploit them. And you spot ways to work around constraints on profitability—or even reshape the forces in your favor.

Industry structure grows out of a set of economic and technical characteristics that determine the strength of each competitive force. We will examine these drivers in the pages that follow, taking the perspective of an incumbent, or a company already present in the industry. The analysis can be readily extended to understand the challenges facing a potential entrant.

Threat of entry

New entrants to an industry bring new capacity and a desire to gain market share that puts pressure on prices, costs, and the rate of investment necessary to compete. Particularly when new entrants

Idea in Practice

By understanding how the five competitive forces influence profitability in your industry, you can develop a strategy for enhancing your company's long-term profits. Porter suggests the following:

Position Your Company Where the Forces Are Weakest

Example: In the heavy-truck industry, many buyers operate large fleets and are highly motivated to drive down truck prices. Trucks are built to regulated standards and offer similar features, so price competition is stiff; unions exercise considerable supplier power; and buyers can use substitutes such as cargo delivery by rail.

To create and sustain long-term profitability within this industry, heavy-truck maker Paccar chose to focus on one customer group where competitive forces are weakest: individual drivers who own their trucks and contract directly with suppliers. These operators have limited clout as buyers and are less price sensitive because of their emotional ties to and economic dependence on their own trucks.

For these customers, Paccar has developed such features as luxurious sleeper cabins, plush leather seats, and sleek exterior styling. Buyers can select from thousands of options to put their personal signature on these built-to-order trucks.

Customers pay Paccar a 10% premium, and the company has been profitable for 68 straight years and earned a long-run return on equity above 20%.

Exploit Changes in the Forces

Example: With the advent of the Internet and digital distribution of music, unauthorized downloading created an illegal but potent substitute for record companies' services. The record companies tried to develop technical platforms for

are diversifying from other markets, they can leverage existing capabilities and cash flows to shake up competition, as Pepsi did when it entered the bottled water industry, Microsoft did when it began to offer internet browsers, and Apple did when it entered the music distribution business.

The threat of entry, therefore, puts a cap on the profit potential of an industry. When the threat is high, incumbents must hold down their prices or boost investment to deter new competitors. In specialty coffee retailing, for example, relatively low entry barriers digital distribution themselves, but major labels didn't want to sell their music through a platform owned by a rival.

Into this vacuum stepped Apple, with its iTunes music store supporting its iPod music player. The birth of this powerful new gatekeeper has whittled down the number of major labels from six in 1997 to four today.

Reshape the Forces in Your Favor

Use tactics designed specifically to reduce the share of profits leaking to other players. For example:

- To neutralize **supplier power,** standardize specifications for parts so your company can switch more easily among vendors.

- To counter **customer power,** expand your services so it's harder for customers to leave you for a rival.

- To temper price wars initiated by **established rivals,** invest more heavily in products that differ significantly from competitors' offerings.

- To scare off **new entrants,** elevate the fixed costs of competing; for instance, by escalating your R&D expenditures.

- To limit the threat of **substitutes,** offer better value through wider product accessibility. Soft-drink producers did this by introducing vending machines and convenience store channels, which dramatically improved the availability of soft drinks relative to other beverages.

mean that Starbucks must invest aggressively in modernizing stores and menus.

The threat of entry in an industry depends on the height of entry barriers that are present and on the reaction entrants can expect from incumbents. If entry barriers are low and newcomers expect little retaliation from the entrenched competitors, the threat of entry is high and industry profitability is moderated. It is the *threat* of entry, not whether entry actually occurs, that holds down profitability.

Barriers to entry. Entry barriers are advantages that incumbents have relative to new entrants. There are seven major sources:

1. *Supply-side economies of scale.* These economies arise when firms that produce at larger volumes enjoy lower costs per unit because they can spread fixed costs over more units, employ more efficient technology, or command better terms from suppliers. Supply-side scale economies deter entry by forcing the aspiring entrant either to come into the industry on a large scale, which requires dislodging entrenched competitors, or to accept a cost disadvantage.

Scale economies can be found in virtually every activity in the value chain; which ones are most important varies by industry.[1] In microprocessors, incumbents such as Intel are protected by scale economies in research, chip fabrication, and consumer marketing. For lawn care companies like Scotts Miracle-Gro, the most important scale economies are found in the supply chain and media advertising. In small-package delivery, economies of scale arise in national logistical systems and information technology.

2. *Demand-side benefits of scale.* These benefits, also known as network effects, arise in industries where a buyer's willingness to pay for a company's product increases with the number of other buyers who also patronize the company. Buyers may trust larger companies more for a crucial product: Recall the old adage that no one ever got fired for buying from IBM (when it was the dominant computer maker). Buyers may also value being in a "network" with a larger number of fellow customers. For instance, online auction participants are attracted to eBay because it offers the most potential trading partners. Demand-side benefits of scale discourage entry by limiting the willingness of customers to buy from a newcomer and by reducing the price the newcomer can command until it builds up a large base of customers.

3. *Customer switching costs.* Switching costs are fixed costs that buyers face when they change suppliers. Such costs may arise because a buyer who switches vendors must, for example, alter product specifications, retrain employees to use a new product, or modify processes or information systems. The larger the switching costs, the harder it will be for an entrant to gain customers. Enterprise resource planning (ERP) software is an example of a product with very high switching costs.

Once a company has installed SAP's ERP system, for example, the costs of moving to a new vendor are astronomical because of embedded data, the fact that internal processes have been adapted to SAP, major retraining needs, and the mission-critical nature of the applications.

4. *Capital requirements.* The need to invest large financial resources in order to compete can deter new entrants. Capital may be necessary not only for fixed facilities but also to extend customer credit, build inventories, and fund start-up losses. The barrier is particularly great if the capital is required for unrecoverable and therefore harder-to-finance expenditures, such as up-front advertising or research and development. While major corporations have the financial resources to invade almost any industry, the huge capital requirements in certain fields limit the pool of likely entrants. Conversely, in such fields as tax preparation services or short-haul trucking, capital requirements are minimal and potential entrants plentiful.

It is important not to overstate the degree to which capital requirements alone deter entry. If industry returns are attractive and are expected to remain so, and if capital markets are efficient, investors will provide entrants with the funds they need. For aspiring air carriers, for instance, financing is available to purchase expensive aircraft because of their high resale value, one reason why there have been numerous new airlines in almost every region.

5. *Incumbency advantages independent of size.* No matter what their size, incumbents may have cost or quality advantages not available to potential rivals. These advantages can stem from such sources as proprietary technology, preferential access to the best raw material sources, preemption of the most favorable geographic locations, established brand identities, or cumulative experience that has allowed incumbents to learn how to produce more efficiently. Entrants try to bypass such advantages. Upstart discounters such as Target and Wal-Mart, for example, have located stores in freestanding sites rather than regional shopping centers where established department stores were well entrenched.

6. *Unequal access to distribution channels.* The new entrant must, of course, secure distribution of its product or service. A new food item, for example, must displace others from the supermarket shelf

The five forces that shape industry competition

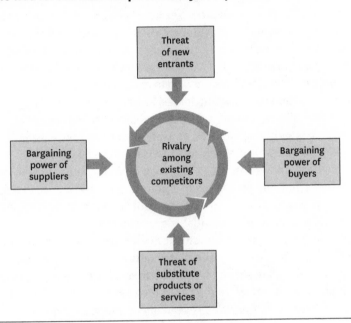

via price breaks, promotions, intense selling efforts, or some other means. The more limited the wholesale or retail channels are and the more that existing competitors have tied them up, the tougher entry into an industry will be. Sometimes access to distribution is so high a barrier that new entrants must bypass distribution channels altogether or create their own. Thus, upstart low-cost airlines have avoided distribution through travel agents (who tend to favor established higher-fare carriers) and have encouraged passengers to book their own flights on the internet.

7. *Restrictive government policy.* Government policy can hinder or aid new entry directly, as well as amplify (or nullify) the other entry barriers. Government directly limits or even forecloses entry into industries through, for instance, licensing requirements and restrictions on foreign investment. Regulated industries like

liquor retailing, taxi services, and airlines are visible examples. Government policy can heighten other entry barriers through such means as expansive patenting rules that protect proprietary technology from imitation or environmental or safety regulations that raise scale economies facing newcomers. Of course, government policies may also make entry easier—directly through subsidies, for instance, or indirectly by funding basic research and making it available to all firms, new and old, reducing scale economies.

Entry barriers should be assessed relative to the capabilities of potential entrants, which may be start-ups, foreign firms, or companies in related industries. And, as some of our examples illustrate, the strategist must be mindful of the creative ways newcomers might find to circumvent apparent barriers.

Expected retaliation. How potential entrants believe incumbents may react will also influence their decision to enter or stay out of an industry. If reaction is vigorous and protracted enough, the profit potential of participating in the industry can fall below the cost of capital. Incumbents often use public statements and responses to one entrant to send a message to other prospective entrants about their commitment to defending market share.

Newcomers are likely to fear expected retaliation if:

- Incumbents have previously responded vigorously to new entrants.

- Incumbents possess substantial resources to fight back, including excess cash and unused borrowing power, available productive capacity, or clout with distribution channels and customers.

- Incumbents seem likely to cut prices because they are committed to retaining market share at all costs or because the industry has high fixed costs, which create a strong motivation to drop prices to fill excess capacity.

- Industry growth is slow so newcomers can gain volume only by taking it from incumbents.

Differences in Industry Profitability

THE AVERAGE RETURN on invested capital varies markedly from industry to industry. Between 1992 and 2006, for example, average return on invested capital in U.S. industries ranged as low as zero or even negative to more than 50%. At the high end are industries like soft drinks and prepackaged software, which have been almost six times more profitable than the airline industry over the period.

Average return on invested capital in U.S. industries, 1992–2006

Return on invested capital (ROIC) is the appropriate measure of profitability for strategy formulation, not to mention for equity investors. Return on sales or the growth rate of profits fail to account for the capital required to compete in the industry. Here, we utilize earnings before interest and taxes divided by average invested capital less excess cash as the measure of ROIC. This measure controls for idiosyncratic differences in capital structure and tax rates across companies and industries.

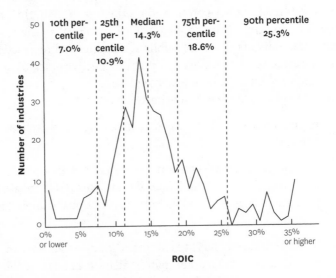

Source: Standard & Poor's, Compustat, and author's calculations

Profitability of selected U.S. industries

Average ROIC, 1992–2006

Industry	ROIC
Security brokers and dealers	40.9%
Soft drinks	37.6%
Prepackaged software	37.6%
Pharmaceuticals	31.7%
Perfume, cosmetics, toiletries	28.6%
Advertising agencies	27.3%
Distilled spirits	26.4%
Semiconductors	21.3%
Medical instruments	21.0%
Men's and boys' clothing	19.5%
Tires	19.5%
Household appliances	19.2%
Malt beverages	19.0%
Child day care services	17.6%
Household furniture	17.0%
Drug stores	16.5%
Grocery stores	16.0%
Iron and steel foundries	15.6%
Cookies and crackers	15.4%
Mobile homes	15.0%
Wine and brandy	13.9%
Bakery products	13.8%
Engines and turbines	13.7%
Book publishing	13.4%
Laboratory equipment	13.4%
Oil and gas machinery	12.6%
Soft drink bottling	11.7%
Knitting mills	10.5%
Hotels	10.4%
Catalog, mail-order houses	5.9%
Airlines	5.9%

Average industry ROIC in the U.S. 14.9%

An analysis of barriers to entry and expected retaliation is obviously crucial for any company contemplating entry into a new industry. The challenge is to find ways to surmount the entry barriers without nullifying, through heavy investment, the profitability of participating in the industry.

The power of suppliers

Powerful suppliers capture more of the value for themselves by charging higher prices, limiting quality or services, or shifting costs to industry participants. Powerful suppliers, including suppliers of labor, can squeeze profitability out of an industry that is unable to pass on cost increases in its own prices. Microsoft, for instance, has contributed to the erosion of profitability among personal computer makers by raising prices on operating systems. PC makers, competing fiercely for customers who can easily switch among them, have limited freedom to raise their prices accordingly.

Companies depend on a wide range of different supplier groups for inputs. A supplier group is powerful if:

- It is more concentrated than the industry it sells to. Microsoft's near monopoly in operating systems, coupled with the fragmentation of PC assemblers, exemplifies this situation.

- The supplier group does not depend heavily on the industry for its revenues. Suppliers serving many industries will not hesitate to extract maximum profits from each one. If a particular industry accounts for a large portion of a supplier group's volume or profit, however, suppliers will want to protect the industry through reasonable pricing and assist in activities such as R&D and lobbying.

- Industry participants face switching costs in changing suppliers. For example, shifting suppliers is difficult if companies have invested heavily in specialized ancillary equipment or in learning how to operate a supplier's equipment (as with Bloomberg terminals used by financial professionals). Or

Industry Analysis in Practice

Good industry analysis looks rigorously at the structural underpinnings of profitability. A first step is to understand the appropriate time horizon. One of the essential tasks in industry analysis is to distinguish temporary or cyclical changes from structural changes. A good guideline for the appropriate time horizon is the full business cycle for the particular industry. For most industries, a three-to-five-year horizon is appropriate, although in some industries with long lead times, such as mining, the appropriate horizon might be a decade or more. It is average profitability over this period, not profitability in any particular year, that should be the focus of analysis.

The point of industry analysis is not to declare the industry attractive or unattractive but to understand the underpinnings of competition and the root causes of profitability. As much as possible, analysts should look at industry structure quantitatively, rather than be satisfied with lists of qualitative factors. Many elements of the five forces can be quantified: the percentage of the buyer's total cost accounted for by the industry's product (to understand buyer price sensitivity); the percentage of industry sales required to fill a plant or operate a logistical network of efficient scale (to help assess barriers to entry); the buyer's switching cost (determining the inducement an entrant or rival must offer customers).

The strength of the competitive forces affects prices, costs, and the investment required to compete; thus the forces are directly tied to the income statements and balance sheets of industry participants. Industry structure defines the gap between revenues and costs. For example, intense rivalry drives down prices or elevates the costs of marketing, R&D, or customer service, reducing margins. How much? Strong suppliers drive up input costs. How much? Buyer power lowers prices or elevates the costs of meeting buyers' demands, such as the requirement to hold more inventory or provide financing. How much? Low barriers to entry or close substitutes limit the level of sustainable prices. How much? It is these economic relationships that sharpen the strategist's understanding of industry competition.

Finally, good industry analysis does not just list pluses and minuses but sees an industry in overall, systemic terms. Which forces are underpinning (or constraining) today's profitability? How might shifts in one competitive force trigger reactions in others? Answering such questions is often the source of true strategic insights.

firms may have located their production lines adjacent to a supplier's manufacturing facilities (as in the case of some beverage companies and container manufacturers). When switching costs are high, industry participants find it hard to play suppliers off against one another. (Note that suppliers may have switching costs as well. This limits their power.)

- Suppliers offer products that are differentiated. Pharmaceutical companies that offer patented drugs with distinctive medical benefits have more power over hospitals, health maintenance organizations, and other drug buyers, for example, than drug companies offering me-too or generic products.

- There is no substitute for what the supplier group provides. Pilots' unions, for example, exercise considerable supplier power over airlines partly because there is no good alternative to a well-trained pilot in the cockpit.

- The supplier group can credibly threaten to integrate forward into the industry. In that case, if industry participants make too much money relative to suppliers, they will induce suppliers to enter the market.

The power of buyers

Powerful customers—the flip side of powerful suppliers—can capture more value by forcing down prices, demanding better quality or more service (thereby driving up costs), and generally playing industry participants off against one another, all at the expense of industry profitability. Buyers are powerful if they have negotiating leverage relative to industry participants, especially if they are price sensitive, using their clout primarily to pressure price reductions.

As with suppliers, there may be distinct groups of customers who differ in bargaining power. A customer group has negotiating leverage if:

- There are few buyers, or each one purchases in volumes that are large relative to the size of a single vendor. Large-volume buyers are particularly powerful in industries with high fixed costs, such as telecommunications equipment, offshore drilling, and bulk chemicals. High fixed costs and low marginal costs amplify the pressure on rivals to keep capacity filled through discounting.

- The industry's products are standardized or undifferentiated. If buyers believe they can always find an equivalent product, they tend to play one vendor against another.

- Buyers face few switching costs in changing vendors.

- Buyers can credibly threaten to integrate backward and produce the industry's product themselves if vendors are too profitable. Producers of soft drinks and beer have long controlled the power of packaging manufacturers by threatening to make, and at times actually making, packaging materials themselves.

A buyer group is price sensitive if:

- The product it purchases from the industry represents a significant fraction of its cost structure or procurement budget. Here buyers are likely to shop around and bargain hard, as consumers do for home mortgages. Where the product sold by an industry is a small fraction of buyers' costs or expenditures, buyers are usually less price sensitive.

- The buyer group earns low profits, is strapped for cash, or is otherwise under pressure to trim its purchasing costs. Highly profitable or cash-rich customers, in contrast, are generally less price sensitive (that is, of course, if the item does not represent a large fraction of their costs).

- The quality of buyers' products or services is little affected by the industry's product. Where quality is very much affected by the industry's product, buyers are generally less price sensitive. When purchasing or renting production quality cameras, for instance, makers of major motion pictures opt for highly reliable equipment with the latest features. They pay limited attention to price.

- The industry's product has little effect on the buyer's other costs. Here, buyers focus on price. Conversely, where an industry's product or service can pay for itself many times over by improving performance or reducing labor, material, or other costs, buyers are usually more interested in quality than in price. Examples include products and services like tax accounting or well logging (which measures below-ground conditions of oil wells) that can save or even make the buyer money. Similarly, buyers tend not to be price sensitive in services such as investment banking, where poor performance can be costly and embarrassing.

Most sources of buyer power apply equally to consumers and to business-to-business customers. Like industrial customers, consumers tend to be more price sensitive if they are purchasing products that are undifferentiated, expensive relative to their incomes, and of a sort where product performance has limited consequences. The major difference with consumers is that their needs can be more intangible and harder to quantify.

Intermediate customers, or customers who purchase the product but are not the end user (such as assemblers or distribution channels), can be analyzed the same way as other buyers, with one important addition. Intermediate customers gain significant bargaining power when they can influence the purchasing decisions of customers downstream. Consumer electronics retailers, jewelry retailers, and agricultural-equipment distributors are examples of distribution channels that exert a strong influence on end customers.

Producers often attempt to diminish channel clout through exclusive arrangements with particular distributors or retailers or by marketing directly to end users. Component manufacturers seek to develop power over assemblers by creating preferences for their components with downstream customers. Such is the case with bicycle parts and with sweeteners. DuPont has created enormous clout by advertising its Stainmaster brand of carpet fibers not only to the carpet manufacturers that actually buy them but also to downstream consumers. Many consumers request Stainmaster carpet even though DuPont is not a carpet manufacturer.

The threat of substitutes

A substitute performs the same or a similar function as an industry's product by a different means. Videoconferencing is a substitute for travel. Plastic is a substitute for aluminum. E-mail is a substitute for express mail. Sometimes, the threat of substitution is downstream or indirect, when a substitute replaces a buyer industry's product. For example, lawn-care products and services are threatened when multifamily homes in urban areas substitute for single-family homes in the suburbs. Software sold to agents is threatened when airline and travel websites substitute for travel agents.

Substitutes are always present, but they are easy to overlook because they may appear to be very different from the industry's product: To someone searching for a Father's Day gift, neckties and power tools may be substitutes. It is a substitute to do without, to purchase a used product rather than a new one, or to do it yourself (bring the service or product in-house).

When the threat of substitutes is high, industry profitability suffers. Substitute products or services limit an industry's profit potential by placing a ceiling on prices. If an industry does not distance itself from substitutes through product performance, marketing, or other means, it will suffer in terms of profitability—and often growth potential.

Substitutes not only limit profits in normal times, they also reduce the bonanza an industry can reap in good times. In emerging economies, for example, the surge in demand for wired telephone lines has been capped as many consumers opt to make a mobile telephone their first and only phone line.

The threat of a substitute is high if:

- It offers an attractive price-performance trade-off to the industry's product. The better the relative value of the substitute, the tighter is the lid on an industry's profit potential. For example, conventional providers of long-distance telephone service have suffered from the advent of inexpensive internet-based phone services such as Vonage and Skype. Similarly, video rental outlets are struggling with the emergence of cable and satellite video-on-demand services, online video rental services such as Netflix, and the rise of internet video sites like Google's YouTube.

- The buyer's cost of switching to the substitute is low. Switching from a proprietary, branded drug to a generic drug usually involves minimal costs, for example, which is why the shift to generics (and the fall in prices) is so substantial and rapid.

Strategists should be particularly alert to changes in other industries that may make them attractive substitutes when they were not before. Improvements in plastic materials, for example, allowed them to substitute for steel in many automobile components. In this way, technological changes or competitive discontinuities in seemingly unrelated businesses can have major impacts on industry profitability. Of course the substitution threat can also shift in favor of an industry, which bodes well for its future profitability and growth potential.

Rivalry among existing competitors

Rivalry among existing competitors takes many familiar forms, including price discounting, new product introductions, advertising campaigns, and service improvements. High rivalry limits the profitability of an industry. The degree to which rivalry drives down an industry's profit potential depends, first, on the *intensity* with which companies compete and, second, on the *basis* on which they compete.

The intensity of rivalry is greatest if:

- Competitors are numerous or are roughly equal in size and power. In such situations, rivals find it hard to avoid poaching business. Without an industry leader, practices desirable for the industry as a whole go unenforced.

- Industry growth is slow. Slow growth precipitates fights for market share.

- Exit barriers are high. Exit barriers, the flip side of entry barriers, arise because of such things as highly specialized assets or management's devotion to a particular business. These barriers keep companies in the market even though they may be earning low or negative returns. Excess capacity remains in use, and the profitability of healthy competitors suffers as the sick ones hang on.

- Rivals are highly committed to the business and have aspirations for leadership, especially if they have goals that go beyond economic performance in the particular industry. High commitment to a business arises for a variety of reasons. For example, state-owned competitors may have goals that include employment or prestige. Units of larger companies may participate in an industry for image reasons or to offer a full line. Clashes of personality and ego have sometimes exaggerated rivalry to the detriment of profitability in fields such as the media and high technology.

- Firms cannot read each other's signals well because of lack of familiarity with one another, diverse approaches to competing, or differing goals.

The strength of rivalry reflects not just the intensity of competition but also the basis of competition. The *dimensions* on which competition takes place, and whether rivals converge to compete on the *same dimensions,* have a major influence on profitability.

Rivalry is especially destructive to profitability if it gravitates solely to price because price competition transfers profits directly from an industry to its customers. Price cuts are usually easy for competitors to see and match, making successive rounds of retaliation likely. Sustained price competition also trains customers to pay less attention to product features and service.

Price competition is most liable to occur if:

- Products or services of rivals are nearly identical and there are few switching costs for buyers. This encourages competitors to cut prices to win new customers. Years of airline price wars reflect these circumstances in that industry.

- Fixed costs are high and marginal costs are low. This creates intense pressure for competitors to cut prices below their average costs, even close to their marginal costs, to steal incremental customers while still making some contribution to covering fixed costs. Many basic-materials businesses, such as paper and aluminum, suffer from this problem, especially if demand is not growing. So do delivery companies with fixed networks of routes that must be served regardless of volume.

- Capacity must be expanded in large increments to be efficient. The need for large capacity expansions, as in the polyvinyl chloride business, disrupts the industry's supply-demand balance and often leads to long and recurring periods of overcapacity and price cutting.

- The product is perishable. Perishability creates a strong temptation to cut prices and sell a product while it still has value. More products and services are perishable than is commonly thought. Just as tomatoes are perishable because they rot, models of computers are perishable because they soon become obsolete, and information may be perishable if it diffuses rapidly or becomes outdated, thereby losing its value. Services such as hotel accommodations are perishable in the sense that unused capacity can never be recovered.

Competition on dimensions other than price—on product features, support services, delivery time, or brand image, for instance—is less likely to erode profitability because it improves customer value and can support higher prices. Also, rivalry focused on such dimensions can improve value relative to substitutes or raise the barriers facing new entrants. While nonprice rivalry sometimes escalates to levels that undermine industry profitability, this is less likely to occur than it is with price rivalry.

As important as the dimensions of rivalry is whether rivals compete on the *same* dimensions. When all or many competitors aim to meet the same needs or compete on the same attributes, the result is zero-sum competition. Here, one firm's gain is often another's loss, driving down profitability. While price competition runs a stronger risk than nonprice competition of becoming zero sum, this may not happen if companies take care to segment their markets, targeting their low-price offerings to different customers.

Rivalry can be positive sum, or actually increase the average profitability of an industry, when each competitor aims to serve the needs of different customer segments, with different mixes of price, products, services, features, or brand identities. Such competition can not only support higher average profitability but also expand the industry, as the needs of more customer groups are better met. The opportunity for positive-sum competition will be greater in industries serving diverse customer groups. With a clear understanding of the structural underpinnings of rivalry, strategists can sometimes take steps to shift the nature of competition in a more positive direction.

Factors, Not Forces

Industry structure, as manifested in the strength of the five competitive forces, determines the industry's long-run profit potential because it determines how the economic value created by the industry is divided—how much is retained by companies in the industry versus bargained away by customers and suppliers, limited by substitutes, or constrained by potential new entrants. By considering all five forces, a strategist keeps overall structure in mind instead of gravitating to any one element. In addition, the strategist's attention remains focused on structural conditions rather than on fleeting factors.

It is especially important to avoid the common pitfall of mistaking certain visible attributes of an industry for its underlying structure. Consider the following:

Industry growth rate

A common mistake is to assume that fast-growing industries are always attractive. Growth does tend to mute rivalry, because an expanding pie offers opportunities for all competitors. But fast growth can put suppliers in a powerful position, and high growth with low entry barriers will draw in entrants. Even without new entrants, a high growth rate will not guarantee profitability if customers are powerful or substitutes are attractive. Indeed, some fast-growth businesses, such as personal computers, have been among the least profitable industries in recent years. A narrow focus on growth is one of the major causes of bad strategy decisions.

Technology and innovation

Advanced technology or innovations are not by themselves enough to make an industry structurally attractive (or unattractive). Mundane, low-technology industries with price-insensitive buyers, high switching costs, or high entry barriers arising from scale economies are often far more profitable than sexy industries, such as software and internet technologies, that attract competitors.[2]

Government

Government is not best understood as a sixth force because government involvement is neither inherently good nor bad for industry profitability. The best way to understand the influence of government on competition is to analyze how specific government policies affect the five competitive forces. For instance, patents raise barriers to entry, boosting industry profit potential. Conversely, government policies favoring unions may raise supplier power and diminish profit potential. Bankruptcy rules that allow failing companies to reorganize rather than exit can lead to excess capacity and intense rivalry. Government operates at multiple levels and through many different policies, each of which will affect structure in different ways.

Complementary products and services

Complements are products or services used together with an industry's product. Complements arise when the customer benefit of two products combined is greater than the sum of each product's value in isolation. Computer hardware and software, for instance, are valuable together and worthless when separated.

In recent years, strategy researchers have highlighted the role of complements, especially in high-technology industries where they are most obvious.[3] By no means, however, do complements appear only there. The value of a car, for example, is greater when the driver also has access to gasoline stations, roadside assistance, and auto insurance.

Complements can be important when they affect the overall demand for an industry's product. However, like government policy, complements are not a sixth force determining industry profitability since the presence of strong complements is not necessarily bad (or good) for industry profitability. Complements affect profitability through the way they influence the five forces.

The strategist must trace the positive or negative influence of complements on all five forces to ascertain their impact on profitability. The presence of complements can raise or lower barriers to entry. In application software, for example, barriers to entry were lowered when producers of complementary operating system software, notably Microsoft, provided tool sets making it easier to write applications. Conversely, the need to attract producers of complements can raise barriers to entry, as it does in video game hardware.

The presence of complements can also affect the threat of substitutes. For instance, the need for appropriate fueling stations makes it difficult for cars using alternative fuels to substitute for conventional vehicles. But complements can also make substitution easier. For example, Apple's iTunes hastened the substitution from CDs to digital music.

Complements can factor into industry rivalry either positively (as when they raise switching costs) or negatively (as when they neutralize product differentiation). Similar analyses can be done for buyer and supplier power. Sometimes companies compete by altering conditions in complementary industries in their favor, such as when videocassette-recorder producer JVC persuaded movie studios to favor its standard in issuing prerecorded tapes even though rival Sony's standard was probably superior from a technical standpoint.

Identifying complements is part of the analyst's work. As with government policies or important technologies, the strategic significance of complements will be best understood through the lens of the five forces.

Changes in Industry Structure

So far, we have discussed the competitive forces at a single point in time. Industry structure proves to be relatively stable, and industry profitability differences are remarkably persistent over time in practice. However, industry structure is constantly undergoing modest adjustment—and occasionally it can change abruptly.

Shifts in structure may emanate from outside an industry or from within. They can boost the industry's profit potential or reduce it. They may be caused by changes in technology, changes in customer needs, or other events. The five competitive forces provide a framework for identifying the most important industry developments and for anticipating their impact on industry attractiveness.

Shifting threat of new entry

Changes to any of the seven barriers described above can raise or lower the threat of new entry. The expiration of a patent, for instance, may unleash new entrants. On the day that Merck's patents for the cholesterol reducer Zocor expired, three pharmaceutical makers entered the market for the drug. Conversely, the proliferation of products in the ice cream industry has gradually filled up the limited freezer space in grocery stores, making it harder for new ice cream makers to gain access to distribution in North America and Europe.

Strategic decisions of leading competitors often have a major impact on the threat of entry. Starting in the 1970s, for example, retailers such as Wal-Mart, Kmart, and Toys "R" Us began to adopt new procurement, distribution, and inventory control technologies with large fixed costs, including automated distribution centers, bar coding, and point-of-sale terminals. These investments increased the economies of scale and made it more difficult for small retailers to enter the business (and for existing small players to survive).

Changing supplier or buyer power

As the factors underlying the power of suppliers and buyers change with time, their clout rises or declines. In the global appliance industry, for instance, competitors including Electrolux, General Electric, and Whirlpool have been squeezed by the consolidation of retail channels (the decline of appliance specialty stores, for instance, and the rise of big-box retailers like Best Buy and Home Depot in the United States). Another example is travel agents, who depend on airlines as a key supplier. When the internet allowed airlines to sell tickets directly to customers, this significantly increased their power to bargain down agents' commissions.

Shifting threat of substitution

The most common reason substitutes become more or less threatening over time is that advances in technology create new substitutes or shift price-performance comparisons in one direction or the other. The earliest microwave ovens, for example, were large and priced above $2,000, making them poor substitutes for conventional ovens. With technological advances, they became serious substitutes. Flash computer memory has improved enough recently to become a meaningful substitute for low-capacity hard-disk drives. Trends in the availability or performance of complementary producers also shift the threat of substitutes.

New bases of rivalry

Rivalry often intensifies naturally over time. As an industry matures, growth slows. Competitors become more alike as industry conventions emerge, technology diffuses, and consumer tastes converge. Industry profitability falls, and weaker competitors are driven from the business. This story has played out in industry after industry; televisions, snowmobiles, and telecommunications equipment are just a few examples.

A trend toward intensifying price competition and other forms of rivalry, however, is by no means inevitable. For example, there has been enormous competitive activity in the U.S. casino industry in recent decades, but most of it has been positive-sum competition directed toward new niches and geographic segments (such as riverboats, trophy properties, Native American reservations, international expansion, and novel customer groups like families). Head-to-head rivalry that lowers prices or boosts the payouts to winners has been limited.

The nature of rivalry in an industry is altered by mergers and acquisitions that introduce new capabilities and ways of competing. Or, technological innovation can reshape rivalry. In the retail brokerage industry, the advent of the internet lowered marginal costs and reduced differentiation, triggering far more intense competition on commissions and fees than in the past.

In some industries, companies turn to mergers and consolidation not to improve cost and quality but to attempt to stop intense competition. Eliminating rivals is a risky strategy, however. The five competitive forces tell us that a profit windfall from removing today's competitors often attracts new competitors and backlash from customers and suppliers. In New York banking, for example, the 1980s and 1990s saw escalating consolidations of commercial and savings banks, including Manufacturers Hanover, Chemical, Chase, and Dime Savings. But today the retail-banking landscape of Manhattan is as diverse as ever, as new entrants such as Wachovia, Bank of America, and Washington Mutual have entered the market.

Implications for Strategy

Understanding the forces that shape industry competition is the starting point for developing strategy. Every company should already know what the average profitability of its industry is and how that has been changing over time. The five forces reveal *why* industry profitability is what it is. Only then can a company incorporate industry conditions into strategy.

The forces reveal the most significant aspects of the competitive environment. They also provide a baseline for sizing up a company's strengths and weaknesses: Where does the company stand versus buyers, suppliers, entrants, rivals, and substitutes? Most importantly, an understanding of industry structure guides managers toward fruitful possibilities for strategic action, which may include any or all of the following: positioning the company to better cope with the current competitive forces; anticipating and exploiting shifts in the forces; and shaping the balance of forces to create a new industry structure that is more favorable to the company. The best strategies exploit more than one of these possibilities.

Positioning the company

Strategy can be viewed as building defenses against the competitive forces or finding a position in the industry where the forces are weakest. Consider, for instance, the position of Paccar in the market for heavy trucks. The heavy-truck industry is structurally challenging. Many buyers operate large fleets or are large leasing companies, with both the leverage and the motivation to drive down the price of one of their largest purchases. Most trucks are built to regulated standards and offer similar features, so price competition is rampant. Capital intensity causes rivalry to be fierce, especially during the recurring cyclical downturns. Unions exercise considerable supplier power. Though there are few direct substitutes for an 18-wheeler, truck buyers face important substitutes for their services, such as cargo delivery by rail.

In this setting, Paccar, a Bellevue, Washington–based company with about 20% of the North American heavy-truck market, has chosen to focus on one group of customers: owner-operators—drivers who own their trucks and contract directly with shippers or serve as subcontractors to larger trucking companies. Such small operators have limited clout as truck buyers. They are also less price sensitive because of their strong emotional ties to and economic dependence on the product. They take great pride in their trucks, in which they spend most of their time.

Paccar has invested heavily to develop an array of features with owner-operators in mind: luxurious sleeper cabins, plush leather seats, noise-insulated cabins, sleek exterior styling, and so on. At the company's extensive network of dealers, prospective buyers use software to select among thousands of options to put their personal signature on their trucks. These customized trucks are built to order, not to stock, and delivered in six to eight weeks. Paccar's trucks also have aerodynamic designs that reduce fuel consumption, and they maintain their resale value better than other trucks. Paccar's roadside assistance program and IT-supported system for distributing spare parts reduce the time a truck is out of service. All these are crucial considerations for an owner-operator. Customers pay Paccar a 10% premium, and its Kenworth and Peterbilt brands are considered status symbols at truck stops.

Paccar illustrates the principles of positioning a company within a given industry structure. The firm has found a portion of its industry where the competitive forces are weaker—where it can avoid buyer power and price-based rivalry. And it has tailored every single part of the value chain to cope well with the forces in its segment. As a result, Paccar has been profitable for 68 years straight and has earned a long-run return on equity above 20%.

In addition to revealing positioning opportunities within an existing industry, the five forces framework allows companies to rigorously analyze entry and exit. Both depend on answering the difficult question: "What is the potential of this business?" Exit is indicated when industry structure is poor or declining and the company has no prospect of a superior positioning. In considering entry into a new industry, creative strategists can use the framework to spot an industry with a good future before this good future is reflected in the prices of acquisition candidates. Five forces analysis may also reveal industries that are not necessarily attractive for the average entrant but in which a company has good reason to believe it can surmount entry barriers at lower cost than most firms or has a unique ability to cope with the industry's competitive forces.

Exploiting industry change

Industry changes bring the opportunity to spot and claim promising new strategic positions if the strategist has a sophisticated understanding of the competitive forces and their underpinnings. Consider, for instance, the evolution of the music industry during the past decade. With the advent of the internet and the digital distribution of music, some analysts predicted the birth of thousands of music labels (that is, record companies that develop artists and bring their music to market). This, the analysts argued, would break a pattern that had held since Edison invented the phonograph: Between three and six major record companies had always dominated the industry. The internet would, they predicted, remove distribution as a barrier to entry, unleashing a flood of new players into the music industry.

A careful analysis, however, would have revealed that physical distribution was not the crucial barrier to entry. Rather, entry was barred by other benefits that large music labels enjoyed. Large labels could pool the risks of developing new artists over many bets, cushioning the impact of inevitable failures. Even more important, they had advantages in breaking through the clutter and getting their new artists heard. To do so, they could promise radio stations and record stores access to well-known artists in exchange for promotion of new artists. New labels would find this nearly impossible to match. The major labels stayed the course, and new music labels have been rare.

This is not to say that the music industry is structurally unchanged by digital distribution. Unauthorized downloading created an illegal but potent substitute. The labels tried for years to develop technical platforms for digital distribution themselves, but major companies hesitated to sell their music through a platform owned by a rival. Into this vacuum stepped Apple with its iTunes music store, launched in 2003 to support its iPod music player. By permitting the creation of a powerful new gatekeeper, the major labels allowed industry structure to shift against them. The number of major record companies has actually declined—from six in 1997 to four today—as companies struggled to cope with the digital phenomenon.

When industry structure is in flux, new and promising competitive positions may appear. Structural changes open up new needs and new ways to serve existing needs. Established leaders may overlook these or be constrained by past strategies from pursuing them. Smaller competitors in the industry can capitalize on such changes, or the void may well be filled by new entrants.

Shaping industry structure

When a company exploits structural change, it is recognizing, and reacting to, the inevitable. However, companies also have the ability to shape industry structure. A firm can lead its industry toward new ways of competing that alter the five forces for the better. In reshaping structure, a company wants its competitors to follow so that the entire industry will be transformed. While many industry participants may benefit in the process, the innovator can benefit most if it can shift competition in directions where it can excel.

An industry's structure can be reshaped in two ways: by redividing profitability in favor of incumbents or by expanding the overall profit pool. Redividing the industry pie aims to increase the share of profits to industry competitors instead of to suppliers, buyers, substitutes, and keeping out potential entrants. Expanding the profit pool involves increasing the overall pool of economic value generated by the industry in which rivals, buyers, and suppliers can all share.

Redividing profitability. To capture more profits for industry rivals, the starting point is to determine which force or forces are currently constraining industry profitability and address them. A company can potentially influence all of the competitive forces. The strategist's goal here is to reduce the share of profits that leak to suppliers, buyers, and substitutes or are sacrificed to deter entrants.

To neutralize supplier power, for example, a firm can standardize specifications for parts to make it easier to switch among suppliers. It can cultivate additional vendors, or alter technology to avoid a powerful supplier group altogether. To counter customer power, companies may expand services that raise buyers' switching costs or find alternative means of reaching customers to neutralize powerful channels. To temper profit-eroding price rivalry, companies can invest more heavily in unique products, as pharmaceutical firms have done, or expand support services to customers. To scare off entrants, incumbents can elevate the fixed cost of competing—for instance, by escalating their R&D or marketing expenditures. To limit the threat of substitutes, companies can offer better value through new features or wider product accessibility. When soft-drink producers introduced vending machines and convenience store channels, for example, they dramatically improved the availability of soft drinks relative to other beverages.

Sysco, the largest food-service distributor in North America, offers a revealing example of how an industry leader can change the structure of an industry for the better. Food-service distributors purchase food and related items from farmers and food processors. They then warehouse and deliver these items to restaurants, hospitals, employer cafeterias, schools, and other food-service institutions. Given low barriers to entry, the food-service distribution industry has historically been highly fragmented, with numerous local competitors. While rivals try to cultivate customer relationships, buyers are price sensitive because food represents a large share of their costs. Buyers can also choose the substitute approaches of purchasing directly from manufacturers or using retail sources, avoiding distributors altogether. Suppliers wield bargaining power: They are often large companies with strong brand names that food preparers and consumers recognize. Average profitability in the industry has been modest.

Sysco recognized that, given its size and national reach, it might change this state of affairs. It led the move to introduce private-label distributor brands with specifications tailored to the food-service market, moderating supplier power. Sysco emphasized value-added services to buyers such as credit, menu planning, and inventory management to shift the basis of competition away from just price. These moves, together with stepped-up investments in information technology and regional distribution centers, substantially raised the bar for new entrants while making the substitutes less attractive. Not surprisingly, the industry has been consolidating, and industry profitability appears to be rising.

Industry leaders have a special responsibility for improving industry structure. Doing so often requires resources that only large players possess. Moreover, an improved industry structure is a public good because it benefits every firm in the industry, not just the company that initiated the improvement. Often, it is more in the interests of an industry leader than any other participant to invest for the common good because leaders will usually benefit the most. Indeed, improving the industry may be a leader's most profitable strategic opportunity, in part because attempts to gain further market share can trigger strong reactions from rivals, customers, and even suppliers.

There is a dark side to shaping industry structure that is equally important to understand. Ill-advised changes in competitive positioning and operating practices can *undermine* industry structure. Faced

Defining the Relevant Industry

DEFINING THE INDUSTRY IN WHICH competition actually takes place is important for good industry analysis, not to mention for developing strategy and setting business unit boundaries. Many strategy errors emanate from mistaking the relevant industry, defining it too broadly or too narrowly. Defining the industry too broadly obscures differences among products, customers, or geographic regions that are important to competition, strategic positioning, and profitability. Defining the industry too narrowly overlooks commonalities and linkages across related products or geographic markets that are crucial to competitive advantage. Also, strategists must be sensitive to the possibility that industry boundaries can shift.

The boundaries of an industry consist of two primary dimensions. First is the *scope of products or services*. For example, is motor oil used in cars part of the same industry as motor oil used in heavy trucks and stationary engines, or are these different industries? The second dimension is *geographic scope*. Most industries are present in many parts of the world. However, is competition contained within each state, or is it national? Does competition take place within regions such as Europe or North America, or is there a single global industry?

The five forces are the basic tool to resolve these questions. If industry structure for two products is the same or very similar (that is, if they have the same buyers, suppliers, barriers to entry, and so forth), then the products are best treated as being part of the same industry. If industry structure differs markedly, however, the two products may be best understood as separate industries.

In lubricants, the oil used in cars is similar or even identical to the oil used in trucks, but the similarity largely ends there. Automotive motor oil is sold to fragmented, generally unsophisticated customers through numerous and often powerful channels, using extensive advertising. Products are packaged

with pressures to gain market share or enamored with innovation for its own sake, managers may trigger new kinds of competition that no incumbent can win. When taking actions to improve their own company's competitive advantage, then, strategists should ask whether they are setting in motion dynamics that will undermine industry structure in the long run. In the early days of the personal computer industry, for instance, IBM tried to make up for its late entry by offering an open in small containers and logistical costs are high, necessitating local production. Truck and power generation lubricants are sold to entirely different buyers in entirely different ways using a separate supply chain. Industry structure (buyer power, barriers to entry, and so forth) is substantially different. Automotive oil is thus a distinct industry from oil for truck and stationary engine uses. Industry profitability will differ in these two cases, and a lubricant company will need a separate strategy for competing in each area.

Differences in the five competitive forces also reveal the geographic scope of competition. If an industry has a similar structure in every country (rivals, buyers, and so on), the presumption is that competition is global, and the five forces analyzed from a global perspective will set average profitability. A single global strategy is needed. If an industry has quite different structures in different geographic regions, however, each region may well be a distinct industry. Otherwise, competition would have leveled the differences. The five forces analyzed for each region will set profitability there.

The extent of differences in the five forces for related products or across geographic areas is a matter of degree, making industry definition often a matter of judgment. A rule of thumb is that where the differences in any one force are large, and where the differences involve more than one force, distinct industries may well be present.

Fortunately, however, even if industry boundaries are drawn incorrectly, careful five forces analysis should reveal important competitive threats. A closely related product omitted from the industry definition will show up as a substitute, for example, or competitors overlooked as rivals will be recognized as potential entrants. At the same time, the five forces analysis should reveal major differences within overly broad industries that will indicate the need to adjust industry boundaries or strategies.

architecture that would set industry standards and attract complementary makers of application software and peripherals. In the process, it ceded ownership of the critical components of the PC—the operating system and the microprocessor—to Microsoft and Intel. By standardizing PCs, it encouraged price-based rivalry and shifted power to suppliers. Consequently, IBM became the temporarily dominant firm in an industry with an enduringly unattractive structure.

Typical Steps in Industry Analysis

Define the relevant industry:

- What products are in it? Which ones are part of another distinct industry?
- What is the geographic scope of competition?

Identify the participants and segment them into groups, if appropriate:

Who are

- the buyers and buyer groups?

- the suppliers and supplier groups?

- the competitors?

- the substitutes?

- the potential entrants?

Assess the underlying drivers of each competitive force to determine which forces are strong and which are weak and why.

Determine overall industry structure, and test the analysis for consistency:

- *Why* is the level of profitability what it is?
- Which are the *controlling* forces for profitability?
- Is the industry analysis consistent with actual long-run profitability?
- Are more-profitable players better positioned in relation to the five forces?

Analyze recent and likely future changes in each force, both positive and negative.

Identify aspects of industry structure that might be influenced by competitors, by new entrants, or by your company.

Expanding the profit pool. When overall demand grows, the industry's quality level rises, intrinsic costs are reduced, or waste is eliminated, the pie expands. The total pool of value available to competitors, suppliers, and buyers grows. The total profit pool expands, for example, when channels become more competitive or when an industry discovers latent buyers for its product that are not currently being served. When soft-drink producers rationalized their independent bottler networks to make them more efficient and effective, both the soft-drink companies and the bottlers benefited. Overall value can also expand when firms work collaboratively with suppliers to improve coordination and limit unnecessary costs incurred in the supply chain. This lowers the inherent cost structure of the industry, allowing higher profit, greater demand through lower prices, or both. Or, agreeing on quality standards can bring up industrywide quality and service levels, and hence prices, benefiting rivals, suppliers, and customers.

Expanding the overall profit pool creates win-win opportunities for multiple industry participants. It can also reduce the risk of destructive rivalry that arises when incumbents attempt to shift bargaining power or capture more market share. However, expanding the pie does not reduce the importance of industry structure. How the expanded pie is divided will ultimately be determined by the five forces. The most successful companies are those that expand the industry profit pool in ways that allow them to share disproportionately in the benefits.

Defining the industry

The five competitive forces also hold the key to defining the relevant industry (or industries) in which a company competes. Drawing industry boundaries correctly, around the arena in which competition actually takes place, will clarify the causes of profitability and the appropriate unit for setting strategy. A company needs a separate strategy for each distinct industry. Mistakes in industry definition made by competitors present opportunities for staking out superior strategic positions. (See the sidebar "Defining the Relevant Industry.")

Competition and Value

The competitive forces reveal the drivers of industry competition. A company strategist who understands that competition extends well beyond existing rivals will detect wider competitive threats

Common Pitfalls

In conducting the analysis avoid the following common mistakes:

- Defining the industry too broadly or too narrowly.

- Making lists instead of engaging in rigorous analysis.

- Paying equal attention to all of the forces rather than digging deeply into the most important ones.

- Confusing effect (price sensitivity) with cause (buyer economics).

- Using static analysis that ignores industry trends.

- Confusing cyclical or transient changes with true structural changes.

- Using the framework to declare an industry attractive or unattractive rather than using it to guide strategic choices.

---

and be better equipped to address them. At the same time, thinking comprehensively about an industry's structure can uncover opportunities: differences in customers, suppliers, substitutes, potential entrants, and rivals that can become the basis for distinct strategies yielding superior performance. In a world of more open competition and relentless change, it is more important than ever to think structurally about competition.

Understanding industry structure is equally important for investors as for managers. The five competitive forces reveal whether an industry is truly attractive, and they help investors anticipate positive or negative shifts in industry structure before they are obvious. The five forces distinguish short-term blips from structural changes and allow investors to take advantage of undue pessimism or optimism. Those companies whose strategies have industry-transforming potential become far clearer. This deeper thinking about competition is a more powerful way to achieve genuine investment success than the financial projections and trend extrapolation that dominate today's investment analysis.

If both executives and investors looked at competition this way, capital markets would be a far more effective force for company success and economic prosperity. Executives and investors would both be focused on the same fundamentals that drive sustained profitability. The conversation between investors and executives would focus on the structural, not the transient. Imagine the improvement in company performance—and in the economy as a whole—if all the energy expended in "pleasing the Street" were redirected toward the factors that create true economic value.

Originally published in January 2008. Reprint R0801E.

Notes

1. For a discussion of the value chain framework, see Michael E. Porter, *Competitive Advantage: Creating and Sustaining Superior Performance* (The Free Press, 1998).

2. For a discussion of how internet technology improves the attractiveness of some industries while eroding the profitability of others, see Michael E. Porter, "Strategy and the Internet" (HBR, March 2001).

3. See, for instance, Adam M. Brandenburger and Barry J. Nalebuff, *Co-opetition* (Currency Doubleday, 1996).

Health Care Needs Real Competition

by Leemore S. Dafny and Thomas H. Lee

HERE'S THE GOOD NEWS: Thanks to the Affordable Care Act, or Obamacare, more Americans have access to health care than ever before. The bad news? The care itself hasn't improved much. Despite the hard work of dedicated providers, our health care system remains chaotic, unreliable, inefficient, and crushingly expensive.

There is no shortage of proposed solutions, many of which have appeared in these pages. But central to the best of them is the idea that health care needs more competition. In other sectors of the economy, competition improves quality and efficiency, spurs innovation, and drives down costs. Health care should be no exception.

Industry executives may think they have more than enough competition already. They spend their days fighting to keep patients from being lured away by competitors, new entrants, and alternative sources of care. Their cost of delivering care continues to climb while hard-bargaining insurers hold the line on reimbursements, or even reduce them. Compounding the problem, the services that account for most of providers' profits, such as radiology and ambulatory surgery, are the ones most vulnerable to poaching. It's hard to sleep at night when every one of Michael Porter's five forces is arrayed against you.

Many health care organizations have sought to stymie competition by consolidating, buying up market share and increasing their bargaining power with insurers and suppliers. From 2005 to 2015, the number of U.S. hospital mergers per year doubled (see the exhibit "Hospital mergers on the rise").

Leaders of proposed health care mergers usually tout their potential to enhance value. But when asked to name a merger that has improved outcomes or lowered prices, they generally fall silent. That shouldn't be a surprise. Years of research by one of us (Dafny) and others show that provider consolidation typically raises prices, with no measurable impact on quality. Indeed, merging with a competitor that has the same fundamental problems you do often increases the scale of problems without creating solutions. State and federal antitrust agencies have successfully quashed some mergers that looked like they would reduce competition, but the government can't possibly challenge every case. It's an endless game of Whac-A-Mole, and providers continue to bet that they'll be among the "moles" to win.

Despite its short-term appeal, consolidation for the purpose of increasing negotiating clout will diminish the potential for the health care sector to create value and thrive in the long run. A new competitive marketplace is emerging in health care today, and organizations must decide whether to continue to deflect competition or make competing on value central to their strategy. In this article, we describe the fundamental shifts that are under way and outline the roles that all key stakeholders—regulators, providers, insurers, employers, and patients themselves—must play to transform health care.

Barriers to Competition

To compete on value, providers must meet patients' needs better or at a lower cost than their competitors do, or both. But this kind of competition has been slow to arrive, because four interrelated barriers have blocked the way.

Limited reimbursement-based incentives
For the most part, providers have not been rewarded financially for delivering value, nor have they been meaningfully penalized for failing to do so. Many hospitals are able to hit their financial targets by

Idea in Brief

The Problem

The U.S. health care system is inefficient, unreliable, and crushingly expensive. In other sectors, competition improves quality and efficiency, spurs innovation, and drives down costs. Yet health care organizations are actively consolidating in order to stymie competition.

The Solution

Health care payers and providers must stop fighting the emergence of a competitive health care marketplace and make competing on value central to their strategy.

The Way Forward

All stakeholders in the health care industry can catalyze change in five ways: Put patients at the center of care, create choice, stop rewarding volume, standardize value-based methods of payment, and make data on outcomes transparent.

competing on the strength of their brand and marketing messages—for example, claiming to have the latest technology, best facilities, or highest magazine rankings. A provider's brand is often unrelated to its actual performance on outcomes, but it can enhance the provider's ability to negotiate favorable reimbursement rates with insurers. Because providers' revenues have not been contingent on the value of the care they deliver, they've had little incentive to compete on that basis.

Limited market-share incentives

Even when providers have improved value, they have not been sufficiently rewarded with increased market share. Consumers have been largely insulated from costs and thus have had little need to bargain hunt—and insurers haven't done it for them—so lowering costs rarely generates an influx of new patients. Nor have providers gained market share by demonstrating improved quality. Most publicly available quality metrics are process measures (such as mammography and cervical cancer screening rates) that vary little among providers. Patients have been only mildly interested in such data—they assume providers are following guidelines—and have been unwilling to switch providers on the basis of them.

Hospital mergers on the rise

Health care providers may seek to blunt competition by consolidating. Over the past decade, the annual number of hospital mergers in the U.S. has doubled.

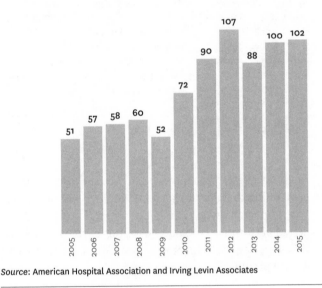

Source: American Hospital Association and Irving Levin Associates

Inadequate data on value

Good data on outcomes and costs is essential to designing and optimizing value-based care; unfortunately, there's very little of it available. To the extent that providers have gathered data on outcomes, their collection and analysis methodologies have rarely been standardized, so the data sets are difficult to use for comparison, competition, or learning. Data on costs, at the level of individual patients or procedures, has been rudimentary at best, the result of a business environment with rampant cross-subsidization. Lucrative commercially insured patients, for example, subsidize lower-paying Medicare and Medicaid patients. Profitable services (such as radiology) subsidize unprofitable services (such as mental health care). Many providers find that using revenue from profitable services and contracts to cover losses elsewhere is simpler than doing the brutal work of measuring service- and patient-level costs and identifying ways to reduce them without compromising quality. In the absence of meaningful data on outcomes and costs, value-focused work has generally gone undetected and thus unrewarded.

Inadequate know-how

Finally, health care has suffered from a simple know-how problem. In the absence of financial incentives to pursue value and without good data to guide leadership, the management skills necessary for transforming care delivery have not developed. Health care leaders have not learned how to achieve consensus quickly, overcome cultural resistance to change, or nurture high-performing teams. They have not mastered the principles of lean management or high-reliability cultures. And they have not gained experience in making tough, data-driven strategic choices in the face of powerful resistance, such as when and where to cut services in order to improve efficiency.

Falling Barriers

These intertwined barriers have blocked competition in health care for decades, but we are at a critical turning point. A combination of market trends, advances in information technology, and a turnover in health care leadership is shifting the environment.

Increasing reimbursement-based incentives

In January 2015, Sylvia Mathews Burwell, the secretary of the U.S. Department of Health and Human Services, announced plans to shift 30% of Medicare fee-for-service payments—$362 billion in 2014—to alternative models that explicitly reward value. That change is slated to take effect by the end of 2016; the figure will rise to 50% by the end of 2018. Under the new contracts, providers that perform well on both quality and cost will see their reimbursements increase; underperformers will see them fall. Soon after Burwell's announcement, Cigna declared that it was committing to the same goals, and other payers are following suit.

Even if insurers fall short of these targets, the message is clear: They've become ever more hostile to fee-for-service payment increases. We spoke with the leaders of a major hospital system about a recent contract negotiation with a commercial insurer. The system sought an 8% increase and were stunned by the insurer's counteroffer: a 20% decrease. After public threats from both sides, the parties agreed on a contract that gave the provider no increase in the first year and small decreases in the next two years.

That provider's leaders and most others we've spoken with agree: Providers can no longer negotiate and cross-subsidize their way out of their financial challenges. As personnel, equipment, and drug costs rise faster than revenues and as the path to higher revenues increasingly depends on better performance, the need for new value-oriented business models has become pressing.

Growing market-share incentives

Until recently, consumers had little reason to seek out value in health care. But as their cost burden rises, their behavior is changing. They're increasingly signing up for lower-cost narrowed networks that limit access to more-expensive providers and choosing high-deductible or tiered insurance products that require them to pay more out of pocket for higher-cost care.

In addition, faster flows of information are allowing insurers to steer patients to similar—but cheaper—options more often and more effectively. For example, a patient who is scheduled for an elective operation might get a phone call from her insurer informing her that she'll pay a lot less out of pocket if she has the same operation by the same surgeon in an ambulatory facility rather than the hospital where it has been scheduled. Presented with options like this, patients tend to call the surgeon—who may be indifferent to where the operation is performed—and the site gets switched.

Thus even if providers manage to renew their contracts with insurers at the same payment levels, they can still lose market share because their customer base is defecting to lower-cost alternatives. Conversations at patients' kitchen tables are becoming as important to providers as their own contract discussions at negotiating tables—perhaps more so.

Meanwhile, increasing numbers of large employers and some insurers are implementing bundled payment programs that provide incentives to patients to get cancer care or major operations at medical centers with outstanding reputations for value. These employers and insurers are figuring out which kinds of patients will travel and how far and tailoring their programs accordingly. The pain from loss of market share is still minimal at most organizations, but the fear of patient defection is real and growing.

Improving data

Two developments are dismantling the data barrier: (1) the emergence of consistent standards and incentives for measuring outcomes and (2) the widespread adoption of technologies that enable data sharing. The National Quality Forum provides a gold standard for quality measures, and the International Consortium for Health Outcomes Measurement is defining minimum sets of outcomes measures for use in evaluating care for common conditions. In addition, Medicare bundled-payment programs increasingly include monetary incentives for publicly reporting outcomes. Given Medicare's prior pattern with patient-experience data (reporting was voluntary at first, then mandatory), we expect a similar trajectory with disclosure of outcomes data.

Outcomes data is also becoming easier to collect and compare, in part because electronic medical records (EMRs) now sit on nearly every clinician's desk. Clinicians have legitimate gripes about EMRs, but their continually improving interoperability across delivery systems has major implications for competition. When clinicians can readily see notes and lab results for patients receiving care in other organizations, they can make informed determinations about which ones provide the greatest value—and favor those providers by referring patients there.

Consider Atrius Health, an organization in the Boston area with nearly 750 physicians and 16 hospital affiliates. Atrius has functional access to EMRs for all those clinicians and providers, so its doctors can coordinate care effectively with them. All those hospitals can—and do—compete for Atrius's business.

Expanding know-how

As the old guard that has long dominated medicine's leadership exits the stage, the know-how barrier is falling. In the past, leaders of health care organizations were physicians who prized autonomy above all else. Today's leaders are younger physicians who value teamwork over autonomy, recognize that managerial skills are essential, and actively seek out opportunities to acquire them.

These emerging leaders are pursuing degrees in management and strategy at business schools and participating in training programs for health care executives. The venerable two-year fellowship at the National Institutes of Health that used to launch physicians into leadership roles has been replaced with stints at consulting firms or management positions in other parts of health care or business. Look at the top ranks of health care organizations, and you'll see 70-year-old physicians being replaced by MD/MBAs in their 40s.

Leaders today are not being picked for their skill in defending the status quo and pushing back at external foes. They are selected for their ability to lead performance improvement—giving organizations the ability to compete and win.

Catalyzing Competition

As barriers to competition crumble, the health care industry must take action to create positive change. There are five ways to accelerate progress.

Put patients first

A central tenet of most businesses is that customers come first. For many providers, though, keeping peace with internal stakeholders (particularly physicians) often takes precedence. But it's only when organizations prioritize patient welfare that they can improve and compete on value.

Consider the initiative launched by the Cleveland Clinic in 2011 to offer same-day appointments to patients. At the time it was common for patients who needed specialty care to wait weeks or even months for appointments, often enduring anxiety during the delays and occasionally suffering complications that might have been averted with more timely care. Providers had little incentive to solve the problem; indeed, at academic medical centers, some physicians famously took pride in the length of their waiting lists. When the Cleveland Clinic began asking patients who called for appointments whether they'd like to be seen that day, other care centers rapidly followed suit. Although waits are still all too common, a web search for "same-day appointments" at academic medical centers now delivers thousands of hits. This simple development underscores the power of a patient-first approach to catalyze competition.

To be sure, reorganizing care delivery to meet patients' needs is not easy. Unlike same-day appointments, which are fairly straightforward to implement, other changes can be highly disruptive. For example, the first step in any customer-centric strategy is segmentation. But segmenting patients into groups with similar needs, and assembling multidisciplinary teams to care for those groups, challenges the entrenched organizational structure of medicine and the flow of money within it. Thus it's often met with resistance, particularly from the old guard.

But even the old guard knows that teams are better than individuals at providing coordinated, integrated, efficient care. And in a value-driven marketplace, teams are not just nice to have—they're essential to competitiveness.

Create choice

For change to take hold in health care, decision makers at every level need real choices: consumers when picking health insurance products, patients when choosing clinicians, and clinicians when selecting the facilities where their patients receive care. When choices exist, clear winners and losers emerge, creating relentless pressure on all providers to improve. Rousing speeches by executives and policymakers can generate some enthusiasm for change, but fear of losing market share to a competitor is uniquely effective in mobilizing organizations. Organizations that are hungry or afraid—be they new entrants or established players—are often the most innovative, generating new choices and stimulating competition.

Take Advocate Health Care, a Chicago-based provider system formed in 1995 in a market dominated by famous academic medical centers like the University of Chicago and Northwestern. Advocate believed that the sustainable strategy in the long run was to offer patients a new choice—a clinically integrated health system focused on increasing quality of care while holding the line on total costs. After the Affordable Care Act was passed, Advocate committed to reorganizing and optimizing patient care in order to succeed under "shared savings" arrangements, which reward providers for beating cost benchmarks while meeting quality goals, and global capitation contracts, which pay providers a fixed amount of revenue per member, per month.

It was a bold move: To succeed, Advocate had to reduce the total cost of care while improving quality and service. But fee-for-service contracts, which dominated the reimbursement landscape at the time, actually punish providers for reducing spending—and fail to compensate them for activities that improve efficiency.

Advocate's gamble paid off. It is thriving under global capitation, which accounts for nearly 40% of its revenues today (up from 11% in 2011), and generates another 30% to 35% of revenues from shared savings arrangements. Advocate has reduced spending growth to below local averages and has partnered with insurers to pass the savings along to consumers through more-affordable, narrow network products. Today Advocate is the largest health system in Illinois and has the state's largest physician network. Growth via acquisitions and affiliations has played a supporting role in Advocate's strategy, but its success derives not from its size but from its commitment to offering patients innovative new choices.

To seriously challenge market leaders, health care needs the kind of hunger demonstrated by Advocate—and by a senior executive we spoke to at the number two provider in another region. "We see [the market leader] as our competition, but they don't think of us as theirs," she told us. "It's perfect. We are eating their lunch, and they are just waking up to it." That provider has launched a wide range of patient-centric initiatives and organizational improvements, some of which have earned the most sincere form of flattery from its rival—imitation.

Stop rewarding volume

Value-based payments may be ramping up, but the vast majority of money in health care still moves through the fee-for-service system, which encourages inefficiency and overutilization. Simply layering modest incentives to offer services that might reduce costs—care coordination, for example—atop a fee-for-service chassis only results in more volume, even if it is better coordinated. Indeed, there's no evidence that overall health care costs go down when the main intervention is adding services, however well intended. So don't hold your breath waiting for savings to accrue from compensating physicians for developing end-of-life care plans with patients, for example. What leads to cost savings is reorganizing care around the delivery of health rather than health care.

One step in the right direction is to pay providers one lump sum to treat a patient's condition over the entire episode of care or a defined period of time. Bundled payments are a prime example. As Michael Porter and Robert Kaplan detail in their July–August 2016 HBR article, "How to Pay for Health Care," bundles are not a new idea, and their ability to drive value improvement in focused areas like transplantation is well established. But for bundles and other non-fee-for-service models to move from theory to practice on a broad scale, the incentives must be compelling and inescapable.

Standardize methods to pay for value

Both public and private payers must do more than push financial risk onto providers. They need to agree on the rules of the game. That means identifying segments of patients with similar needs—typically groups with the same condition (such as heart failure or prostate cancer)—and agreeing on the outcomes measures that will be used to assess the quality of care for the conditions. Payers should propose common methods for collecting and analyzing data, using input from providers, government agencies, and health care IT experts. And they should agree on a common payment structure for episodes of care so that providers can focus on improving care delivery rather than navigating the reimbursement maze. Insurers,

Catalysts for competition

Five interrelated actions can spur value-based competition in health care.

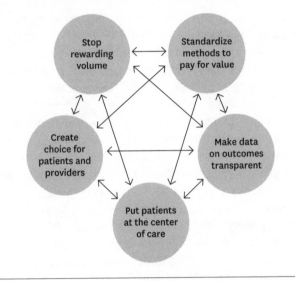

meanwhile, can use the standardized data to identify and reward the highest-value providers.

While patients can't be perfectly divided into all-inclusive, mutually exclusive categories, some movement in this direction is surely better than none. Working with providers, payers can change the game in health care by defining some rules.

Make outcomes transparent

Even when health care providers collect data on outcomes, and even when the data is standardized, providers often resist sharing results publicly. But real competition will emerge only if outcomes data is made available to decision makers, be they patients, payers, or other providers. Data transparency has already driven improvement in clinical outcomes in transplantation, cardiac surgery, in vitro fertilization, and patient experience. Consumers may initially pay the data little heed, but providers will still vie to earn the highest marks, and payers and referring physicians will ultimately shift volume toward those that do.

Such transparency unnerves many providers, who worry that factors beyond their control will negatively impact their results and that reported data will be misinterpreted. For example, "safety net" institutions that serve poorer populations and teaching hospitals that attract the sickest patients can look worse than those with healthier patient populations. Although risk adjustment methodologies can mitigate the effects of differences among patient populations, transparency will sometimes lead to rankings of providers that are not fair. Nevertheless, transparency can be more effective than financial incentives in driving quality improvement—and it's often cheaper.

Stakeholder Roles

As the competitive marketplace emerges, no one wants to be the last to embrace the rapid changes under way. Here are some of the ways key stakeholders—governments, providers, payers, employers, and consumers—could be (and in many cases are) responding to the new landscape.

Government as regulator

Governments and their myriad agencies perform important regulatory functions, ranging from establishing and enforcing insurer-solvency requirements to specifying which health care facilities need backup electricity generators. But government also has a vital role to play in protecting and promoting competition. In particular, the Federal Trade Commission, the antitrust division of the Department of Justice, and state attorneys general all have a mandate to enforce competition law. However, the volume of health care mergers and the pace of change in business practices exceed the resources available to investigate them.

Increasing funding for these agencies is a wise long-term investment in the productivity of the health care sector. Entrenched anti-competitive practices—such as Blue Cross Blue Shield's "exclusive territory" agreements, which preclude affiliates from competing against one another in most geographies—are difficult to challenge and undo. Dissolving mergers that prove anticompetitive is costly and exceedingly difficult as well. It is much more effective to get ahead of the gamesmanship.

Governmental agencies can also promote competition by monitoring and reporting on changes—particularly prospective mergers—in local health care markets. This will require new resources, but the business adage about spending money to make money (or in this case, to save it) applies.

One agency playing this role is the Massachusetts Health Policy Commission (HPC), established and funded by state legislation enacted in 2012. The HPC requires all providers to disclose merger and acquisition plans and conducts analyses of sizeable transactions. Merging entities may be asked to describe how their deals will benefit consumers and, after the fact, to report publicly on their progress toward goals. The HPC also set a target of 3.6% for the annual growth rate of total health care spending over the period 2013 through 2017—a figure that matched the projected growth in state GDP from 2013 to 2015. Providers complained that this target was arbitrary, but it had the intended effect: In contract negotiations with insurers, providers shifted their demands for reimbursement increases downward to reflect the goal.

Finally, regulators should seek to lower barriers for new entrants into payer and provider marketplaces. State legislatures can repeal (or not enact) laws that protect incumbents rather than consumers. Such laws are common: Texas, for example, requires that patients see a physician face-to-face in order to pursue a telehealth consultation, even when there are no legitimate health or safety justifications for such a requirement. Some states have created similar obstacles for retail health clinics that otherwise could safely and effectively serve patients. These barriers to competition reflect the tendency of state medical societies to resist challenges to traditional health-care-delivery models and demonstrate the need for government to ramp up efforts to promote delivery innovations, particularly in regions where competition among traditional providers is weak.

Government as payer

Medicare and Medicaid have emerged as potent leaders of change—developing innovative payment mechanisms, setting ambitious targets, and using their sheer scale to move the marketplace. Consider Medicare's Comprehensive Care for Joint Replacement (CJR) program under which hospitals in 67 regions receive a lump sum for the entire episode of care involving total hip and knee replacements, rather than individual payments for discrete services (radiology, anesthesia, surgery, and so on). The key difference between the CJR and Medicare's earlier bundled payment initiatives is that prior programs were voluntary; the CJR is mandatory.

Instead of meeting to discuss *whether* to participate in the CJR, hospital leaders now meet to discuss *how* to do so. Hospitals that organize to improve quality and efficiency can expect to share in the savings; those that do not should be prepared to lose money. In July, the Centers for Medicare & Medicaid Services announced plans to implement the approach for acute myocardial infarction, coronary artery bypass graft surgery, and femur fracture surgery. Those programs are slated to launch in July 2017.

Medicaid is becoming a change agent on a state-by-state basis as well. In Arkansas, Tennessee, and Ohio, Medicaid programs have recently implemented mandatory bundled payment programs that cover more than a dozen conditions, including asthma, pregnancy, attention deficit disorder, and congestive heart failure. Regulations in Arizona, Pennsylvania, and South Carolina require that commercial insurers covering Medicaid enrollees generate 20% to 30% of their revenues from value-based payment methods over the next three years. New York State has declared that 80% to 90% of Medicaid payments must be delivered through value-based models by 2020.

The incentive for providers to comply with these mandates is compelling. In many states, the Medicaid-covered share of the population is now pushing 25%. If those patients go elsewhere, many providers won't have the critical mass they need to stay afloat. A decade ago, the idea of providers actively pursuing Medicaid patients would have defied credulity; the fact that they are now competing fiercely to hold onto that market share is a sign of the magnitude of the change under way.

Providers

Health care providers must be the protagonists in this unfolding story. Boards of directors have to ask questions at the heart of strategy: "What is our goal? How are we going to differentiate ourselves?"

Providers instinctively avoid new payment models, but they need to recognize the writing on the wall and embrace models that reward value, despite their risks and imperfections. They should work with other providers as well as insurers to develop new care-delivery schemes such as bundles and to engage in the open-ended work of making them better. Where a provider's rivals are paralyzed, there is a competitive opportunity both to redesign care delivery so that it improves value and to reshape the payment models that reward it.

The emergence of the Health Care Transformation Task Force, a consortium of patients, payers, providers, and purchasers committed to improving health care, is compelling evidence that the landscape is changing. The task force includes 26 provider organizations that have committed to generating more than 75% of their revenues via payment arrangements that hold them accountable for cost and quality by 2020. The providers have also declared their support for voluntary reporting on outcomes for patients undergoing surgery as part of Medicare's CJR bundle program.

These are not small providers under the spell of charismatic leaders. They include enormous delivery systems, such as Trinity Health, Advocate Health Care, Ascension, Dignity Health, Partners HealthCare, and Providence Health & Services. Nor are they merely paying lip service to the need for change: Task force providers and payers reported that 41% of their business was in new value-based payment models at the end of 2015—an increase from 30% at the end of 2014.

One path providers should *not* pursue is consolidation that does not directly lead to improved value for patients. Some providers argue that the Affordable Care Act encourages mergers as a means to create larger organizations that are more resilient in the face of financial risk. However, the real goal of health care reform is to encourage alliances that are better, not just bigger. There has been a good deal of horizontal consolidation (among competing hospitals, for example), but these deals often change little about the way care is delivered. In contrast, vertical integration (for example, between hospitals and nonacute facilities) may have greater potential to improve quality and efficiency—and in many cases can be achieved via joint ventures rather than mergers.

Too often, providers seek to grow by searching for targets with similar values and complementary geographic footprints. Instead, providers seeking growth should first consider how they can serve patients better, and only then ask if an acquisition is the way to do it. If managers can't explain how an acquisition will improve the value of care, boards should question whether to pursue it.

Commercial insurers

Private insurers historically have battled with providers to secure the lowest reimbursement for each service. A better way for insurers to keep prices low is to foster and reward competition among providers on value.

First, commercial insurers should align themselves with the Centers for Medicare & Medicaid Services in making value-based payment the norm and adopt a similar structure for bundled payments. Early experience with bundles suggests that providers are more likely to be successful when they reorganize care delivery for all patients, not just those of a single payer, and when they implement bundles for multiple conditions, not just one. For this reason, commercial insurers should work together to create common definitions and outcomes measures for bundles and other value-based payment models.

At the same time, insurers should compete vigorously with one another for market share on the basis of creative new product offerings. Like providers, they should engage in more market segmentation (for example, creating insurance plans designed for families with young children). Simply getting bigger is not a strategy. The insurance industry is already highly consolidated; meanwhile, the pace of new-product design and levels of customer satisfaction are disappointing, to say the least.

Commercial insurers should continue to resist fee-for-service payment increases. This will keep a lid on costs and compel providers to focus on value rather than volume. Insurers should also combat provider consolidation by creating programs that effectively expand the market, such as offering patients incentives to travel to other regions to get quality care at a lower cost and negotiating prices on the basis of regional or national benchmarks.

Patients and employers

Consumers can energize the marketplace by creating real consequences for the winners and losers. If patients choose to receive care from high-value providers, which may mean traveling farther, then providers will focus their energy on improving care delivery. Patients should no longer settle for care that is not coordinated, compassionate, safe, and technically excellent. When it falls short, they should be vocal—or leave. Consumers should also demand a broader set of insurance choices from their employers—perhaps via private insurance exchanges—so that they can vote with their feet and switch to products that best suit their needs. Only then will payers find it profitable to introduce easy-to-navigate plans that reward low-cost, high-quality providers.

Employers also wield considerable influence. Major corporations such as Walmart are already collaborating with providers and insurers to create programs that encourage employees to seek out high-value care. Other entities that work on behalf of employees are proving similarly catalytic. The California Public Employees' Retirement System (CalPERS), which provides health insurance coverage for 1.3 million people, is a case in point. CalPERS was seeing wide variation in prices for many procedures its members received, depending on where they got their care. For example, it was paying anywhere from $12,000 to $75,000 for joint replacement surgery, although there was no clear difference in the quality of the services. To address the problem, CalPERS introduced a "reference price" of $30,000—the maximum it would pay—and assembled a list of high-quality providers willing to accept it. Patients who chose to go to more expensive providers had to pay the difference out of pocket.

Patients responded by shifting their business to lower-cost providers. Faced with the threat of losing market share, most providers cut their prices. From 2011 to 2015, the number of California hospitals charging less than $30,000 for joint replacement increased nearly 60%, from 46 to 72. That kind of change could never have been achieved at the negotiating table; it took the fear of losing business to focus providers' attention. Once it was clear that some well-regarded hospitals in California could meet CalPERS's price, it did not take long for others to follow.

We don't underestimate the turmoil that the health care sector faces in the years ahead. We know that every scenario for transforming the sector will yield unpleasant or unintended consequences for some stakeholders. But the consequences of failing to compete on value will be worse: chaotic, costly care of uneven quality, with a growing toll on individuals and the economy. Real competition must be the path forward. Health care organizations that try to deflect competition are on the wrong side of history and the wrong side of strategy.

Originally published in December 2016. Reprint R1612F

Building Your Company's Vision

by Jim Collins and Jerry I. Porras

We shall not cease from exploration/And the end of all our explor-
ing/Will be to arrive where we started/And know the place for the
first time.
—T.S. Eliot, *Four Quartets*

COMPANIES THAT ENJOY ENDURING success have core values and a
core purpose that remain fixed while their business strategies and
practices endlessly adapt to a changing world. The dynamic of preserving the core while stimulating progress is the reason that companies such as Hewlett-Packard, 3M, Johnson & Johnson, Procter &
Gamble, Merck, Sony, Motorola, and Nordstrom became elite institutions able to renew themselves and achieve superior long-term performance. Hewlett-Packard employees have long known that radical
change in operating practices, cultural norms, and business strategies
does not mean losing the spirit of the HP Way—the company's core
principles. Johnson & Johnson continually questions its structure
and revamps its processes while preserving the ideals embodied in
its credo. In 1996, 3M sold off several of its large mature businesses—
a dramatic move that surprised the business press—to refocus on its
enduring core purpose of solving unsolved problems innovatively.
We studied companies such as these in our research for *Built to Last:*
Successful Habits of Visionary Companies and found that they have
outperformed the general stock market by a factor of 12 since 1925.

Truly great companies understand the difference between what should never change and what should be open for change, between what is genuinely sacred and what is not. This rare ability to manage continuity and change—requiring a consciously practiced discipline—is closely linked to the ability to develop a vision. Vision provides guidance about what core to preserve and what future to stimulate progress toward. But *vision* has become one of the most overused and least understood words in the language, conjuring up different images for different people: of deeply held values, outstanding achievement, societal bonds, exhilarating goals, motivating forces, or raisons d'être. We recommend a conceptual framework to define vision, add clarity and rigor to the vague and fuzzy concepts swirling around that trendy term, and give practical guidance for articulating a coherent vision within an organization. It is a prescriptive framework rooted in six years of research and refined and tested by our ongoing work with executives from a great variety of organizations around the world.

A well-conceived vision consists of two major components: *core ideology* and *envisioned future*. (See the exhibit "Articulating a vision.") Core ideology, the yin in our scheme, defines what we stand for and why we exist. Yin is unchanging and complements yang, the envisioned future. The envisioned future is what we aspire to become, to achieve, to create—something that will require significant change and progress to attain.

Core Ideology

Core ideology defines the enduring character of an organization—a consistent identity that transcends product or market life cycles, technological breakthroughs, management fads, and individual leaders. In fact, the most lasting and significant contribution of those who build visionary companies is the core ideology. As Bill Hewlett said about his longtime friend and business partner David Packard upon Packard's death not long ago, "As far as the company is concerned, the greatest thing he left behind him was a code of ethics known as the HP Way." HP's core ideology, which has guided the company since its inception more than 50 years ago, includes a deep respect for the individual, a

Idea in Brief

Hewlett-Packard. 3M. Sony. Companies with exceptionally durable visions that are "built to last." What distinguishes their visions from most others, those empty muddles that get revised with every passing business fad, but never prompt anything more than a yawn? Enduring companies have clear plans for how they will advance into an uncertain future. But they are equally clear about how they will remain steadfast, about the values and purposes they will always stand for. This *Harvard Business Review* article describes the two components of any lasting vision: **core ideology** and an **envisioned future.**

dedication to affordable quality and reliability, a commitment to community responsibility (Packard himself bequeathed his $4.3 billion of Hewlett-Packard stock to a charitable foundation), and a view that the company exists to make technical contributions for the advancement and welfare of humanity. Company builders such as David Packard, Masaru Ibuka of Sony, George Merck of Merck, William McKnight of 3M, and Paul Galvin of Motorola understood that it is more important to know who you are than where you are going, for where you are going will change as the world around you changes. Leaders die, products become obsolete, markets change, new technologies emerge, and management fads come and go, but core ideology in a great company endures as a source of guidance and inspiration.

Core ideology provides the glue that holds an organization together as it grows, decentralizes, diversifies, expands globally, and develops workplace diversity. Think of it as analogous to the principles of Judaism that held the Jewish people together for centuries without a homeland, even as they spread throughout the Diaspora. Or think of the truths held to be self-evident in the Declaration of Independence, or the enduring ideals and principles of the scientific community that bond scientists from every nationality together in the common purpose of advancing human knowledge. Any effective vision must embody the core ideology of the organization, which in turn consists of two distinct parts: core values, a system of guiding principles and tenets; and core purpose, the organization's most fundamental reason for existence.

Idea in Practice

A company's practices and strategies should change continually; its core ideology should not. Core ideology defines a company's timeless character. It's the glue that holds the enterprise together even when everything else is up for grabs. Core ideology is something you *discover*—by looking inside. It's not something you can invent, much less fake.

A core ideology has two parts:

1. **Core values are the handful of guiding principles by which a company navigates.** They require no external justification. For example, Disney's core values of imagination and wholesomeness stem from the founder's belief that these should be nurtured for their own sake, not merely to capitalize on a business opportunity. Instead of changing its core values, a great company will change its markets—seek out different customers—in order to remain true to its core values.

2. **Core purpose is an organization's most fundamental reason for being.** It should not be confused with the company's current product lines or customer segments. Rather, it reflects people's idealistic motivations for doing the company's work. Disney's core purpose is to make people happy—not to build theme parks and make cartoons.

An envisioned future, the second component of an effective vision, has two elements:

1. **Big, Hairy, Audacious Goals (BHAGs) are ambitious plans that rev up the entire organization.** They typically require 10 to 30 years' work to complete.

2. **Vivid descriptions paint a picture of what it will be like to achieve the BHAGs.** They make the goals vibrant, engaging—and tangible.

Example: In the 1950s, Sony's goal was to "become the company most known for changing the worldwide poor-quality image of Japanese products." It made this BHAG vivid by adding, "Fifty years from now, our brand name will be as well known as any in the world . . . and will signify innovation and quality. . . . 'Made in Japan' will mean something fine, not something shoddy."

Don't confuse your company's core ideology with its envisioned future—in particular, don't confuse a BHAG with a core purpose. A BHAG is a clearly articulated goal that is reachable within 10 to 30 years. But your core purpose can never be completed.

Core values

Core values are the essential and enduring tenets of an organization. A small set of timeless guiding principles, core values require no external justification; they have *intrinsic* value and importance to those inside the organization. The Walt Disney Company's core values of imagination and wholesomeness stem not from market requirements but from the founder's inner belief that imagination and wholesomeness should be nurtured for their own sake. William Procter and James Gamble didn't instill in P&G's culture a focus on product excellence merely as a strategy for success but as an almost religious tenet. And that value has been passed down for more than 15 decades by P&G people. Service to the customer—even to the point of subservience—is a way of life at Nordstrom that traces its roots back to 1901, eight decades before customer service programs became stylish. For Bill Hewlett and David Packard, respect for the individual was first and foremost a deep personal value; they didn't get it from a book or hear it from a management guru. And Ralph S. Larsen, CEO of Johnson & Johnson, puts it this way: "The core values embodied in our credo might be a competitive advantage, but that is not *why* we have them. We have them because they define for us what we stand for, and we would hold them even if they became a competitive *dis*advantage in certain situations."

The point is that a great company decides for itself what values it holds to be core, largely independent of the current environment, competitive requirements, or management fads. Clearly, then, there is no universally right set of core values. A company need not have as its core value customer service (Sony doesn't) or respect for the individual (Disney doesn't) or quality (Wal-Mart Stores doesn't) or market focus (HP doesn't) or teamwork (Nordstrom doesn't). A company might have operating practices and business strategies around those qualities without having them at the essence of its being. Furthermore, great companies need not have likable or humanistic core values, although many do. The key is not *what* core values an organization has but that it has core values at all.

Companies tend to have only a few core values, usually between three and five. In fact, we found that none of the visionary companies we studied in our book had more than five: most had only three or four. (See the sidebar "Core Values Are a Company's Essential Tenets.") And, indeed, we should expect that. Only a few values can be truly *core*—that is, so fundamental and deeply held that they will change seldom, if ever.

To identify the core values of your own organization, push with relentless honesty to define what values are truly central. If you articulate more than five or six, chances are that you are confusing core values (which do not change) with operating practices, business strategies, or cultural norms (which should be open to change). Remember, the values must stand the test of time. After you've drafted a preliminary list of the core values, ask about each one, If the circumstances changed and *penalized* us for holding this core value, would we still keep it? If you can't honestly answer yes, then the value is not core and should be dropped from consideration.

A high-technology company wondered whether it should put quality on its list of core values. The CEO asked, "Suppose in ten years quality doesn't make a hoot of difference in our markets.

Articulating a vision

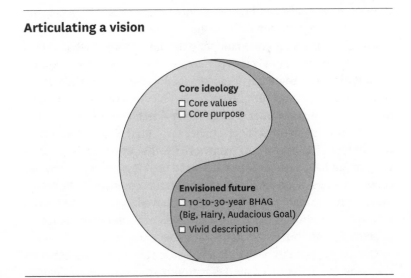

Suppose the only thing that matters is sheer speed and horsepower but not quality. Would we still want to put quality on our list of core values?" The members of the management team looked around at one another and finally said no. Quality stayed in the *strategy* of the company, and quality-improvement programs remained in place as a mechanism for stimulating progress; but quality did not make the list of core values.

The same group of executives then wrestled with leading-edge innovation as a core value. The CEO asked, "Would we keep innovation on the list as a core value, no matter how the world around us changed?" This time, the management team gave a resounding yes. The managers' outlook might be summarized as, "We always want to do leading-edge innovation. That's who we are. It's really important to us and always will be. No matter what. And if our current markets don't value it, we will find markets that do." Leading-edge innovation went on the list and will stay there. A company should not change its core values in response to market changes; rather, it should change markets, if necessary, to remain true to its core values.

Who should be involved in articulating the core values varies with the size, age, and geographic dispersion of the company, but in many situations we have recommended what we call a *Mars Group*. It works like this: Imagine that you've been asked to re-create the very best attributes of your organization on another planet but you have seats on the rocket ship for only five to seven people. Whom should you send? Most likely, you'll choose the people who have a gut-level understanding of your core values, the highest level of credibility with their peers, and the highest levels of competence. We'll often ask people brought together to work on core values to nominate a Mars Group of five to seven individuals (not necessarily all from the assembled group). Invariably, they end up selecting highly credible representatives who do a super job of articulating the core values precisely because they are exemplars of those values—a representative slice of the company's genetic code.

Even global organizations composed of people from widely diverse cultures can identify a set of shared core values. The secret is to work from the individual to the organization. People involved in

Core Values Are a Company's Essential Tenets

Merck

- Corporate social responsibility
- Unequivocal excellence in all aspects of the company
- Science-based innovation
- Honesty and integrity
- Profit, but profit from work that benefits humanity

Nordstrom

- Service to the customer above all else
- Hard work and individual productivity
- Never being satisfied
- Excellence in reputation; being part of something special

Philip Morris

- The right to freedom of choice
- Winning—beating others in a good fight
- Encouraging individual initiative
- Opportunity based on merit; no one is entitled to anything
- Hard work and continuous self-improvement

Sony

- Elevation of the Japanese culture and national status
- Being a pioneer—not following others; doing the impossible
- Encouraging individual ability and creativity

Walt Disney

- No cynicism
- Nurturing and promulgation of "wholesome American values"
- Creativity, dreams, and imagination
- Fanatical attention to consistency and detail
- Preservation and control of the Disney magic

articulating the core values need to answer several questions: What core values do you personally bring to your work? (These should be so fundamental that you would hold them regardless of whether or not they were rewarded.) What would you tell your children are the core values that you hold at work and that you hope *they* will hold when they become working adults? If you awoke tomorrow morning with enough money to retire for the rest of your life, would you continue to live those core values? Can you envision them being as valid for you 100 years from now as they are today? Would you want to hold those core values, even if at some point one or more of them became a com-petitive *dis*advantage? If you were to start a new organization tomor-row in a different line of work, what core values would you build into the new organization regardless of its industry? The last three questions are particularly important because they make the crucial distinction between enduring core values that should not change and practices and strategies that should be changing all the time.

Core purpose

Core purpose, the second part of core ideology, is the organization's reason for being. An effective purpose reflects people's idealistic motivations for doing the company's work. It doesn't just describe the organization's output or target customers; it captures the soul of the organization. (See the sidebar "Core Purpose Is a Company's Reason for Being.") Purpose, as illustrated by a speech David Packard gave to HP employees in 1960, gets at the deeper reasons for an orga-nization's existence beyond just making money. Packard said,

> I want to discuss why a company exists in the first place. In other words, why are we here? I think many people assume, wrongly, that a company exists simply to make money. While this is an important result of a company's existence, we have to go deeper and find the real reasons for our being. As we investigate this, we inevitably come to the conclusion that a group of people get together and exist as an institution that we call a company so they are able to accomplish something collectively that they could not accomplish separately—they make a contribution to

society, a phrase which sounds trite but is fundamental . . . You can look around [in the general business world and] see people who are interested in money and nothing else, but the underlying drives come largely from a desire to do something else: to make a product, to give a service—generally to do something which is of value.[1]

Purpose (which should last at least 100 years) should not be confused with specific goals or business strategies (which should change many times in 100 years). Whereas you might achieve a goal or complete a strategy, you cannot fulfill a purpose; it is like a guiding star on the horizon—forever pursued but never reached. Yet although purpose itself does not change, it does inspire change. The very fact that purpose can never be fully realized means that an organization can never stop stimulating change and progress.

In identifying purpose, some companies make the mistake of simply describing their current product lines or customer segments. We do not consider the following statement to reflect an effective purpose: "We exist to fulfill our government charter and participate in the secondary mortgage market by packaging mortgages into investment securities." The statement is merely descriptive. A far more effective statement of purpose would be that expressed by the executives of the Federal National Mortgage Association, Fannie Mae: "To strengthen the social fabric by continually democratizing home ownership." The secondary mortgage market as we know it might not even exist in 100 years, but strengthening the social fabric by continually democratizing home ownership can be an enduring purpose, no matter how much the world changes. Guided and inspired by this purpose, Fannie Mae launched in the early 1990s a series of bold initiatives, including a program to develop new systems for reducing mortgage underwriting costs by 40% in five years; programs to eliminate discrimination in the lending process (backed by $5 billion in underwriting experiments); and an audacious goal to provide, by the year 2000, $1 trillion targeted at 10 million families that had traditionally been shut out of home ownership—minorities, immigrants, and low-income groups.

Similarly, 3M defines its purpose not in terms of adhesives and abrasives but as the perpetual quest to solve unsolved problems innovatively—a purpose that is always leading 3M into new fields. McKinsey & Company's purpose is not to do management consulting but to help corporations and governments be more successful: in 100 years, it might involve methods other than consulting. Hewlett-Packard doesn't exist to make electronic test and measurement equipment but to make technical contributions that improve people's lives—a purpose that has led the company far afield from its origins in electronic instruments. Imagine if Walt Disney had conceived of his company's purpose as to make cartoons, rather than to make people happy; we probably wouldn't have Mickey Mouse, Disneyland, EPCOT Center, or the Anaheim Mighty Ducks Hockey Team.

One powerful method for getting at purpose is the *five whys*. Start with the descriptive statement We make X products or We deliver X services, and then ask, Why is that important? five times. After a few whys, you'll find that you're getting down to the fundamental purpose of the organization.

We used this method to deepen and enrich a discussion about purpose when we worked with a certain market-research company. The executive team first met for several hours and generated the following statement of purpose for their organization: To provide the best market-research data available. We then asked the following question: Why is it important to provide the best market-research data available? After some discussion, the executives answered in a way that reflected a deeper sense of their organization's purpose: To provide the best market-research data available so that our customers will understand their markets better than they could otherwise. A further discussion let team members realize that their sense of self-worth came not just from helping customers understand their markets better but also from making a *contribution* to their customers' success. This introspection eventually led the company to identify its purpose as: To contribute to our customers' success by helping them understand their markets. With this purpose in mind, the company now frames its product decisions not with the question Will it sell? but with the question Will it make a contribution to our customers' success?

Core Purpose Is a Company's Reason for Being

3M: To solve unsolved problems innovatively

Cargill: To improve the standard of living around the world

Fannie Mae: To strengthen the social fabric by continually democratizing home ownership

Hewlett-Packard: To make technical contributions for the advancement and welfare of humanity

Lost Arrow Corporation: To be a role model and a tool for social change

Pacific Theatres: To provide a place for people to flourish and to enhance the community

Mary Kay Cosmetics: To give unlimited opportunity to women

McKinsey & Company: To help leading corporations and governments be more successful

Merck: To preserve and improve human life

Nike: To experience the emotion of competition, winning, and crushing competitors

Sony: To experience the joy of advancing and applying technology for the benefit of the public

Telecare Corporation: To help people with mental impairments realize their full potential

Wal-Mart: To give ordinary folk the chance to buy the same things as rich people

Walt Disney: To make people happy

The five whys can help companies in any industry frame their work in a more meaningful way. An asphalt and gravel company might begin by saying, We make gravel and asphalt products. After a few whys, it could conclude that making asphalt and gravel is important because the quality of the infrastructure plays a vital role in people's safety and experience; because driving on a pitted road is annoying and dangerous; because 747s cannot land safely on runways built with poor workmanship or inferior concrete; because buildings with substandard materials weaken with time and crumble in earthquakes. From such introspection may emerge this purpose: To make people's lives better by improving the quality of man-made structures. With a sense of purpose very much along those lines, Granite Rock Company of Watsonville, California, won the Malcolm Baldrige National Quality Award—not an easy feat for a small rock quarry and asphalt company. And Granite Rock has gone on to be one of the most progressive and exciting companies we've encountered in *any* industry.

Notice that none of the core purposes fall into the category "maximize shareholder wealth." A primary role of core purpose is to guide and inspire. Maximizing shareholder wealth does not inspire people at all levels of an organization, and it provides precious little guidance. Maximizing shareholder wealth is the standard off-the-shelf purpose for those organizations that have not yet identified their true core purpose. It is a substitute—and a weak one at that.

When people in great organizations talk about their achievements, they say very little about earnings per share. Motorola people talk about impressive quality improvements and the effect of the products they create on the world. Hewlett-Packard people talk about their technical contributions to the marketplace. Nordstrom people talk about heroic customer service and remarkable individual performance by star salespeople. When a Boeing engineer talks about launching an exciting and revolutionary new aircraft, she does not say, "I put my heart and soul into this project because it would add 37 cents to our earnings per share."

One way to get at the purpose that lies beyond merely maximizing shareholder wealth is to play the "Random Corporate Serial Killer" game. It works like this: Suppose you could sell the company to someone who would pay a price that everyone inside and outside the company agrees is more than fair (even with a very generous set of assumptions about the expected future cash flows of the company). Suppose further that this buyer would guarantee stable employment for all employees at the same pay scale after the purchase but with no guarantee that those jobs would be in the same industry. Finally, suppose the buyer plans to kill the company after the purchase—its products or services would be discontinued, its operations would be shut down, its brand names would be shelved forever, and so on. The company would utterly and completely cease to exist. Would you accept the offer? Why or why not? What would be lost if the company ceased to exist? Why is it important that the company continue to exist? We've found this exercise to be very powerful for helping hard-nosed, financially focused executives reflect on their organization's deeper reasons for being.

Another approach is to ask each member of the Mars Group, How could we frame the purpose of this organization so that if you woke up tomorrow morning with enough money in the bank to retire, you would nevertheless keep working here? What deeper sense of purpose would motivate you to continue to dedicate your precious creative energies to this company's efforts?

As they move into the twenty-first century, companies will need to draw on the full creative energy and talent of their people. But why should people give full measure? As Peter Drucker has pointed out, the best and most dedicated people are ultimately volunteers, for they have the opportunity to do something else with their lives. Confronted with an increasingly mobile society, cynicism about corporate life, and an expanding entrepreneurial segment of the economy, companies more than ever need to have a clear understanding of their purpose in order to make work meaningful and thereby attract, motivate, and retain outstanding people.

Discovering Core Ideology

You do not create or set core ideology. You *discover* core ideology. You do not deduce it by looking at the external environment. You understand it by looking inside. Ideology has to be authentic. You cannot fake it. Discovering core ideology is not an intellectual exercise. Do not ask, What core values should we hold? Ask instead, What core values do we truly and passionately hold? You should not confuse values that you think the organization ought to have— but does not—with authentic core values. To do so would create cynicism throughout the organization. ("Who're they trying to kid? We all know that isn't a core value around here!") Aspirations are more appropriate as part of your envisioned future or as part of your strategy, not as part of the core ideology. However, authentic core values that have weakened over time can be considered a legitimate part of the core ideology—as long as you acknowledge to the organization that you must work hard to revive them.

Also be clear that the role of core ideology is to guide and inspire, not to differentiate. Two companies can have the same core values or purpose. Many companies could have the purpose to make technical contributions, but few live it as passionately as Hewlett-Packard. Many companies could have the purpose to preserve and improve human life, but few hold it as deeply as Merck. Many companies could have the core value of heroic customer service, but few create as intense a culture around that value as Nordstrom. Many companies could have the core value of innovation, but few create the powerful alignment mechanisms that stimulate the innovation we see at 3M. The authenticity, the discipline, and the consistency with which the ideology is lived—not the content of the ideology—differentiate visionary companies from the rest of the pack.

Core ideology needs to be meaningful and inspirational only to people inside the organization; it need not be exciting to outsiders. Why not? Because it is the people inside the organization who need to commit to the organizational ideology over the long term. Core ideology can also play a role in determining who *is* inside and who is not. A clear and well-articulated ideology attracts to the company people whose personal values are compatible with the company's core values; conversely, it repels those whose personal values are incompatible. You cannot impose new core values or purpose on people. Nor are core values and purpose things people can buy into. Executives often ask, How do we get people to share our core ideology? You don't. You can't. Instead, find people who are predisposed to share your core values and purpose; attract and retain those people; and let those who do not share your core values go elsewhere. Indeed, the very process of articulating core ideology may cause some people to leave when they realize that they are not personally compatible with the organization's core. Welcome that outcome. It is certainly desirable to retain within the core ideology a diversity of people and viewpoints. People who share the same core values and purpose do not necessarily all think or look the same.

Don't confuse core ideology itself with core-ideology statements. A company can have a very strong core ideology without a formal statement. For example, Nike has not (to our knowledge) formally articulated a statement of its core purpose. Yet, according to our observations, Nike has a powerful core purpose that permeates the entire organization: to experience the emotion of competition, winning, and crushing competitors. Nike has a campus that seems more like a shrine to the competitive spirit than a corporate office complex. Giant photos of Nike heroes cover the walls, bronze plaques of Nike athletes hang along the Nike Walk of Fame, statues of Nike athletes stand alongside the running track that rings the campus, and buildings honor champions such as Olympic marathoner Joan Benoit, basketball superstar Michael Jordan, and tennis pro John McEnroe. Nike people who do not feel stimulated by the competitive spirit and the urge to be ferocious simply do not last long in the culture. Even the company's name reflects a sense of competition: Nike is the Greek goddess of victory. Thus, although Nike has not formally articulated its purpose, it clearly has a strong one.

Identifying core values and purpose is therefore not an exercise in wordsmithery. Indeed, an organization will generate a variety of statements over time to describe the core ideology. In Hewlett-Packard's archives, we found more than half a dozen distinct versions of the HP Way, drafted by David Packard between 1956 and 1972. All versions stated the same principles, but the words used varied depending on the era and the circumstances. Similarly, Sony's core ideology has been stated many different ways over the company's history. At its founding, Masaru Ibuka described two key elements of Sony's ideology: "We shall welcome technical difficulties and focus on highly sophisticated technical products that have great usefulness for society regardless of the quantity involved; we shall place our main emphasis on ability, performance, and personal character so that each individual can show the best in ability and skill."[2] Four decades later, this same concept appeared in a statement of core ideology called Sony Pioneer Spirit: "Sony is a pioneer and never intends to follow others. Through progress, Sony wants to serve the whole world. It shall be always a seeker of the unknown. . . . Sony has a principle of respecting and encouraging one's ability . . . and always tries to bring out the best in a person. This is the vital force of Sony."[3] Same core values, different words.

You should therefore focus on getting the content right—on capturing the essence of the core values and purpose. The point is not to create a perfect statement but to gain a deep understanding of your organization's core values and purpose, which can then be expressed in a multitude of ways. In fact, we often suggest that once the core has been identified, managers should generate their own statements of the core values and purpose to share with their groups.

Finally, don't confuse core ideology with the concept of core competence. Core competence is a strategic concept that defines your organization's capabilities—what you are particularly good at— whereas core ideology captures what you stand for and why you exist. Core competencies should be well aligned with a company's core ideology and are often rooted in it; but they are not the same thing. For example, Sony has a core competence of miniaturization— a strength that can be strategically applied to a wide array of products and markets. But it does not have a core *ideology* of miniaturization. Sony might not even have miniaturization as part of its strategy in 100 years, but to remain a great company, it will still have the same core values described in the Sony Pioneer Spirit and the same fundamental reason for being—namely, to advance technology for the benefit of the general public. In a visionary company like Sony, core competencies change over the decades, whereas core ideology does not.

Once you are clear about the core ideology, you should feel free to change absolutely *anything* that is not part of it. From then on, whenever someone says something should not change because "it's part of our culture" or "we've always done it that way" or any such excuse, mention this simple rule: If it's not core, it's up for change.

The strong version of the rule is, *If it's not core, change it!* Articulating core ideology is just a starting point, however. You also must determine what type of progress you want to stimulate.

Envisioned Future

The second primary component of the vision framework is *envisioned future*. It consists of two parts: a 10-to-30-year audacious goal plus vivid descriptions of what it will be like to achieve the goal. We recognize that the phrase *envisioned future* is somewhat paradoxical. On the one hand, it conveys concreteness—something visible, vivid, and real. On the other hand, it involves a time yet unrealized—with its dreams, hopes, and aspirations.

Vision-level BHAG

We found in our research that visionary companies often use bold missions—or what we prefer to call *BHAGs* (pronounced BEE-hags and shorthand for Big, Hairy, Audacious Goals)—as a powerful way to stimulate progress. All companies have goals. But there is a difference between merely having a goal and becoming committed to a huge, daunting challenge—such as climbing Mount Everest. A true BHAG is clear and compelling, serves as a unifying focal point of effort, and acts as a catalyst for team spirit. It has a clear finish line, so the organization can know when it has achieved the goal; people like to shoot for finish lines. A BHAG engages people—it reaches out and grabs them. It is tangible, energizing, highly focused. People get it right away; it takes little or no explanation. For example, NASA's 1960s moon mission didn't need a committee of wordsmiths to spend endless hours turning the goal into a verbose, impossible-to-remember mission statement. The goal itself was so easy to grasp—so compelling in its own right—that it could be said 100 different ways yet be easily understood by everyone. Most corporate statements we've seen do little to spur forward movement because they do not contain the powerful mechanism of a BHAG.

Although organizations may have many BHAGs at different levels operating at the same time, vision requires a special type of BHAG—a vision-level BHAG that applies to the entire organization and requires 10 to 30 years of effort to complete. Setting the BHAG that far into the future requires thinking beyond the current capabilities of the organization and the current environment. Indeed, inventing such a goal forces an executive team to be visionary, rather than just strategic or tactical. A BHAG should not be a sure bet—it will have perhaps only a 50% to 70% probability of success—but the organization must believe that it can reach the goal anyway. A BHAG should require extraordinary effort and perhaps a little luck. We have helped companies create a vision-level BHAG by advising them to think in terms of four broad categories: target BHAGs, common-enemy BHAGs, role-model BHAGs, and internal-transformation BHAGs. (See the sidebar "Big, Hairy, Audacious Goals Aid Long-Term Vision.")

Vivid description

In addition to vision-level BHAGs, an envisioned future needs what we call vivid description—that is, a vibrant, engaging, and specific description of what it will be like to achieve the BHAG. Think of it as translating the vision from words into pictures, of creating an image that people can carry around in their heads. It is a question of painting a picture with your words. Picture painting is essential for making the 10-to-30-year BHAG tangible in people's minds.

For example, Henry Ford brought to life the goal of democratizing the automobile with this vivid description: "I will build a motor car for the great multitude. . . . It will be so low in price that no man making a good salary will be unable to own one and enjoy with his family the blessing of hours of pleasure in God's great open spaces. . . . When I'm through, everybody will be able to afford one, and everyone will have one. The horse will have disappeared from our highways, the automobile will be taken for granted . . . [and we will] give a large number of men employment at good wages."

The components-support division of a computer-products company had a general manager who was able to describe vividly the goal of becoming one of the most sought-after divisions in the company: "We will be respected and admired by our peers. . . . Our solutions will be actively sought by the end-product divisions, who will achieve

Big, Hairy, Audacious Goals Aid Long-Term Vision

Target BHAGs can be quantitative or qualitative

- Become a $125 billion company by the year 2000 (Wal-Mart, 1990)
- Democratize the automobile (Ford Motor Company, early 1900s)
- Become the company most known for changing the worldwide poor-quality image of Japanese products (Sony, early 1950s)
- Become the most powerful, the most serviceable, the most far-reaching world financial institution that has ever been (City Bank, predecessor to Citicorp, 1915)
- Become the dominant player in commercial aircraft and bring the world into the jet age (Boeing, 1950)

Common-enemy BHAGs involve David-versus-Goliath thinking

- Knock off RJR as the number one tobacco company in the world (Philip Morris, 1950s)
- Crush Adidas (Nike, 1960s)
- *Yamaha wo tsubusu!* We will destroy Yamaha! (Honda, 1970s)

Role-model BHAGs suit up-and-coming organizations

- Become the Nike of the cycling industry (Giro Sport Design, 1986)
- Become as respected in 20 years as Hewlett-Packard is today (Watkins-Johnson, 1996)
- Become the Harvard of the West (Stanford University, 1940s)

Internal-transformation BHAGs suit large, established organizations

- Become number one or number two in every market we serve and revolutionize this company to have the strengths of a big company combined with the leanness and agility of a small company (General Electric Company, 1980s)
- Transform this company from a defense contractor into the best diversified high-technology company in the world (Rockwell, 1995)
- Transform this division from a poorly respected internal products supplier to one of the most respected, exciting, and sought-after divisions in the company (Components Support Division of a computer products company, 1989)

significant product 'hits' in the marketplace largely because of our technical contribution. . . . We will have pride in ourselves. . . . The best up-and-coming people in the company will seek to work in our division. . . . People will give unsolicited feedback that they love what they are doing. . . . [Our own] people will walk on the balls of their feet. . . . [They] will willingly work hard because they want to. . . . Both employees and customers will feel that our division has contributed to their life in a positive way."

In the 1930s, Merck had the BHAG to transform itself from a chemical manufacturer into one of the preeminent drug-making companies in the world, with a research capability to rival any major university. In describing this envisioned future, George Merck said at the opening of Merck's research facility in 1933, "We believe that research work carried on with patience and persistence will bring to industry and commerce new life; and we have faith that in this new laboratory, with the tools we have supplied, science will be advanced, knowledge increased, and human life win ever a greater freedom from suffering and disease. . . . We pledge our every aid that this enterprise shall merit the faith we have in it. Let your light so shine—that those who seek the Truth, that those who toil that this world may be a better place to live in, that those who hold aloft that torch of science and knowledge through these social and economic dark ages, shall take new courage and feel their hands supported."

Passion, emotion, and conviction are essential parts of the vivid description. Some managers are uncomfortable expressing emotion about their dreams, but that's what motivates others. Churchill understood that when he described the BHAG facing Great Britain in 1940. He did not just say, "Beat Hitler." He said, "Hitler knows he will have to break us on this island or lose the war. If we can stand up to him, all Europe may be free, and the life of the world may move forward into broad, sunlit uplands. But if we fail, the whole world, including the United States, including all we have known and cared for, will sink into the abyss of a new Dark Age, made more sinister and perhaps more protracted by the lights of perverted science. Let us therefore brace ourselves to our duties and so bear ourselves that if the British Empire and its Commonwealth last for a thousand years, men will still say, 'This was their finest hour.'"

A few key points

Don't confuse core ideology and envisioned future. In particular, don't confuse core purpose and BHAGs. Managers often exchange one for the other, mixing the two together or failing to articulate both as distinct items. Core purpose—not some specific goal—is the reason why the organization exists. A BHAG is a clearly articulated goal. Core purpose can never be completed, whereas the BHAG is reachable in 10 to 30 years. Think of the core purpose as the star on the horizon to be chased forever; the BHAG is the mountain to be climbed. Once you have reached its summit, you move on to other mountains.

Identifying core ideology is a discovery process, but setting the envisioned future is a creative process. We find that executives often have a great deal of difficulty coming up with an exciting BHAG. They want to analyze their way into the future. We have found, therefore, that some executives make more progress by starting first with the vivid description and backing from there into the BHAG. This approach involves starting with questions such as, We're sitting here in 20 years; what would we love to see? What should this company look like? What should it feel like to employees? What should it have achieved? If someone writes an article for a major business magazine about this company in 20 years, what will it say? One biotechnology company we worked with had trouble envisioning its future. Said one member of the executive team, "Every time we come up with something for the entire company, it is just too generic to be exciting—something banal like 'advance biotechnology worldwide.'" Asked to paint a picture of the company in 20 years, the executives mentioned such things as "on the cover of *Business Week* as a model success story . . . the *Fortune* most admired top-ten list . . . the best science and business graduates want to work here . . . people on airplanes rave about one of our products to seatmates . . . 20 consecutive years of profitable growth . . . an entrepreneurial culture that has spawned half a dozen new divisions from within . . . management gurus use us as an example of excellent management and progressive thinking," and so on. From this, they were able to set the goal of becoming as well respected as Merck or as Johnson & Johnson in biotechnology.

It makes no sense to analyze whether an envisioned future is the right one. With a creation—and the task is creation of a future, not prediction—there can be no right answer. Did Beethoven create the right Ninth Symphony? Did Shakespeare create the right *Hamlet*? We can't answer these questions; they're nonsense. The envisioned future involves such essential questions as Does it get our juices flowing? Do we find it stimulating? Does it spur forward momentum? Does it get people going? The envisioned future should be so exciting in its own right that it would continue to keep the organization motivated even if the leaders who set the goal disappeared. City Bank, the predecessor of Citicorp, had the BHAG "to become the most powerful, the most serviceable, the most far-reaching world financial institution that has ever been"—a goal that generated excitement through multiple generations until it was achieved. Similarly, the NASA moon mission continued to galvanize people even though President John F. Kennedy (the leader associated with setting the goal) died years before its completion.

To create an effective envisioned future requires a certain level of unreasonable confidence and commitment. Keep in mind that a BHAG is not just a goal; it is a Big, Hairy, Audacious Goal. It's not reasonable for a small regional bank to set the goal of becoming "the most powerful, the most serviceable, the most far-reaching world financial institution that has ever been," as City Bank did in 1915. It's not a tepid claim that "we will democratize the automobile," as Henry Ford said. It was almost laughable for Philip Morris—as the sixth-place player with 9% market share in the 1950s—to take on the goal of defeating Goliath RJ Reynolds Tobacco Company and becoming number one. It was hardly modest for Sony, as a small, cash-strapped venture, to proclaim the goal of changing the poor-quality image of Japanese products around the world. (See the sidebar "Putting It All Together: Sony in the 1950s.") Of course, it's not only the audacity of the goal but also the level of commitment to the goal that counts. Boeing didn't just envision a future dominated by its commercial jets; it bet the company on the 707 and, later, on the

Putting It All Together: Sony in the 1950s

Core Ideology
Core Values
- Elevation of the Japanese culture and national status
- Being a pioneer—not following others; doing the impossible
- Encouraging individual ability and creativity

Purpose
To experience the sheer joy of innovation and the application of technology for the benefit and pleasure of the general public

Envisioned Future
BHAG
Become the company most known for changing the worldwide poor-quality image of Japanese products

Vivid Description
We will create products that become pervasive around the world. . . . We will be the first Japanese company to go into the U.S. market and distribute directly. . . . We will succeed with innovations that U.S. companies have failed at—such as the transistor radio. . . . Fifty years from now, our brand name will be as well known as any in the world . . . and will signify innovation and quality that rival the most innovative companies anywhere. . . . "Made in Japan" will mean something fine, not something shoddy.

747. Nike's people didn't just talk about the idea of crushing Adidas; they went on a crusade to fulfill the dream. Indeed, the envisioned future should produce a bit of the "gulp factor": when it dawns on people what it will take to achieve the goal, there should be an almost audible gulp.

But what about failure to realize the envisioned future? In our research, we found that the visionary companies displayed a remarkable ability to achieve even their most audacious goals. Ford did democratize the automobile; Citicorp did become the most far-reaching bank in the world; Philip Morris did rise from sixth to first and beat RJ Reynolds worldwide; Boeing did become the dominant commercial aircraft company; and it looks like Wal-Mart will achieve its $125 billion goal, even without Sam Walton. In contrast, the comparison companies in our research frequently did not achieve their

BHAGs, if they set them at all. The difference does not lie in setting easier goals: the visionary companies tended to have even more audacious ambitions. The difference does not lie in charismatic, visionary leadership: the visionary companies often achieved their BHAGs without such larger-than-life leaders at the helm. Nor does the difference lie in better strategy: the visionary companies often realized their goals more by an organic process of "let's try a lot of stuff and keep what works" than by well-laid strategic plans. Rather, their success lies in building the strength of their organization as their primary way of creating the future.

Why did Merck become the preeminent drug-maker in the world? Because Merck's architects built the best pharmaceutical research and development organization in the world. Why did Boeing become the dominant commercial aircraft company in the world? Because of its superb engineering and marketing organization, which had the ability to make projects like the 747 a reality. When asked to name the most important decisions that have contributed to the growth and success of Hewlett-Packard, David Packard answered entirely in terms of decisions to build the strength of the organization and its people.

Finally, in thinking about the envisioned future, beware of the We've Arrived Syndrome—a complacent lethargy that arises once an organization has achieved one BHAG and fails to replace it with another. NASA suffered from that syndrome after the successful moon landings. After you've landed on the moon, what do you do for an encore? Ford suffered from the syndrome when, after it succeeded in democratizing the automobile, it failed to set a new goal of equal significance and gave General Motors the opportunity to jump ahead in the 1930s. Apple Computer suffered from the syndrome after achieving the goal of creating a computer that non-techies could use. Start-up companies frequently suffer from the We've Arrived Syndrome after going public or after reaching a stage in which survival no longer seems in question. An envisioned future helps an organization only as long as it hasn't yet been achieved. In our work with companies, we frequently hear executives say, "It's just not as exciting around here as it used to be; we seem to have lost our momentum." Usually, that kind of remark signals that the organization has climbed one mountain and not yet picked a new one to climb.

Many executives thrash about with mission statements and vision statements. Unfortunately, most of those statements turn out to be a muddled stew of values, goals, purposes, philosophies, beliefs, aspirations, norms, strategies, practices, and descriptions. They are usually a boring, confusing, structurally unsound stream of words that evoke the response "True, but who cares?" Even more problematic, seldom do these statements have a direct link to the fundamental dynamic of visionary companies: preserve the core and stimulate progress. That dynamic, not vision or mission statements, is the primary engine of enduring companies. Vision simply provides the context for bringing this dynamic to life. Building a visionary company requires 1% vision and 99% alignment. When you have superb alignment, a visitor could drop in from outer space and infer your vision from the operations and activities of the company without ever reading it on paper or meeting a single senior executive.

Creating alignment may be your most important work. But the first step will always be to recast your vision or mission into an effective context for building a visionary company. If you do it right, you shouldn't have to do it again for at least a decade.

Originally published in September 1996. Reprint 96501

Reprinted with permission from Jim Collins and Jerry I. Porras.

Notes

1. David Packard, speech given to Hewlett-Packard's training group on March 8, 1960; courtesy of Hewlett-Packard Archives.

2. See Nick Lyons, *The Sony Vision* (New York: Crown Publishers, 1976). We also used a translation by our Japanese student Tsuneto Ikeda.

3. Akio Morita, *Made in Japan* (New York: E.P. Dutton, 1986), p. 147.

Reinventing Your Business Model

by Mark W. Johnson, Clayton M. Christensen, and Henning Kagermann

IN 2003, APPLE INTRODUCED the iPod with the iTunes store, revolutionizing portable entertainment, creating a new market, and transforming the company. In just three years, the iPod/iTunes combination became a nearly $10 billion product, accounting for almost 50% of Apple's revenue. Apple's market capitalization catapulted from around $1 billion in early 2003 to over $150 billion by late 2007.

This success story is well known; what's less well known is that Apple was not the first to bring digital music players to market. A company called Diamond Multimedia introduced the Rio in 1998. Another firm, Best Data, introduced the Cabo 64 in 2000. Both products worked well and were portable and stylish. So why did the iPod, rather than the Rio or Cabo, succeed?

Apple did something far smarter than take a good technology and wrap it in a snazzy design. It took a good technology and wrapped it in a great business model. Apple's true innovation was to make downloading digital music easy and convenient. To do that, the company built a groundbreaking business model that combined hardware, software, and service. This approach worked like Gillette's famous blades-and-razor model in reverse: Apple essentially gave away the "blades" (low-margin iTunes music) to lock in purchase of the "razor" (the high-margin iPod). That model defined value in a new way and provided game-changing convenience to the consumer.

A Bit of Context

In the "When a New Business Model Is Needed" section of this article, the authors describe the strategic circumstances that require business model change. Leaders of health care organizations may find some of them uncomfortably familiar, such as the threatened loss of large groups of potential customers for whom existing solutions are too expensive or too complex—for example, the growing number of consumers signing up for "narrowed network" insurance products that are more affordable. Or the threat posed to financial margins of existing organizations by "low-end" disruptors, such as freestanding and lower-cost radiology or ambulatory surgery centers. Or a change in the basis of the competition, such as the increasing number of employers and insurers that are steering patients toward "centers of excellence" ready to take bundled payments and compete on outcomes.

In part, the importance of this article for health care leaders is in highlighting the need to shift from a mind-set in which they are "weathering a storm" to one in which they are building a better boat and truly innovating their business models. The authors emphasize at the outset that success starts with focusing on the needs of the true customer: in our case, the patient. Those outside the health care industry are often surprised that this orientation requires a departure from business as usual, but the industry as a whole is only now shifting its basis of competition from meeting the needs of physicians to meeting the needs of patients.

In the last century, health care was organized around the expertise and the activities of physicians, who mastered specific areas of medical science (for example, cardiology, oncology) and saw patients in structures organized around those areas of expertise. Provider organizations received revenue based on the activities of those physicians, so it made sense that organizations such as hospitals saw physicians as their true customers. Keep physicians happy, patients would come in the door,

Business model innovations have reshaped entire industries and redistributed billions of dollars of value. Retail discounters such as Wal-Mart and Target, which entered the market with pioneering business models, now account for 75% of the total valuation of the retail sector. Low-cost U.S. airlines grew from a blip on the radar screen to 55% of the market value of all carriers. Fully 11 of the 27 companies and payments would soon follow. However, as we described in the introduction to this book, value from the perspective of patients is emerging as the imperative of health care. If the clinical outcomes are not good or the care is not affordable, patients are not going to come, no matter how glowing the credentials of physicians.

To thrive in this new world, providers and payers need to offer patients something better than their competitors. Thus, the business model innovation that this article describes: finding a way to consider the value proposition from the perspective of patients, and how to bring them that value in a way in which the providers can profit. Once you identify the new model and then the organizational structure, operational choices about technology follow.

A good example of this kind of innovation is Providence Express Care, a new offering of the Providence Health system in the western United States. The goal of the offering is to meet patients' needs effectively and conveniently. If you want to be seen in an urgent care clinic, you can see which ones nearby have appointments when convenient for you and book a slot with a click. If you are in Southern California, you can order a house call; a nurse practitioner will come to your home, office, or hotel on the same day you put in your request (for a fee, although insurance will often cover most of the price). And if you need treatment for a simple problem and want to stay home or at work, you can have a secure virtual visit with a provider from your phone, tablet, or computer (for an even lower fee)—basically FaceTime with a doctor. This kind of "telemedicine" is not a business model in and of itself; the technology enables the business model to work.

It's no accident that the leader of these innovations at Providence came from Amazon. This kind of creativity is accelerating throughout health care and bodes well for the overall system. But it also creates urgency for leaders of existing organizations to understand when to change their business models and how to begin that work.

—Thomas H. Lee

born in the last quarter century that grew their way into the *Fortune* 500 in the past 10 years did so through business model innovation.

Stories of business model innovation from well-established companies like Apple, however, are rare. An analysis of major innovations within existing corporations in the past decade shows that precious few have been business-model related. And a recent

American Management Association study determined that no more than 10% of innovation investment at global companies is focused on developing new business models.

Yet everyone's talking about it. A 2005 survey by the Economist Intelligence Unit reported that over 50% of executives believe business model innovation will become even more important for success than product or service innovation. A 2008 IBM survey of corporate CEOs echoed these results. Nearly all of the CEOs polled reported the need to adapt their business models; more than two-thirds said that extensive changes were required. And in these tough economic times, some CEOs are already looking to business model innovation to address permanent shifts in their market landscapes.

Senior managers at incumbent companies thus confront a frustrating question: Why is it so difficult to pull off the new growth that business model innovation can bring? Our research suggests two problems. The first is a lack of definition: Very little formal study has been done into the dynamics and processes of business model development. Second, few companies understand their existing business model well enough—the premise behind its development, its natural interdependencies, and its strengths and limitations. So they don't know when they can leverage their core business and when success requires a new business model.

After tackling these problems with dozens of companies, we have found that new business models often look unattractive to internal and external stakeholders—at the outset. To see past the borders of what is and into the land of the new, companies need a road map.

Ours consists of three simple steps. The first is to realize that success starts by not thinking about business models at all. It starts with thinking about the opportunity to satisfy a real customer who needs a job done. The second step is to construct a blueprint laying out how your company will fulfill that need at a profit. In our model, that plan has four elements. The third is to compare that model to your existing model to see how much you'd have to change it to capture the opportunity. Once you do, you will know if you can use your existing model and organization or need to separate out a new unit

Idea in Brief

When Apple introduced the iPod, it did something far smarter than wrap a good technology in a snazzy design. It wrapped a good technology in a **great business model**. Combining hardware, software, and service, the model provided game-changing convenience for consumers *and* record-breaking profits for Apple.

Great business models can reshape industries and drive spectacular growth. Yet many companies find business-model innovation difficult. Managers don't understand their existing model well enough to know when it needs changing—or how.

To determine whether your firm should alter its business model, Johnson, Christensen, and Kagermann advise these steps:

1. Articulate what makes your existing model successful. For example, what customer problem does it solve? How does it make money for your firm?

2. Watch for signals that your model needs changing, such as tough new competitors on the horizon.

3. Decide whether reinventing your model is worth the effort. The answer's yes only if the new model changes the industry or market.

to execute a new model. Every successful company is already fulfilling a real customer need with an effective business model, whether that model is explicitly understood or not. Let's take a look at what that entails.

Business Model: A Definition

A business model, from our point of view, consists of four interlocking elements that, taken together, create and deliver value. The most important to get right, by far, is the first.

Customer value proposition (CVP)

A successful company is one that has found a way to create value for customers—that is, a way to help customers get an important job done. By "job" we mean a fundamental problem in a given situation that needs a solution. Once we understand the job and all its dimensions, including the full process for how to get it done, we can

Idea in Practice

Understand Your Current Business Model

A successful model has these components:

- **Customer value proposition.** The model helps customers perform a specific "job" that alternative offerings don't address.

Example: MinuteClinics enable people to visit a doctor's office without appointments by making nurse practitioners available to treat minor health issues.

- **Profit formula.** The model generates value for your company through factors such as revenue model, cost structure, margins, and inventory turnover.

Example: The Tata Group's inexpensive car, the Nano, is profitable because the company has reduced many cost structure elements, accepted lower-than-standard gross margins, and sold the Nano in large volumes to its target market: first-time car buyers in emerging markets.

- **Key resources and processes.** Your company has the people, technology, products, facilities, equipment, and brand required to deliver the value proposition to your targeted customers. And it has processes (training, manufacturing, service) to leverage those resources.

Example: For Tata Motors to fulfill the requirements of the Nano's profit formula, it had to reconceive how a car is designed, manufactured, and distributed. It redefined its supplier strategy, choosing to outsource a remarkable 85% of the Nano's components and to use nearly 60% fewer vendors than normal to reduce transaction costs.

Identify When a New Model May Be Needed

These circumstances often require business model change:

design the offering. The more important the job is to the customer, the lower the level of customer satisfaction with current options for getting the job done, and the better your solution is than existing alternatives at getting the job done (and, of course, the lower the price), the greater the CVP. Opportunities for creating a CVP are at their most potent, we have found, when alternative products and services have not been designed with the real job in mind and you can design an offering that gets that job—and only that job—done perfectly. We'll come back to that point later.

An opportunity to . . .	Example
Address needs of large groups who find existing solutions too expensive or complicated.	The Nano's goal is to open car ownership to low-income consumers in emerging markets.
Capitalize on new technology, or leverage existing technologies in new markets.	A company develops a commercial application for a technology originally developed for military use.
Bring a job-to-be-done focus where it doesn't exist.	FedEx focused on performing customers' unmet "job": Receive packages faster and more reliably than any other service could.

A need to . . .	Example
Fend off low-end disruptors.	Mini-mills threatened the integrated steel mills a generation ago by making steel at significantly lower prices.
Respond to shifts in competition.	Power-tool maker Hilti switched from selling to renting its tools in part because "good enough" low-end entrants had begun chipping away at the market for selling high-quality tools.

Profit formula

The profit formula is the blueprint that defines how the company creates value for itself while providing value to the customer. It consists of the following:

- *Revenue model:* price x volume

- *Cost structure:* direct costs, indirect costs, economies of scale. Cost structure will be predominantly driven by the cost of the key resources required by the business model.

- *Margin model:* given the expected volume and cost structure, the contribution needed from each transaction to achieve desired profits.

- *Resource velocity:* how fast we need to turn over inventory, fixed assets, and other assets—and, overall, how well we need to utilize resources—to support our expected volume and achieve our anticipated profits.

People often think the terms "profit formulas" and "business models" are interchangeable. But how you make a profit is only one piece of the model. We've found it most useful to start by setting the price required to deliver the CVP and then work backwards from there to determine what the variable costs and gross margins must be. This then determines what the scale and resource velocity needs to be to achieve the desired profits.

Key resources

The key resources are assets such as the people, technology, products, facilities, equipment, channels, and brand required to deliver the value proposition to the targeted customer. The focus here is on the *key* elements that create value for the customer and the company, and the way those elements interact. (Every company also has generic resources that do not create competitive differentiation.)

Key processes

Successful companies have operational and managerial processes that allow them to deliver value in a way they can successfully repeat and increase in scale. These may include such recurrent tasks as training, development, manufacturing, budgeting, planning, sales, and service. Key processes also include a company's rules, metrics, and norms.

These four elements form the building blocks of any business. The customer value proposition and the profit formula define value for the customer and the company, respectively; key resources and key processes describe how that value will be delivered to both the customer and the company.

As simple as this framework may seem, its power lies in the complex interdependencies of its parts. Major changes to any of these four elements affect the others and the whole. Successful businesses devise a more or less stable system in which these elements bond to one another in consistent and complementary ways.

How Great Models Are Built

To illustrate the elements of our business model framework, we will look at what's behind two companies' game-changing business model innovations.

Creating a customer value proposition

It's not possible to invent or reinvent a business model without first identifying a clear customer value proposition. Often, it starts as a quite simple realization. Imagine, for a moment, that you are standing on a Mumbai road on a rainy day. You notice the large number of motor scooters snaking precariously in and out around the cars. As you look more closely, you see that most bear whole families—both parents and several children. Your first thought might be "That's crazy!" or "That's the way it is in developing countries—people get by as best they can."

When Ratan Tata of Tata Group looked out over this scene, he saw a critical job to be done: providing a safer alternative for scooter families. He understood that the cheapest car available in India cost easily five times what a scooter did and that many of these families could not afford one. Offering an affordable, safer, all-weather alternative for scooter families was a powerful value proposition, one with the potential to reach tens of millions of people who were not yet part of the car-buying market. Ratan Tata also recognized that Tata Motors' business model could not be used to develop such a product at the needed price point.

At the other end of the market spectrum, Hilti, a Liechtenstein-based manufacturer of high-end power tools for the construction industry, reconsidered the real job to be done for many of its current customers. A contractor makes money by finishing projects; if the required tools aren't available and functioning properly, the job

The Elements of a Successful Business Model

EVERY SUCCESSFUL COMPANY ALREADY operates according to an effective business model. By systematically identifying all of its constituent parts, executives can understand how the model fulfills a potent value proposition in a profitable way using certain key resources and key processes. With that understanding, they can then judge how well the same model could be used to fulfill a radically different CVP—and what they'd need to do to construct a new one, if need be, to capitalize on that opportunity.

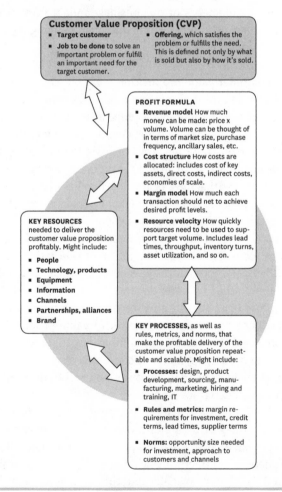

Customer Value Proposition (CVP)

- **Target customer**
- **Job to be done** to solve an important problem or fulfill an important need for the target customer.
- **Offering**, which satisfies the problem or fulfills the need. This is defined not only by what is sold but also by how it's sold.

PROFIT FORMULA

- **Revenue model** How much money can be made: price x volume. Volume can be thought of in terms of market size, purchase frequency, ancillary sales, etc.
- **Cost structure** How costs are allocated: includes cost of key assets, direct costs, indirect costs, economies of scale.
- **Margin model** How much each transaction should net to achieve desired profit levels.
- **Resource velocity** How quickly resources need to be used to support target volume. Includes lead times, throughput, inventory turns, asset utilization, and so on.

KEY RESOURCES needed to deliver the customer value proposition profitably. Might include:

- People
- Technology, products
- Equipment
- Information
- Channels
- Partnerships, alliances
- Brand

KEY PROCESSES, as well as rules, metrics, and norms, that make the profitable delivery of the customer value proposition repeatable and scalable. Might include:

- **Processes:** design, product development, sourcing, manufacturing, marketing, hiring and training, IT
- **Rules and metrics:** margin requirements for investment, credit terms, lead times, supplier terms
- **Norms:** opportunity size needed for investment, approach to customers and channels

doesn't get done. Contractors don't make money by *owning* tools; they make it by using them as efficiently as possible. Hilti could help contractors get the job done by selling tool *use* instead of the tools themselves—managing its customers' tool inventory by providing the best tool at the right time and quickly furnishing tool repairs, replacements, and upgrades, all for a monthly fee. To deliver on that value proposition, the company needed to create a fleet-management program for tools and in the process shift its focus from manufacturing and distribution to service. That meant Hilti had to construct a new profit formula and develop new resources and new processes.

The most important attribute of a customer value proposition is its precision: how perfectly it nails the customer job to be done—and nothing else. But such precision is often the most difficult thing to achieve. Companies trying to create the new often neglect to focus on *one* job; they dilute their efforts by attempting to do lots of things. In doing lots of things, they do nothing *really* well.

One way to generate a precise customer value proposition is to think about the four most common barriers keeping people from getting particular jobs done: insufficient wealth, access, skill, or time. Software maker Intuit devised QuickBooks to fulfill small-business owners' need to avoid running out of cash. By fulfilling that job with greatly simplified accounting software, Intuit broke the *skills barrier* that kept untrained small-business owners from using more-complicated accounting packages. MinuteClinic, the drugstore-based basic health care provider, broke the *time barrier* that kept people from visiting a doctor's office with minor health issues by making nurse practitioners available without appointments.

Designing a profit formula
Ratan Tata knew the only way to get families off their scooters and into cars would be to break the *wealth barrier* by drastically decreasing the price of the car. "What if I can change the game and make a car for one lakh?" Tata wondered, envisioning a price point of around US$2,500, less than half the price of the cheapest car available. This, of course, had dramatic ramifications for the profit

formula: It required both a significant drop in gross margins and a radical reduction in many elements of the cost structure. He knew, however, he could still make money if he could increase sales volume dramatically, and he knew that his target base of consumers was potentially huge.

For Hilti, moving to a contract management program required shifting assets from customers' balance sheets to its own and generating revenue through a lease/subscription model. For a monthly fee, customers could have a full complement of tools at their fingertips, with repair and maintenance included. This would require a fundamental shift in all major components of the profit formula: the revenue stream (pricing, the staging of payments, and how to think about volume), the cost structure (including added sales development and contract management costs), and the supporting margins and transaction velocity.

Identifying key resources and processes

Having articulated the value proposition for both the customer and the business, companies must then consider the key resources and processes needed to deliver that value. For a professional services firm, for example, the key resources are generally its people, and the key processes are naturally people related (training and development, for instance). For a packaged goods company, strong brands and well-selected channel retailers might be the key resources, and associated brand-building and channel-management processes among the critical processes.

Oftentimes, it's not the individual resources and processes that make the difference but their relationship to one another. Companies will almost always need to integrate their key resources and processes in a unique way to get a job done perfectly for a set of customers. When they do, they almost always create enduring competitive advantage. Focusing first on the value proposition and the profit formula makes clear how those resources and processes need to interrelate. For example, most general hospitals offer a value proposition that might be described as, "We'll do anything for anybody." Being all things to all people requires these hospitals to have

Hilti Sidesteps Commoditization

HILTI IS CAPITALIZING ON a game-changing opportunity to increase profitability by turning products into a service. Rather than sell tools (at lower and lower prices), it's selling a "just-the-tool-you-need-when-you-need-it, no-repair-or-storage-hassles" service. Such a radical change in customer value proposition required a shift in all parts of its business model.

Traditional power tool company		Hilti's tool fleet management service
Sales of industrial and professional power tools and accessories	**Customer value proposition**	Leasing a comprehensive fleet of tools to increase contractors's on-site productivity
Low margins, high inventory turnover	**Profit formula**	Higher margins; asset heavy; monthly payments for tool maintenance, repair, and replacement
Distribution channel, low-cost manufacturing plants in developing countries, R&D	**Key resources and processes**	Strong direct-sales approach, contract management, IT systems for inventory management and repair, warehousing

a vast collection of resources (specialists, equipment, and so on) that can't be knit together in any proprietary way. The result is not just a lack of differentiation but dissatisfaction.

By contrast, a hospital that focuses on a specific value proposition can integrate its resources and processes in a unique way that delights customers. National Jewish Health in Denver, for example, is organized around a focused value proposition we'd characterize as, "If you have a disease of the pulmonary system, bring it here. We'll define its root cause and prescribe an effective therapy." Narrowing its focus has allowed National Jewish to develop processes that integrate the ways in which its specialists and specialized equipment work together.

For Tata Motors to fulfill the requirements of its customer value proposition and profit formula for the Nano, it had to reconceive how a car is designed, manufactured, and distributed. Tata built a small team of fairly young engineers who would not, like the company's more-experienced designers, be influenced and constrained in their thinking by the automaker's existing profit formulas. This team dramatically minimized the number of parts in the vehicle, resulting in a significant cost saving. Tata also reconceived its supplier strategy, choosing to outsource a remarkable 85% of the Nano's components and use nearly 60% fewer vendors than normal to reduce transaction costs and achieve better economies of scale.

At the other end of the manufacturing line, Tata is envisioning an entirely new way of assembling and distributing its cars. The ultimate plan is to ship the modular components of the vehicles to a combined network of company-owned and independent entrepreneur-owned assembly plants, which will build them to order. The Nano will be designed, built, distributed, and serviced in a radically new way—one that could not be accomplished without a new business model. And while the jury is still out, Ratan Tata may solve a traffic safety problem in the process.

For Hilti, the greatest challenge lay in training its sales representatives to do a thoroughly new task. Fleet management is not a half-hour sale; it takes days, weeks, even months of meetings to persuade customers to buy a program instead of a product. Suddenly, field reps accustomed to dealing with crew leaders and on-site purchasing managers in mobile trailers found themselves staring down CEOs and CFOs across conference tables.

Additionally, leasing required new resources—new people, more robust IT systems, and other new technologies—to design and develop the appropriate packages and then come to an agreement on monthly payments. Hilti needed a process for maintaining large arsenals of tools more inexpensively and effectively than its customers had. This required warehousing, an inventory management system, and a supply of replacement tools. On the customer management side, Hilti developed a website that enabled construction managers to view all the tools in their fleet and their usage rates. With that information readily available, the managers could easily handle the cost accounting associated with those assets.

Rules, norms, and metrics are often the last element to emerge in a developing business model. They may not be fully envisioned until the new product or service has been road tested. Nor should they be. Business models need to have the flexibility to change in their early years.

When a New Business Model Is Needed

Established companies should not undertake business-model innovation lightly. They can often create new products that disrupt competitors without fundamentally changing their own business model. Procter & Gamble, for example, developed a number of what it calls "disruptive market innovations" with such products as the Swiffer disposable mop and duster and Febreze, a new kind of air freshener. Both innovations built on P&G's existing business model and its established dominance in household consumables.

There are clearly times, however, when creating new growth requires venturing not only into unknown market territory but also into unknown business model territory. When? The short answer is "When significant changes are needed to all four elements of your existing model." But it's not always that simple. Management judgment is clearly required. That said, we have observed five strategic circumstances that often require business model change:

1. The opportunity to address through disruptive innovation the needs of large groups of potential customers who are shut out of a market entirely because existing solutions are too expensive or complicated for them. This includes the opportunity to democratize products in emerging markets (or reach the bottom of the pyramid), as Tata's Nano does.

2. The opportunity to capitalize on a brand-new technology by wrapping a new business model around it (Apple and MP3 players) or the opportunity to leverage a tested technology by bringing it to a whole new market (say, by offering military technologies in the commercial space or vice versa).

3. The opportunity to bring a job-to-be-done focus where one does not yet exist. That's common in industries where companies focus on products or customer segments, which leads

them to refine existing products more and more, increasing commoditization over time. A jobs focus allows companies to redefine industry profitability. For example, when FedEx entered the package delivery market, it did not try to compete through lower prices or better marketing. Instead, it concentrated on fulfilling an entirely unmet customer need to receive packages far, far faster, and more reliably, than any service then could. To do so, it had to integrate its key processes and resources in a vastly more efficient way. The business model that resulted from this job-to-be-done emphasis gave FedEx a significant competitive advantage that took UPS many years to copy.

4. The need to fend off low-end disrupters. If the Nano is successful, it will threaten other automobile makers, much as mini-mills threatened the integrated steel mills a generation ago by making steel at significantly lower cost.

5. The need to respond to a shifting basis of competition. Inevitably, what defines an acceptable solution in a market will change over time, leading core market segments to commoditize. Hilti needed to change its business model in part because of lower global manufacturing costs; "good enough" low-end entrants had begun chipping away at the market for high-quality power tools.

Of course, companies should not pursue business model reinvention unless they are confident that the opportunity is large enough to warrant the effort. And, there's really no point in instituting a new business model unless it's not only new to the company but in some way new or game-changing to the industry or market. To do otherwise would be a waste of time and money.

These questions will help you evaluate whether the challenge of business model innovation will yield acceptable results. Answering "yes" to all four greatly increases the odds of successful execution:

- Can you nail the job with a focused, compelling customer value proposition?

Dow Corning Embraces the Low End

TRADITIONALLY HIGH-MARGIN DOW CORNING found new opportunities in low-margin offerings by setting up a separate business unit that operates in an entirely different way. By fundamentally differentiating its low-end and high-end offerings, the company avoided cannibalizing its traditional business even as it found new profits at the low end.

Established business		New business unit
Customized solutions, negotiated contracts	**Customer value proposition**	No frills, bulk prices, sold through the internet
High-margin, high-overhead retail prices pay for value-added services	**Profit formula**	Spot-market pricing, low overhead to accommodate lower margins, high throughput
R&D, sales, and services orientation	**Key resources and processes**	IT system, lowest-cost processes, maximum automation

- Can you devise a model in which all the elements—the customer value proposition, the profit formula, the key resources, and the key processes—work together to get the job done in the most efficient way possible?

- Can you create a new business development process unfettered by the often negative influences of your core business?

- Will the new business model disrupt competitors?

Creating a new model for a new business does not mean the current model is threatened or should be changed. A new model often reinforces and complements the core business, as Dow Corning discovered.

How Dow Corning Got Out of Its Own Way

When business model innovation is clearly called for, success lies not only in getting the model right but also in making sure the incumbent business doesn't in some way prevent the new model

When the Old Model Will Work

YOU DON'T ALWAYS NEED a new business model to capitalize on a game-changing opportunity. Sometimes, as P&G did with its Swiffer, a company finds that its current model is revolutionary in a new market. When will the old model do? When you can fulfill the new customer value proposition:

- With your current profit formula
- Using most, if not all, of your current key resources and processes
- Using the same core metrics, rules, and norms you now use to run your business

---

from creating value or thriving. That was a problem for Dow Corning when it built a new business unit—with a new profit formula—from scratch.

For many years, Dow Corning had sold thousands of silicone-based products and provided sophisticated technical services to an array of industries. After years of profitable growth, however, a number of product areas were stagnating. A strategic review uncovered a critical insight: Its low-end product segment was commoditizing. Many customers experienced in silicone application no longer needed technical services; they needed basic products at low prices. This shift created an opportunity for growth, but to exploit that opportunity Dow Corning had to figure out a way to serve these customers with a lower-priced product. The problem was that both the business model and the culture were built on high-priced, innovative product and service packages. In 2002, in pursuit of what was essentially a commodity business for low-end customers, Dow Corning CEO Gary Anderson asked executive Don Sheets to form a team to start a new business.

The team began by formulating a customer value proposition that it believed would fulfill the job to be done for these price-driven customers. It determined that the price point had to drop 15% (which for a commoditizing material was a huge reduction). As the team analyzed what that new customer value proposition would require, it realized reaching that point was going to take a lot more than merely eliminating services. Dramatic price reduction would call for a different profit formula with a fundamentally lower cost structure, which depended heavily on developing a new IT system. To sell more products faster, the company would need to use the internet to automate processes and reduce overhead as much as possible.

Breaking the rules

As a mature and successful company, Dow Corning was full of highly trained employees used to delivering its high-touch, customized value proposition. To automate, the new business would have to be far more standardized, which meant instituting different and, over- all, much stricter rules. For example, order sizes would be limited to a few, larger-volume options; order lead times would fall between two and four weeks (exceptions would cost extra); and credit terms would be fixed. There would be charges if a purchaser required customer service. The writing was on the wall: The new venture would be low-touch, self-service, and standardized. To succeed, Dow Corning would have to break the rules that had previously guided its success.

Sheets next had to determine whether this new venture, with its new rules, could succeed within the confines of Dow Corning's core enterprise. He set up an experimental war game to test how exist- ing staff and systems would react to the requirements of the new customer value proposition. He got crushed as entrenched habits and existing processes thwarted any attempt to change the game. It became clear that the corporate antibodies would kill the initiative before it got off the ground. The way forward was clear: The new venture had to be free from existing rules and free to decide what rules would be appropriate in order for the new commodity line of business to thrive. To nurture the opportunity—and also protect the existing model—a new business unit with a new brand identity was needed. Xiameter was born.

Identifying new competencies

Following the articulation of the new customer value proposi- tion and new profit formula, the Xiameter team focused on the new competencies it would need, its key resources and processes. Information technology, just a small part of Dow Corning's core

What Rules, Norms, and Metrics Are Standing in Your Way?

IN ANY BUSINESS, a fundamental understanding of the core model often fades into the mists of institutional memory, but it lives on in rules, norms, and metrics put in place to protect the status quo (for example, "Gross margins must be at 40%"). They are the first line of defense against any new model's taking root in an existing enterprise.

Financial

- Gross margins
- Opportunity size
- Unit pricing
- Unit margin
- Time to breakeven
- Net present value calculations
- Fixed cost investment
- Credit items

Operational

- End-product quality
- Supplier quality
- Owned versus outsourced manufacturing
- Customer service
- Channels
- Lead times
- Throughput

Other

- Pricing
- Performance demands
- Product-development life cycles
- Basis for individuals' rewards and incentives
- Brand parameters

competencies at that time, emerged as an essential part of the now web-enabled business. Xiameter also needed employees who could make smart decisions very quickly and who would thrive in a fast-changing environment, filled initially with lots of ambiguity. Clearly, new abilities would have to be brought into the business.

Although Xiameter would be established and run as a separate business unit, Don Sheets and the Xiameter team did not want to give up the incumbency advantage that deep knowledge of the industry and of their own products gave them. The challenge was to tap into the expertise without importing the old-rules mind-set. Sheets conducted a focused HR search within Dow Corning for risk takers. During the interview process, when he came across candidates with the right skills, he asked them to take the job on the spot, before they left the room. This approach allowed him to cherry-pick those who could make snap decisions and take big risks.

The secret sauce: patience

Successful new businesses typically revise their business models four times or so on the road to profitability. While a well-considered business-model-innovation process can often shorten this cycle, successful incumbents must tolerate initial failure and grasp the need for course correction. In effect, companies have to focus on learning and adjusting as much as on executing. We recommend companies with new business models be patient for growth (to allow the market opportunity to unfold) but impatient for profit (as an early validation that the model works). A profitable business is the best early indication of a viable model.

Accordingly, to allow for the trial and error that naturally accompanies the creation of the new while also constructing a development cycle that would produce results and demonstrate feasibility with minimal resource outlay, Dow Corning kept the scale of Xiameter's operation small but developed an aggressive timetable for launch and set the goal of becoming profitable by the end of year one.

Xiameter paid back Dow Corning's investment in just three months and went on to become a major, transformative success. Beforehand, Dow Corning had had no online sales component; now

30% of sales originate online, nearly three times the industry average. Most of these customers are new to the company. Far from cannibalizing existing customers, Xiameter has actually supported the main business, allowing Dow Corning's salespeople to more easily enforce premium pricing for their core offerings while providing a viable alternative for the price-conscious.

Established companies' attempts at transformative growth typically spring from product or technology innovations. Their efforts are often characterized by prolonged development cycles and fitful attempts to find a market. As the Apple iPod story that opened this article suggests, truly transformative businesses are never exclusively about the discovery and commercialization of a great technology. Their success comes from enveloping the new technology in an appropriate, powerful business model.

Bob Higgins, the founder and general partner of Highland Capital Partners, has seen his share of venture success and failure in his 20 years in the industry. He sums up the importance and power of business model innovation this way: "I think historically where we [venture capitalists] fail is when we back technology. Where we succeed is when we back new business models."

Originally published in December 2008. Reprint R0812C

Will Disruptive Innovations Cure Health Care?

by Clayton M. Christensen, Richard Bohmer, and John Kenagy

IMAGINE A PORTABLE, LOW-INTENSITY X-RAY MACHINE that can be wheeled between offices on a small cart. It creates images of such clarity that pediatricians, internists, and nurses can detect cracks in bones or lumps in tissue in their offices, not in a hospital. It works through a patented "nanocrystal" process, which uses night-vision technology borrowed from the military. At 10% of the cost of a conventional X-ray machine, it could save patients, their employers, and insurance companies hundreds of thousands of dollars every year. Great innovation, right? Guess again. When the entrepreneur who developed the machine tried to license the technology to established health care companies, he couldn't even get his foot in the door. Large-scale X-ray equipment suppliers wanted no part of it. Why? Because it threatened their business models.

What happened to the X-ray entrepreneur is all too common in the health care industry. Powerful institutional forces fight simpler alternatives to expensive care because those alternatives threaten their livelihoods. And those opponents to low-cost change are usually lined up three or four deep. Imagine for a moment that our entrepreneur was able to license the technology. Even then, he would probably face insuperable barriers. Regulators, afraid of putting

A Bit of Context

This article made the competitive threats and opportunities in health care explicit when it was published in 2000. Its messages are now even more compelling, as competition on value rather than brand is increasingly driving the health care marketplace, and as a wired world enhances the feasibility of meeting patients' needs in so many new, more convenient, and less expensive ways. If in-office care is a potential disruptor, as portrayed in this article's well-known graph, "Disruptions of Health Care Institutions," the race is on to develop models that make the office visit a secondary or even more later option in meeting patients' needs.

The authors' "disruptive innovation" framework also helps explain why health care leaders must recognize that fighting against the outward trend of health care services is a losing battle, as they shift from the high-cost centers where many were invented, toward lower-cost and more convenient sites of care. The natural sequence goes like this: An academic medical center where expert clinicians and researchers work shoulder to shoulder develops a new test or procedure. Its value is proven in research studies. At first, patients flock to the one or several medical centers that offer it, but once the bugs are worked out, other well-trained clinicians can perform it. Soon, community hospitals offer

patients at risk, would withhold approvals. Radiologists, who establish the licensing standards that regulators enforce, don't want to lose their jobs, so they'd fight it, too. Insurance companies, which approve only established licensed procedures, would refuse to reimburse for it. And hospitals, with their large investments in radiology and emergency departments, want injuries to flow to them—so they, too, would join the forces holding back change.

This resistance to low-cost alternatives is understandable, but it's not in the best interests of the industry or of the patients it serves. Quite the reverse—the health care industry desperately needs to open its doors to market forces. Health care professionals often shudder when they hear that phrase "market forces." But when we use it, we're not talking about letting insurance companies micromanage doctors as they practice medicine or about putting the test or procedure. Then doctors' offices. And then, in some cases, other settings, including patients' homes.

If you are a leader in an academic medical center or any of the other stopping places along this path—but *only* one stopping place—you naturally don't want the expertise to migrate outward. You want the patients (and the revenue) to stay with your organization. So you resist, using tactics such as pushing for regulations that make it difficult for the test or procedure to be performed in other settings. In doing so, you are setting yourself up to be a casualty of the disruptive innovation that will inevitably arise—somewhere else.

Instead, recognizing these dynamics at work, many health care organizations are merging vertically, that is, acquiring the downstream, lower-cost sites to which they would otherwise inevitably lose business. Moving to own more of the options is a step in the right direction, as it at least reduces the reflexive resistance to movement outward. But, to compete successfully and thrive in today's marketplaces, more is needed than these opportunistic mergers. Health care leaders should read the last sections ("Solutions to the Crisis" and "The Need for Leadership") with care, and ask how disruptive innovation represents a threat they are at risk for ignoring *and* an opportunity that they should seize as they compete to improve the value of care.

—Thomas H. Lee

profits above patient care. Rather, we're talking about being open to disruptive technologies and business models that may threaten the status quo but will ultimately raise the quality of health care for everyone.

Make no mistake: the U.S. health care industry is in crisis. Prestigious teaching hospitals lose millions of dollars every year. Health care delivery is convoluted, expensive, and often deeply dissatisfying to consumers. Managed care, which evolved to address some of these problems, seems increasingly to contribute to them— and some of the best managed-care agencies are on the brink of insolvency. We believe that a whole host of disruptive innovations, small and large, could end the crisis—but only if the entrenched powers get out of the way and let market forces play out. If the natural process of disruption is allowed to proceed, we'll be able to build a new system

that's characterized by lower costs, higher quality, and greater convenience than could ever be achieved under the old system.

What's Wrong with Health Care

In any industry, a disruptive innovation sneaks in from below. While
the dominant players are focused on improving their products or services to the point where the average consumer doesn't even know
what she's using (think overengineered computers), they miss simpler,
more convenient, and less costly offerings initially designed to appeal
to the low end of the market. Over time, the simpler offerings get
better—so much better that they meet the needs of the vast majority
of users. We've seen this happen recently in the telecommunications
industry, where routers—initially dismissed by leading makers of the
faster, more reliable circuit switches—came to take over the market.

The graph "The progress of disruptive innovation" illustrates
this dynamic. The top solid line depicts the pace of technological
innovation—the improvement an industry creates as it introduces
new and more-advanced products to serve the more-sophisticated
customers at the high end of the market. We call these *sustaining
innovations*. The shaded area outlines the rate of improvement consumers can absorb over the same time. The pace of sustaining innovation nearly always outstrips the ability of customers to absorb it.
That creates the potential for upstart companies to introduce *disruptive innovations*—cheaper, simpler, more convenient products
or services that start by meeting the needs of less-demanding customers. The progress of these disruptive innovations is shown by
the bottom solid line. Disruptive technologies have caused many of
history's best companies to plunge into crisis and ultimately fail.[1]

This phenomenon of overshooting the needs of average customers and creating the potential for disruption quite accurately
describes the health care industry. If we were to draw a graph to
illustrate health care specifically, we would measure the complexity
of diagnosing and treating various disorders on the vertical axis. The
least-demanding tiers of the market are patients with disorders such
as simple infectious diseases. The most-demanding tiers include

Idea in Brief

The U.S. health care industry is ailing. The symptoms? Expensive, inconvenient delivery systems that leave more and more consumers dissatisfied. Why? Major health care institutions have "overshot" the level of care most patients need. Researchers and practitioners focus on the most complicated diseases, while paying insufficient attention to the needs of patients with more common ailments.

The cure? All health care industry players must embrace **disruptive innovations:** cheaper, simpler, more convenient products or services that ultimately let less expensive professionals provide sophisticated service in affordable settings. Consider angioplasty, used by cardiologists with patients who not long ago would have needed invasive, costly surgery by open-heart specialists. Or the latest blood glucose meters, which allow diabetic patients to monitor their own health—accurately, conveniently, and inexpensively.

We need many more of these disruptive innovations to revitalize the health care industry. Companies that develop them will grow profitably with less investment. Hospitals and managed-care institutions will stem their financial hemorrhaging. When industry players and consumers join forces to promote affordable, high-quality medical services, everyone will win.

patients with complex, interactive problems such as an elderly man with a broken hip complicated by poor health from long-standing diabetes, hypertension, and heart disease—situations in which multiple systems of the body are involved, and cause and effect are difficult to disentangle.

Our major health care institutions—medical schools, groups of specialist physicians, general hospitals, research organizations—have together overshot the level of care actually needed or used by the vast majority of patients. Indeed, most players in today's health care system are in a lockstep march toward the most scientifically demanding challenges. Between 1960 and now, for example, our medical schools and residency programs have churned out specialists and subspecialists with extraordinary capabilities. But most of the things that afflict us are relatively straightforward disorders whose diagnoses and treatments tap but a small fraction of what our medical schools have prepared

Idea in Practice

Disruptive innovations in other industries offer lessons for transforming health care:

- **Create a system that matches clinicians' skill levels to the level of medical difficulty.** Use technology to channel simple problems (e.g., strep throat) to clinicians who can follow predictable rules for diagnosis and treatment. For example, expand nurse practitioners' role as primary care providers and provide tools that allow them to accurately refer more complicated conditions to physicians with more sophisticated diagnostic abilities.

- **Invest more money in technologies that simplify complex problems, and less in high-end technologies.** Today most R&D dollars go to complex solutions for complex problems. But more venture capital must flow to projects focused on technologies that simplify diagnosis and treatment—especially of common diseases. By launching a series of such disruptive business ventures, major health care companies (Johnson & Johnson, Baxter, Merck) could spur significant growth—with less investment.

- **Don't be afraid to invent the institution that could put you out of business.** We'll always need some general hospitals for critical care (just as we still need mainframe computers after PCs transformed that industry). But most health care needs can be better met through specialized institutions that provide state-of-the-art care for a single category of disorders, such as cardiac or renal illnesses.

- **Overcome the inertia of regulation.** Instead of working to preserve the existing system at all costs, regulators should be asking, "How can we enable disruptive innovations to emerge?"

Example: An entrepreneur creates a portable X-ray machine for use in medical offices rather than in hospitals—promising significant cost savings. Regulators could support the new technology and address any concerns about possible risks. How? Require that all images interpreted by nonradiologists be transmitted via Internet to a second-opinion center. There, skilled radiologists could check or confirm initial diagnoses.

The progress of disruptive innovation

Dominant players in most markets focus on sustaining innovations—on improving their products and services to meet the needs of the profitable high-end customers. Soon, those improvements overshoot the needs of the vast majority of customers. That makes a market ripe for upstart companies seeking to introduce disruptive innovations—cheaper, simpler, more convenient products or services aimed at the lower end of the market. Over time, those products improve to meet the needs of most of the market, a phenomenon that has caused many of history's best companies to plunge into crisis.

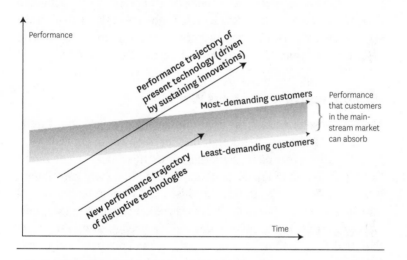

physicians to do. Similarly, the vast majority of research funding from the National Institutes of Health is aimed at learning to cure diseases that historically have been incurable. Much less is being spent on learning how to provide the health care that most of us need most of the time in a way that is simpler, more convenient, and less costly.

General hospitals—especially teaching hospitals—have likewise overshot the needs of most patients. Their impressive technological ability to deliver care enables them to address the needs of a relatively small population of very sick patients. But in the process of adding and incurring the costs of such capabilities, they have come to overserve the needs of the much larger population of patients with less serious disorders. Most types of patients that occupied hospital beds 20 years ago are not there today; they're being treated in lower cost, more-focused settings. As the stand-alone cardiac care centers, outpatient surgery centers, and other focused institutions get better and better, they become the price setters. As a consequence, the old high-cost institutions can't compete financially; nor are there enough really sick people to sustain them. Last year not a single teaching hospital in Massachusetts made money.

As a group, the medical schools, specialist physicians, hospitals, and equipment suppliers have done an exceptional job of learning to treat and resolve difficult, intractable problems at the high end. We stand in awe of what they have accomplished. But precisely because of their achievements, health care is now ripe for disruption.

How Disruptive Innovations Work

To get a sense of what those disruptions might be, let's look briefly at what has happened in other industries. Many of the most powerful innovations that disrupted other industries did so by enabling a larger population of less-skilled people to do in a more convenient, less expensive setting things that historically could be performed only by expensive specialists in centralized, inconvenient locations.

For example, in the 1960s when people needed computing help, they had to take their punched cards to the corporate mainframe computer center and wait in line for the data-processing specialists to run the job for them. Minicomputers and then personal computers were disruptive technologies to the mainframe makers. At the outset, they weren't nearly as capable as mainframes, and as a consequence the professionals who operated the sophisticated computers, and the companies that supplied them, discounted their value. But minicomputers enabled engineers to solve problems for themselves that had required centralized computing facilities. And personal computers enabled the unwashed masses—less-skilled people like the rest of us—to compute in the convenience of their offices and homes.

Nearly every disruptive innovation in history has had the same impact. George Eastman's camera made amateur photography widespread. Bell's telephone let people communicate without the need for professional telegraph operators. Photocopying enabled office workers to do things that historically only professional printers could do. Online brokerages have made investing so inexpensive and convenient that even college students now actively manage their own portfolios. Indeed, disruptive technologies have been one of the fundamental mechanisms through which the quality of our lives has improved. In each of these cases, the disruption left consumers far better off than they had been—we don't yearn to return to the days of the corporate mainframe center, for example.

Disruptions of health care professions

As specialist physicians continue to concentrate on curing the most incurable of illnesses for the sickest of patients, less-skilled practitioners could take on more complex roles than they are currently being allowed to do. Already, a host of over-the-counter drugs allow patients to administer care that used to require a doctor's prescription. Nurse practitioners are capable of treating many ailments that used to require a physician's care. And new procedures like angioplasty are allowing cardiologists to treat patients that in the past would have needed the services of open-heart surgeons.

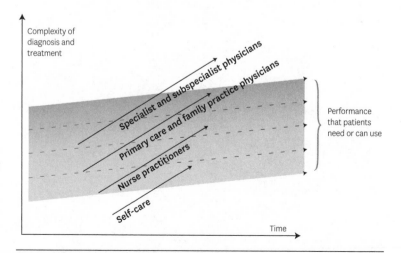

Our health care system needs to be transformed in the same way. Rather than ask complex, high-cost institutions and expensive, specialized professionals to move down-market, we need to look at the problem in a very different way. Managers and technologies need to focus instead on enabling less expensive professionals to do progressively more sophisticated things in less expensive settings.

We need diagnostic and therapeutic advances that allow nurse practitioners to treat diseases that used to require a physician's care, for example, or primary care physicians to treat conditions that used to require specialists. Similarly, we need innovations that enable procedures to be done in less expensive, more convenient settings—for doctors to provide services in their offices that used to be done during a hospital stay, for example. The graphs "Disruptions

Disruptions of health care institutions

Teaching hospitals incur great costs to develop the ability to treat difficult, intractable illnesses at the high end. In the process, they have come to overserve the needs of the much larger population of patients whose disorders are becoming more and more routine. Most types of patients that occupied hospital beds 20 years ago are now being treated in more-focused care centers and outpatient clinics, doctors' offices, and even at home.

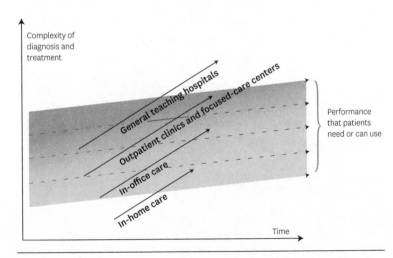

of health care professions" and "Disruptions of health care institutions" suggest the patterns by which these disruptive innovations might transform health care.

Some innovations of exactly this sort have transformed pockets of the health care system, and where they have happened, higher quality, greater convenience, and lower cost actually have been achieved. Before 1980, for example, patients with diabetes could only know whether they had abnormal levels of glucose in their blood indirectly; they used an often inaccurate urine test or visited a doctor who drew a blood sample and then measured its glucose content on an expensive piece of laboratory equipment. Today, patients pack miniature blood glucose meters with them wherever they go; they themselves now manage most aspects of a disease that previously had required much more professional involvement. They get far higher quality care far more conveniently. No patient or professional pines for the good old days—even though the companies that made the large laboratory blood-glucose testers were all driven from the market, and endocrinologists now face significantly reduced demand for their services.

Angioplasty is another example. Before the early 1980s, patients with coronary artery disease were treated through bypass surgery. It required a complex, technologically sophisticated surgical team, as well as multiple specialists in several disciplines, complicated equipment, days in the hospital, and weeks in recovery. The far simpler angioplasty uses a balloon to dilate narrowed arteries, causing less pain and disability. It enables less expensive or specialized practitioners to treat more people with coronary artery disease in lower cost settings. Initially, angioplasty was used in only the easiest cases and was much less effective than surgery. Experts viewed the procedure with skepticism because of all the things it and its practitioners couldn't do. But over time the disruptive innovation improved. Increasing skill and experience, together with sustaining technological innovations such as stents, have allowed angioplasty to supplant surgery in many cases. Angioplasty can now be reliably performed in stand-alone cardiac care centers, which aren't burdened with the tremendous overhead costs of hospitals.

By enabling less expensive practitioners to treat diabetes and coronary artery disease in less costly locations, these disruptive innovations have made health care more efficient. But more important, no compromises in quality were made. On the contrary, more patients get more care. When care is complex, expensive, and inconvenient, many afflictions simply go untreated. Before the disruption of angioplasty, for example, many people with coronary artery disease were not treated. Patients had to be disabled with chest pain or at risk of heart attack to justify the expense and inconvenience of open-heart surgery.

We need many more such disruptions—and today we have them within our reach. Unfortunately, the people and institutions whose livelihoods they threaten often resist them. We saw such resistance in the story of the portable X-ray machine. Here's another example. An English entrepreneur has developed a system for customizing eyeglasses quickly and efficiently. The patient puts on a pair of eyeglasses with seemingly flat lenses and an odd-looking rubber bulb attached to each stem. Looking at a vision-test chart and covering one eye, she squeezes the bulb on the right stem until she can read the fine print on the chart. A monomer in the bulb shapes the lens until that eye can see perfectly. She repeats the process for the other eye. Within two minutes, she has perfectly tailored eyeglasses—at a cost of about $5. This is a disruptive technology. It lets patients do for themselves something that historically required the skill of professionals.

Predictably, the established professions quickly mobilized to discredit the entrepreneur's technology, asserting that dangers such as glaucoma might go undetected if patients corrected their own vision and that for the long-term well-being of patients, care of the eyes must be left in the hands of professionals. Of course this is a reasonable concern. But it frames the problem incorrectly. The problem should be, instead, let's find a way to allow patients to correct vision for themselves while finding new ways for professionals to catch potentially serious disorders at an early stage.

Such resistance affects not only technology but people as well. Take nurse practitioners and physicians' assistants. Because of advances in diagnostic and therapeutic technologies, these clinicians can now competently, reliably diagnose and treat simple disorders that would have required the training and judgment of a physician only a few years ago. Accurate new tests, for example, allow physicians' assistants to diagnose diseases as simple as strep infections and as serious as diabetes. In addition, studies have shown that nurse practitioners typically devote more time to patients during consultations than physicians do and emphasize prevention and health maintenance to a greater degree.[2] But many states have regulations that prevent nurse practitioners from diagnosing diseases or from prescribing treatment that they are fully capable of handling.

The flawed rationale behind such policies is that because nurse practitioners are not as highly trained as physicians, they are not capable of providing care of comparable quality. This is the same logic that minicomputer makers used to discredit the personal computer. When a physician diagnoses a simple infectious disease, the patient uses only that fraction of the physician's training that relates to simple infectious diseases. Studies have shown that nurse practitioners with comparable training in simple infectious diseases can provide care of comparable quality in that tier of the market—even though they lack training in more complex disorders.[3]

Some nearsighted advocates of patients' rights assert that nurse practitioners might not have the judgment to recognize when a disorder is beyond their expertise. But family practice doctors recognize when they can treat a disorder and when it merits referral to a specialist. Surely nurse practitioners, working at even simpler tiers of the market, can be equipped to do the same thing. The real reason for blocking such disruption, we suspect, is the predictable desire of physicians to preserve their traditional market hegemony.

Instead of working to enable the natural upmarket migration that is an intrinsic part of economic progress, today's managed care organizations, insurers, and regulators have done just the opposite. They have forced highly trained physicians down-market to diagnose ear infections and bronchitis and have prevented nurse practitioners from doing things that technology enables them to do perfectly well. The result of this policy is perverse. To maintain their incomes, primary care physicians are forced to churn patients at an alarming

Patient Welfare in Disruptive Times

HOW MIGHT PATIENTS FARE AMIDST health care disruptions? The answer depends on whether competitive markets are allowed to work efficiently. If clinicians or patients are forced to use less expensive technologies, disaster will result. But if consumers and providers are given choices, the use of disruptive technologies will migrate to those applications where they create real value.

Consider Sonosite, a Seattle-area company that makes a small, highly portable, inexpensive ultrasound machine. The machine is good, but it is disruptive—it lacks the analytical features and the degree of resolution found in more expensive ultrasound equipment. If a managed care organization forced echocardiologists and OB-GYN physicians to use these less expensive devices for situations in which they previously have used traditional equipment, a specialist could risk missing something important, and the patient's well-being could be compromised. But suppose instead that because Sonosite's technology now makes ultrasound accessible and affordable to generalist clinicians, they could begin to provide better, more accurate care within the low-cost and more convenient context of their offices. Instead of conducting exams in which they hypothesize about what's going on inside a patient's body by listening through a stethoscope or by using their fingers to probe for irregularities, they could use this simple ultrasound device that would let them see inside the body. By enabling generalists to diagnose more quickly and with greater precision, disruptive technologies such as Sonosite's can improve, not compromise, the cost, quality, and convenience of care.

Ultimately, we would expect that the disruptive portable machines will improve to the point that they will supplant the more expensive traditional ultrasound equipment in established applications as well. But the true transformative impact of such technologies in health care will come as they allow less expensive professionals to provide better care.

If history is any guide, the established high-end providers of products and services are likely to be articulate and assertive about preserving existing systems in order to ensure patient well-being. Very often, however, their eloquence reflects concerns about their own well-being. Customers have almost always emerged from disruptive transitions better off—as long as the disruptions are not forced into an old mode, but instead enable better service to be delivered in a less-costly, more convenient context.

rate—frequently spending only a few minutes with each patient. That reduces the quality and convenience of care.

This practice, which has become pervasive in most managed care organizations, is akin to what would have happened if some regulatory body in the early 1980s had decreed that because microprocessors were inferior in computing power to wired logic circuits, all personal computers had to be equipped with wired logic boards, not microprocessors. Such a regulation would have halted the industry's progress. The fact that we were able to use microprocessor-based computers for the jobs they were capable of handling, and wired-logic-based machines for the jobs for which microprocessors weren't suited, has been a key to the creation of high-quality, convenient, cost-effective computing for all of us. Enabling less expensive people to do things that were previously unimaginable has been one of the fundamental engines of economic progress—and the established health care institutions have fought that engine tooth and nail.

Solutions to the Crisis

The crisis in health care is deep, to be sure. But the history of other disruptive revolutions offers a number of suggestions for how a systemic transformation might be managed. We describe some of these here:

Create—then embrace—a system where the clinician's skill level is matched to the difficulty of the medical problem

Medical problems range from the very simple to the very complex, as we've said. Let's look more closely at that range for a moment. In the simplest tiers, diagnosis and treatment can be rule-based: accurate data yield an unambiguous diagnosis, indicating a proven therapeutic strategy. Many infectious diseases fall into this category. In the middle tiers, diagnosis and treatment occur through pattern recognition—no single piece of data yields an answer, but multiple data points lead to a definitive diagnosis. The onset of Type I diabetes, for example, is diagnosed when a pattern is observed—blurry vision, incessant thirst, weight loss, and frequent urination. Once a diagnosis is confirmed, relatively standardized treatment protocols

CHRISTENSEN, BOHMER, AND KENAGY

often exist. In the most complex disorders, diagnosis and treatment occur in a problem-solving mode. These problems require the collective experience and judgment of a team of clinical investigators and often involve cycles of testing, hypotheses, and experimentation.

By now it's clear that the simplest tiers can be reliably treated and diagnosed by less highly skilled clinicians—and also that institutional forces will fight that reality. We cannot allow such opposition to arrest reform. Instead, we must invent processes that can channel complex problems, which can't be solved in a rule-based mode, to clinicians whose skills are appropriate to a pattern-recognition or a problem-solving mode.

Scientific progress moves disorders that used to be dealt with in a problem-solving mode toward a pattern-recognition mode and those that had to be addressed through pattern recognition toward a rule-based regime. Mapping the human genome will accelerate this process. Not long ago, for example, leukemia was thought to be a single disease. Diagnosing and treating it was complex—no two patients responded identically to the same therapy, and treatment required the experience, intuition, and problem-solving skills of the best oncologists. Our improved understanding of the human genetic code, however, has helped researchers see that what we previously called leukemia is really at least six different diseases. Each is characterized by a specific genetic pattern, and patients can be precisely diagnosed by matching their patterns to a template.

Where once therapy used to be applied experimentally, such precise definition of the disease will allow for precise treatment protocols. Disruptive technologies such as this are precisely what are needed to reform health care. They will continue to enable less-experienced caregivers to make more precise diagnoses and provide higher quality care than they could have in problem-solving mode.

It's in physicians' interest to embrace this change. Rather than fight the nurse practitioners who are invading their turf, primary care physicians should move upmarket themselves, using advances in diagnostic and therapeutic technologies to perform many of the services they now refer to costly hospitals and specialists. They should, in other words, disrupt those above them rather than fight a reactionary and ultimately futile battle with disrupters from below.[4] Let us be clear. Many managed care organizations today give primary care physicians a financial incentive *not* to refer patients to specialists—to continue treating patients they are not competent to care for. Inviting them to move incompetently upmarket is a recipe for disaster. Disruptive technologies such as those we have described will enable these caregivers to move *competently* upward. These innovations are the sort that will reform health care. This strategy—unlike the one that pushes these physicians down-market or encourages them upward without enabling technology—is consistent with the way technological progress and customer needs interact.

Invest less money in high-end, complex technologies and more in technologies that simplify complex problems

Equity markets have not been generous to companies making health care products and equipment in recent years. Other sectors of the economy are perceived to exhibit greater growth and profit potential. One reason for this, we believe, is that much of the energy and capital spent in the development of new health care products and services have been targeted at the high end—at sustaining technologies that enable the most skilled practitioners to solve problems that could not be solved before. We do not contest the value of these innovations—but they will not transform health care. The great growth opportunities exist in the simpler tiers of the market. History tells us that major new growth markets coalesce when products, processes, and information technologies let less highly paid groups of people do things in more convenient settings. To truly disrupt the health care system, venture capital, entrepreneurial energy, and technology development need to flow toward these enabling initiatives. Rather than focus on complex solutions for complex problems, research and development need to focus on simplification.

It's not entirely clear why more venture capital hasn't flowed in this direction. One possible reason is that individual entrepreneurial companies don't get to pick fights with individual Goliaths—more often, they face an army of giants. Because regulators, litigators, insurers, physicians, hospitals, and medical schools have such powerful interlocking interests in the status quo, disruption might require the concerted strategic focus of major health care companies such as Johnson & Johnson, Baxter, Medtronic, or Merck. Over time, they could overcome the inertia of entrenched institutions. A series of disruptive business ventures launched by these companies would create far greater growth for them, with less investment, than would continued pursuit of sustaining technologies that enable specialists to push further into high-end complexities.

Create new organizations to do the disrupting

The health care industry today is trying to preserve outmoded institutions. Yet the history of disruptive innovations tells us that those institutions will be replaced, soon enough, with new institutions whose business models are appropriate to the new technologies and markets.

When disruptive innovations have invaded the mainstream markets of other industries, a difficult period typically has preceded the arrival of truly convenient, lower cost, higher quality products and services. Between 1988 and 1993, for example, as networked personal computers became the dominant information technology architecture, the former industry leaders fell into disarray. Together, the mainframe and minicomputer makers logged $20 billion in operating losses during that period. None of these companies was able to adapt its business model to compete in the personal computer world. Instead, they seemed able only to tighten the thumbscrews on their existing processes, attacking costs through mergers and layoffs, as they withered away. During this period, it wasn't the computer industry that was in crisis—only its traditional institutions were. Disruptive innovators such as Intel, Sun, Microsoft, and Dell were creating extraordinary value.

The massive financial losses that hospitals and managed care institutions are suffering today mirror exactly what happened to the dominant players in other disrupted industries. And they are responding in the same way—by tightening controls on their existing business models. They are merging, closing facilities, laying off workers, forming buying groups, delaying payments, adding layers of control-oriented overhead workers, and hiring consultants—while going about their work in a fundamentally unchanged way. In fact, the billions of dollars large general hospitals are spending to build information technology systems and to create integrated feeder systems of physicians' group practices and primary-, secondary-, and tertiary-care hospitals are designed to preserve, rather than displace, the existing institutions.

We will always need some general hospitals to provide intensive and critical care to the sickest patients, just as we still need IBM and Hitachi to make mainframe computers for the most complex computing applications. But it is very likely that the care of disorders that primarily involve one system in the body—from earaches to cardiac and renal illnesses—will migrate to focused institutions whose scope enables them to provide better care with less complexity-driven overhead. If history is any guide, the health care system can be transformed only by creating new institutions that can capably deliver the vast majority of such care, rather than attempting a tortuous transformation of existing institutions that were designed for other purposes.

Leaders of today's hospital and managed care companies might profit from comparing the approaches that S. S. Kresge and F. W. Woolworth took toward disruptive discount retailing, beginning in the early 1960s, as recounted in Clayton Christensen's *The Innovator's Dilemma*. Kresge addressed the disruption by systematically closing 10% of its variety stores every year and funneling all its cash into its disruptive start-up, Kmart. Woolworth, by contrast, tried to maintain its pace of investment in its traditional stores while building its discount-retailing arm, Woolco. Despite the fact that Woolworth was far larger and had much deeper pockets, Woolco—and ultimately all of Woolworth's variety stores—folded. The lessons for today's medical institutions: don't be scared to invent the institution that could put you out of business, and stop investing in dying business models.

Overcome the inertia of regulation

Attempts to use regulation to stave off disruptive attacks are quite common. The U.S. automakers, for example, relied on import quotas as long as they could to keep disruptive Toyota and Honda at bay.

Unfortunately, regulators are inclined to be even more protective of the entrenched professions and institutions in health care than they were of the U.S. automakers. The links between those institutions, federal and state regulators, and insurance companies are strong; they are wielded to preserve the status quo. (Nothing else could explain why nurse practitioners are forbidden from diagnosing simple illnesses in so many states.)

Instead of working to preserve the existing system, regulators need to frame their jobs differently. They need to ask how they can enable disruptive innovations to emerge. Let's return to the example we began with—the low-cost X-ray machine. Suppose the regulators wanted to see this disruptive innovation work in doctors' offices but were concerned about potential risks. They might require that all images interpreted in a physician's office by a non-radiologist be transmitted via the Internet to a second-opinion center, where skilled radiologists could confirm those initial diagnoses. Admittedly, that would require a massive change in the way regulators do their work.

The Need for Leadership

Once an industry is in crisis, individual leaders often become paralyzed. They're incapable of embracing disruptive approaches because the profitability of the institutions they lead has been so eroded. Typically, not only do they ignore the potential disruptions, they actively work to discredit and oppose them. Thus far, this pattern has held true in the health care industry as well.

Successful disruptive revolution of this system will unfold more quickly, and far less painfully for everyone, if leaders at regional and national levels work together—not to regulate the existing system but to coordinate the removal of the barriers that have prevented disruptions from happening. Unfortunately, in this presidential election year, the proposals from both leading parties for dealing with the crisis in health care have been molded within the established system. These proposals can be divided into three categories of solutions: control costs by consuming less health care; impose reimbursement controls that force high-end providers to become more efficient; and use government money to subsidize the high costs of health care for targeted segments of the population. None of these proposals addresses the fundamental causes of the dilemmas that the health care system faces.

Government and health care industry leaders need to step forward—to help insurers, regulators, managed care organizations, hospitals, and health professionals work together to facilitate disruption instead of uniting to prevent it. If they do, some of the established institutions will fail. But many more health care providers will realize the opportunities for growth that come with disruption— because disruption is the fundamental mechanism through which we will build a higher quality, more convenient, and lower cost health care system. If leaders with such vision do indeed step forward, we will all have access to more health care, not less.

Originally published in September–October 2000. Reprint R0050I

Notes

The authors express appreciation to Jeff Elton and his staff at Integral, Incorporated for their contributions to this article.

1. Clayton M. Christensen, *The Innovator's Dilemma: When New Technologies Cause Great Firms to Fail* (Harvard Business School Press, 1997).

2. See James Lardner, "For Nurses, a Barrier Is Broken," *U.S. News & World Report,* July 1998.

3. Richard A. Cooper, MD, et al. "Roles of Non-physician Clinicians as Autonomous Providers of Patient Care," *JAMA,* September 2, 1998. These market forces are already at work. It is estimated that by the year 2005, the number of nurse practitioners in clinical practice will equal the number of family physicians. Between 1992 and 1997, the number of schools offering qualification programs for NPs more than doubled, from less than 100 to approximately 250. During that same time, the number of students pursuing NP degrees quintupled, from 4,000 to over 20,000.

4. Evidence that specialists are already being disrupted in this manner can be found in a 1995 report by the Council of Graduate Medical Education, which predicted an excess of 115,000 specialists by the year 2000. See Stephen M. Shortell et al., *Remaking Health Care in America: Building Organized Delivery Systems* (Jossey-Bass Publishers, 1996), p. 298.

Blue Ocean Strategy

by W. Chan Kim and Renée Mauborgne

A ONETIME ACCORDION PLAYER, stilt walker, and fire-eater, Guy
Laliberté is now CEO of one of Canada's largest cultural exports,
Cirque du Soleil. Founded in 1984 by a group of street performers,
Cirque has staged dozens of productions seen by some 40 million
people in 90 cities around the world. In 20 years, Cirque has achieved
revenues that Ringling Bros. and Barnum & Bailey—the world's leading circus—took more than a century to attain.

Cirque's rapid growth occurred in an unlikely setting. The circus
business was (and still is) in long-term decline. Alternative forms of
entertainment—sporting events, TV, and video games—were casting
a growing shadow. Children, the mainstay of the circus audience,
preferred PlayStations to circus acts. There was also rising senti-
ment, fueled by animal rights groups, against the use of animals, traditionally an integral part of the circus. On the supply side, the star
performers that Ringling and the other circuses relied on to draw in
the crowds could often name their own terms. As a result, the industry was hit by steadily decreasing audiences and increasing costs.
What's more, any new entrant to this business would be competing
against a formidable incumbent that for most of the last century had
set the industry standard.

How did Cirque profitably increase revenues by a factor of 22 over
the last ten years in such an unattractive environment? The tagline
for one of the first Cirque productions is revealing: "We reinvent the
circus." Cirque did not make its money by competing within the confines of the existing industry or by stealing customers from Ringling

and the others. Instead it created uncontested market space that made the competition irrelevant. It pulled in a whole new group of customers who were traditionally noncustomers of the industry—adults and corporate clients who had turned to theater, opera, or ballet and were, therefore, prepared to pay several times more than the price of a conventional circus ticket for an unprecedented entertainment experience.

To understand the nature of Cirque's achievement, you have to realize that the business universe consists of two distinct kinds of space, which we think of as red and blue oceans. Red oceans represent all the industries in existence today—the known market space. In red oceans, industry boundaries are defined and accepted, and the competitive rules of the game are well understood. Here, companies try to outperform their rivals in order to grab a greater share of existing demand. As the space gets more and more crowded, prospects for profits and growth are reduced. Products turn into commodities, and increasing competition turns the water bloody.

Blue oceans denote all the industries *not* in existence today—the unknown market space, untainted by competition. In blue oceans, demand is created rather than fought over. There is ample opportunity for growth that is both profitable and rapid. There are two ways to create blue oceans. In a few cases, companies can give rise to completely new industries, as eBay did with the online auction industry. But in most cases, a blue ocean is created from within a red ocean when a company alters the boundaries of an existing industry. As will become evident later, this is what Cirque did. In breaking through the boundary traditionally separating circus and theater, it made a new and profitable blue ocean from within the red ocean of the circus industry.

Cirque is just one of more than 150 blue ocean creations that we have studied in over 30 industries, using data stretching back more than 100 years. We analyzed companies that created those blue oceans and their less successful competitors, which were caught in red oceans. In studying these data, we have observed a consistent pattern of strategic thinking behind the creation of new markets and industries, what we call blue ocean strategy. The logic behind blue

Idea in Brief

The best way to drive profitable growth? Stop competing in overcrowded industries. In those **red oceans,** companies try to outperform rivals to grab bigger slices of existing demand. As the space gets increasingly crowded, profit and growth prospects shrink. Products become commoditized. Ever-more-intense competition turns the water bloody.

How to avoid the fray? Kim and Mauborgne recommend creating **blue oceans**—uncontested market spaces where the competition is irrelevant. In blue oceans, you invent and capture new demand, and you offer customers a leap in value while also streamlining your costs. Results? Handsome profits, speedy growth—and brand equity that lasts for decades while rivals scramble to catch up.

Consider Cirque du Soleil—which invented a new industry that combined elements from traditional circus with elements drawn from sophisticated theater. In just 20 years, Cirque raked in revenues that Ringling Bros. and Barnum & Bailey—the world's leading circus—needed more than a century to attain.

ocean strategy parts with traditional models focused on competing in existing market space. Indeed, it can be argued that managers' failure to realize the differences between red and blue ocean strategy lies behind the difficulties many companies encounter as they try to break from the competition.

In this article, we present the concept of blue ocean strategy and describe its defining characteristics. We assess the profit and growth consequences of blue oceans and discuss why their creation is a rising imperative for companies in the future. We believe that an understanding of blue ocean strategy will help today's companies as they struggle to thrive in an accelerating and expanding business universe.

Blue and Red Oceans

Although the term may be new, blue oceans have always been with us. Look back 100 years and ask yourself which industries known today were then unknown. The answer: Industries as basic as automobiles, music recording, aviation, petrochemicals,

Idea in Practice

How to begin creating blue oceans? Kim and Mauborgne offer these suggestions:

Understand the Logic Behind Blue Ocean Strategy

The logic behind blue ocean strategy is counterintuitive:

- **It's not about technology innovation.** Blue oceans seldom result from technological innovation. Often, the underlying technology already exists—and blue ocean creators link it to what buyers value. Compaq, for example, used existing technologies to create its ProSignia server, which gave buyers twice the file and print capability of the minicomputer at one-third the price.

- **You don't have to venture into distant waters to create blue oceans.** Most blue oceans are created from within, not beyond, the red oceans of existing industries. Incumbents often create blue oceans within their core businesses. Consider the megaplexes introduced by AMC—an established player in the movie-theater industry. Megaplexes provided movie-goers spectacular viewing experiences in stadium-size theater complexes at lower costs to theater owners.

Apply Blue Ocean Strategic Moves

To apply blue ocean strategic moves:

- **Never use the competition as a benchmark.** Instead, make the competition irrelevant by creating a leap in value for both yourself and your

pharmaceuticals, and management consulting were unheard-of or had just begun to emerge. Now turn the clock back only 30 years and ask yourself the same question. Again, a plethora of multibillion-dollar industries jump out: mutual funds, cellular telephones, biotechnology, discount retailing, express package delivery, snow-boards, coffee bars, and home videos, to name a few. Just three decades ago, none of these industries existed in a meaningful way.

This time, put the clock forward 20 years. Ask yourself: How many industries that are unknown today will exist then? If history is any predictor of the future, the answer is many. Companies have a huge capacity to create new industries and re-create existing ones, customers. Ford did this with the Model T. Ford could have tried besting the fashionable, customized cars that wealthy people bought for weekend jaunts in the countryside. Instead, it offered a car for everyday use that was far more affordable, durable, and easy to use and fix than rivals' offerings. Model T sales boomed, and Ford's market share surged from 9% in 1908 to 61% in 1921.

- **Reduce your costs while also offering customers more value.** Cirque du Soleil omitted costly elements of traditional circus, such as animal acts and aisle concessions. Its reduced cost structure enabled it to provide sophisticated elements from theater that appealed to adult audiences—such as themes, original scores, and enchanting sets, all of which change year to year. The added value lured adults who had not gone to a circus for years and enticed them to come back more frequently—thereby increasing revenues. By offering the best of circus and theater, Cirque created a market space that, as yet, has no name—and no equals.

a fact that is reflected in the deep changes that have been necessary in the way industries are classified. The half-century-old Standard Industrial Classification (SIC) system was replaced in 1997 by the North American Industry Classification System (NAICS). The new system expanded the ten SIC industry sectors into 20 to reflect the emerging realities of new industry territories—blue oceans. The services sector under the old system, for example, is now seven sectors ranging from information to health care and social assistance. Given that these classification systems are designed for standardization and continuity, such a replacement shows how significant a source of economic growth the creation of blue oceans has been.

Looking forward, it seems clear to us that blue oceans will remain the engine of growth. Prospects in most established market spaces—red oceans—are shrinking steadily. Technological advances have substantially improved industrial productivity, permitting suppliers to produce an unprecedented array of products and services. And as trade barriers between nations and regions fall and information on products and prices becomes instantly and globally available, niche markets and monopoly havens are continuing to disappear. At the same time, there is little evidence of any increase in demand, at least in the developed markets, where recent United Nations statistics even point to declining populations. The result is that in more and more industries, supply is overtaking demand.

This situation has inevitably hastened the commoditization of products and services, stoked price wars, and shrunk profit margins. According to recent studies, major American brands in a variety of product and service categories have become more and more alike. And as brands become more similar, people increasingly base purchase choices on price. People no longer insist, as in the past, that their laundry detergent be Tide. Nor do they necessarily stick to Colgate when there is a special promotion for Crest, and vice versa. In overcrowded industries, differentiating brands becomes harder both in economic upturns and in downturns.

The Paradox of Strategy

Unfortunately, most companies seem becalmed in their red oceans. In a study of business launches in 108 companies, we found that 86% of those new ventures were line extensions—incremental improvements to existing industry offerings—and a mere 14% were aimed at creating new markets or industries. While line extensions did account for 62% of the total revenues, they delivered only 39% of the total profits. By contrast, the 14% invested in creating new markets and industries delivered 38% of total revenues and a startling 61% of total profits.

So why the dramatic imbalance in favor of red oceans? Part of the explanation is that corporate strategy is heavily influenced by its roots in military strategy. The very language of strategy is deeply imbued with military references—chief executive "officers" in "headquarters," "troops" on the "front lines." Described this way, strategy is all about red ocean competition. It is about confronting an opponent and driving him off a battlefield of limited territory. Blue ocean strategy, by contrast, is about doing business where there is no competitor. It is about creating new land, not dividing up existing land. Focusing on the red ocean therefore means accepting the key constraining factors of war—limited terrain and the need to beat an enemy to succeed. And it means denying the distinctive strength of the business world—the capacity to create new market space that is uncontested.

The tendency of corporate strategy to focus on winning against rivals was exacerbated by the meteoric rise of Japanese companies in the 1970s and 1980s. For the first time in corporate history, customers were deserting Western companies in droves. As competition mounted in the global marketplace, a slew of red ocean strategies emerged, all arguing that competition was at the core of corporate success and failure. Today, one hardly talks about strategy without using the language of competition. The term that best symbolizes this is "competitive advantage." In the competitive-advantage worldview, companies are often driven to outperform rivals and capture greater shares of existing market space.

Of course competition matters. But by focusing on competition, scholars, companies, and consultants have ignored two very important—and, we would argue, far more lucrative—aspects of strategy: One is to find and develop markets where there is little or no competition—blue oceans—and the other is to exploit and protect blue oceans. These challenges are very different from those to which strategists have devoted most of their attention.

Toward Blue Ocean Strategy

What kind of strategic logic is needed to guide the creation of blue oceans? To answer that question, we looked back over 100 years of data on blue ocean creation to see what patterns could be discerned.

A snapshot of blue ocean creation

This table identifies the strategic elements that were common to blue ocean creations in three different industries in different eras. It is not intended to be comprehensive in coverage or exhaustive in content. We chose to show American industries because they represented the largest and least-regulated market during our study period. The pattern of blue ocean creations exemplified by these three industries is consistent with what we observed in the other industries in our study.

Key blue ocean creations	Was the blue ocean created by a new entrant or an incumbent?	Was it driven by technology pioneering or value pioneering?	At the time of the blue ocean creation, was the industry attractive or unattractive?
Automobiles			
Ford Model T Unveiled in 1908, the Model T was the first mass-produced car, priced so that many Americans could afford it.	New entrant	Value pioneering* (mostly existing technologies)	Unattractive
GM's "car for every purse and purpose" GM created a blue ocean in 1924 by injecting fun and fashion into the car.	Incumbent	Value pioneering (some new technologies)	Attractive
Japanese fuel-efficient autos Japanese automakers created a blue ocean in the mid-1970s with small, reliable lines of cars.	Incumbent	Value pioneering (some new technologies)	Unattractive
Chrysler minivan With its 1984 minivan, Chrysler created a new class of automobile that was as easy to use as a car but had the passenger space of a van.	Incumbent	Value pioneering (mostly existing technologies)	Unattractive

*Driven by value pioneering does not mean that technologies were not involved. Rather, it means that the defining technologies used had largely been in existence, whether in that industry or elsewhere.

Key blue ocean creations	Was the blue ocean created by a new entrant or an incumbent?	Was it driven by technology pioneering or value pioneering?	At the time of the blue ocean creation, was the industry attractive or unattractive?
Computers			
CTR's tabulating machine In 1914, CTR created the business machine industry by simplifying, modularizing, and leasing tabulating machines. CTR later changed its name to IBM.	Incumbent	Value pioneering (some new technologies)	Unattractive
IBM 650 electronic computer and System/360 In 1952, IBM created the business computer industry by simplifying and reducing the power and price of existing technology. And it exploded the blue ocean created by the 650 when in 1964 it unveiled the System/360, the first modularized computer system.	Incumbent	Value pioneering (650: mostly existing technologies) Value and technology pioneering (System/360: new and existing technologies)	Nonexistent
Apple personal computer Although it was not the first home computer, the all-in-one, simple-to-use Apple II was a blue ocean creation when it appeared in 1978.	New entrant	Value pioneering (mostly existing technologies)	Unattractive
Compaq PC servers Compaq created a blue ocean in 1992 with its ProSignia server, which gave buyers twice the file and print capability of the minicomputer at one-third the price.	Incumbent	Value pioneering (mostly existing technologies)	Nonexistent

(continued)

175

Key blue ocean creations	Was the blue ocean created by a new entrant or an incumbent?	Was it driven by technology pioneering or value pioneering?	At the time of the blue ocean creation, was the industry attractive or unattractive?
Dell built-to-order computers In the mid-1990s, Dell created a blue ocean in a highly competitive industry by creating a new purchase and delivery experience for buyers.	New entrant	Value pioneering (mostly existing technologies)	Unattractive
Movie theaters			
Nickelodeon The first Nickelodeon opened its doors in 1905, showing short films around-the-clock to working-class audiences for five cents.	New entrant	Value pioneering (mostly existing technologies)	Nonexistent
Palace theaters Created by Roxy Rothapfel in 1914, these theaters provided an operalike environment for cinema viewing at an affordable price.	Incumbent	Value pioneering (mostly existing technologies)	Attractive
AMC multiplex In the 1960s, the number of multiplexes in America's suburban shopping malls mushroomed. The multiplex gave viewers greater choice while reducing owners' costs.	Incumbent	Value pioneering (mostly existing technologies)	Unattractive
AMC megaplex Megaplexes, introduced in 1995, offered every current blockbuster and provided spectacular viewing experiences in theater complexes as big as stadiums, at a lower cost to theater owners.	Incumbent	Value pioneering (mostly existing technologies)	Unattractive

Some of our data are presented in "A snapshot of blue ocean creation." It shows an overview of key blue ocean creations in three industries that closely touch people's lives: autos—how people get to work; computers—what people use at work; and movie theaters—where people go after work for enjoyment. We found that:

Blue oceans are not about technology innovation

Leading-edge technology is sometimes involved in the creation of blue oceans, but it is not a defining feature of them. This is often true even in industries that are technology intensive. As the exhibit reveals, across all three representative industries, blue oceans were seldom the result of technological innovation per se; the underlying technology was often already in existence. Even Ford's revolutionary assembly line can be traced to the meatpacking industry in America. Like those within the auto industry, the blue oceans within the computer industry did not come about through technology innovations alone but by linking technology to what buyers valued. As with the IBM 650 and the Compaq PC server, this often involved simplifying the technology.

Incumbents often create blue oceans—and usually within their core businesses

GM, the Japanese automakers, and Chrysler were established players when they created blue oceans in the auto industry. So were CTR and its later incarnation, IBM, and Compaq in the computer industry. And in the cinema industry, the same can be said of palace theaters and AMC. Of the companies listed here, only Ford, Apple, Dell, and Nickelodeon were new entrants in their industries; the first three were start-ups, and the fourth was an established player entering an industry that was new to it. This suggests that incumbents are not at a disadvantage in creating new market spaces. Moreover, the blue oceans made by incumbents were usually within their core businesses. In fact, as the exhibit shows, most blue oceans are created from within, not beyond, red oceans of existing industries. This challenges the view that new markets are in distant waters. Blue oceans are right next to you in every industry.

Company and industry are the wrong units of analysis

The traditional units of strategic analysis—company and industry—have little explanatory power when it comes to analyzing how and why blue oceans are created. There is no consistently excellent company; the same company can be brilliant at one time and wrongheaded at another. Every company rises and falls over time. Likewise, there is no perpetually excellent industry; relative attractiveness is driven largely by the creation of blue oceans from within them.

The most appropriate unit of analysis for explaining the creation of blue oceans is the strategic move—the set of managerial actions and decisions involved in making a major market-creating business offering. Compaq, for example, is considered by many people to be "unsuccessful" because it was acquired by Hewlett-Packard in 2001 and ceased to be a company. But the firm's ultimate fate does not invalidate the smart strategic move Compaq made that led to the creation of the multibillion-dollar market in PC servers, a move that was a key cause of the company's powerful comeback in the 1990s.

Creating blue oceans builds brands

So powerful is blue ocean strategy that a blue ocean strategic move can create brand equity that lasts for decades. Almost all of the companies listed in the exhibit are remembered in no small part for the blue oceans they created long ago. Very few people alive today were around when the first Model T rolled off Henry Ford's assembly line in 1908, but the company's brand still benefits from that blue ocean move. IBM, too, is often regarded as an "American institution" largely for the blue oceans it created in computing; the 360 series was its equivalent of the Model T.

Our findings are encouraging for executives at the large, established corporations that are traditionally seen as the victims of new market space creation. For what they reveal is that large R&D budgets are not the key to creating new market space. The key is making the right strategic moves. What's more, companies that understand what drives a good strategic move will be well placed to create multiple blue oceans over time, thereby continuing to deliver high growth and profits over a sustained period. The creation of blue oceans, in other words, is a product of strategy and as such is very much a product of managerial action.

The Defining Characteristics

Our research shows several common characteristics across strategic moves that create blue oceans. We found that the creators of blue oceans, in sharp contrast to companies playing by traditional rules, never use the competition as a benchmark. Instead they make it irrelevant by creating a leap in value for both buyers and the company itself. (The exhibit "Red ocean versus blue ocean strategy" compares the chief characteristics of these two strategy models.)

Perhaps the most important feature of blue ocean strategy is that it rejects the fundamental tenet of conventional strategy: that a trade-off exists between value and cost. According to this thesis, companies can either create greater value for customers at a higher cost or create reasonable value at a lower cost. In other words, strategy is essentially a choice between differentiation and low cost. But when it comes to creating blue oceans, the evidence shows that successful companies pursue differentiation and low cost simultaneously.

To see how this is done, let us go back to Cirque du Soleil. At the time of Cirque's debut, circuses focused on benchmarking one another and maximizing their shares of shrinking demand by tweaking traditional circus acts. This included trying to secure more and better-known clowns and lion tamers, efforts that raised circuses' cost structure without substantially altering the circus experience. The result was rising costs without rising revenues and a downward spiral in overall circus demand. Enter Cirque. Instead of following the conventional logic of outpacing the competition by offering a better solution to the given problem—creating a circus with even greater fun and thrills—it redefined the problem itself by offering people the fun and thrill of the circus *and* the intellectual sophistication and artistic richness of the theater.

In designing performances that landed both these punches, Cirque had to reevaluate the components of the traditional circus

Red ocean versus blue ocean strategy

The imperatives for red ocean and blue ocean strategies are starkly different.

Red ocean strategy	Blue ocean strategy
Compete in existing market space.	Create uncontested market space.
Beat the competition.	Make the competition irrelevant.
Exploit existing demand.	Create and capture new demand.
Make the value/cost trade-off.	Break the value/cost trade-off.
Align the whole system of a company's activities with its strategic choice of differentiation *or* low cost.	Align the whole system of a company's activities in pursuit of differentiation *and* low cost.

offering. What the company found was that many of the elements considered essential to the fun and thrill of the circus were unnecessary and in many cases costly. For instance, most circuses offer animal acts. These are a heavy economic burden, because circuses have to shell out not only for the animals but also for their training, medical care, housing, insurance, and transportation. Yet Cirque found that the appetite for animal shows was rapidly diminishing because of rising public concern about the treatment of circus animals and the ethics of exhibiting them.

Similarly, although traditional circuses promoted their performers as stars, Cirque realized that the public no longer thought of circus artists as stars, at least not in the movie star sense. Cirque did away with traditional three-ring shows, too. Not only did these create confusion among spectators forced to switch their attention from one ring to another, they also increased the number of performers needed, with obvious cost implications. And while aisle concession sales appeared to be a good way to generate revenue, the high prices discouraged parents from making purchases and made them feel they were being taken for a ride.

Cirque found that the lasting allure of the traditional circus came down to just three factors: the clowns, the tent, and the classic acrobatic acts. So Cirque kept the clowns, while shifting their humor away from slapstick to a more enchanting, sophisticated style. It glamorized the tent, which many circuses had abandoned in favor of rented venues. Realizing that the tent, more than anything else, captured the magic of the circus, Cirque designed this classic symbol with a glorious external finish and a high level of audience comfort. Gone were the sawdust and hard benches. Acrobats and other thrilling performers were retained, but Cirque reduced their roles and made their acts more elegant by adding artistic flair.

Even as Cirque stripped away some of the traditional circus offerings, it injected new elements drawn from the world of theater. For instance, unlike traditional circuses featuring a series of unrelated acts, each Cirque creation resembles a theater performance in that it has a theme and story line. Although the themes are intentionally vague, they bring harmony and an intellectual element to the acts. Cirque also borrows ideas from Broadway. For example, rather than putting on the traditional "once and for all" show, Cirque mounts multiple productions based on different themes and story lines. As with Broadway productions, too, each Cirque show has an original musical score, which drives the performance, lighting, and timing of the acts, rather than the other way around. The productions feature abstract and spiritual dance, an idea derived from theater and ballet. By introducing these factors, Cirque has created highly sophisticated entertainments. And by staging multiple productions, Cirque gives people reason to come to the circus more often, thereby increasing revenues.

Cirque offers the best of both circus and theater. And by eliminating many of the most expensive elements of the circus, it has been able to dramatically reduce its cost structure, achieving both differentiation and low cost. (For a depiction of the economics underpinning blue ocean strategy, see "The simultaneous pursuit of differentiation and low cost.")

By driving down costs while simultaneously driving up value for buyers, a company can achieve a leap in value for both itself and its customers. Since buyer value comes from the utility and price a company offers, and a company generates value for itself through cost structure and price, blue ocean strategy is achieved only when the whole system of a company's utility, price, and cost activities is properly aligned. It is this whole-system approach that makes the creation of blue oceans a sustainable strategy. Blue ocean strategy integrates the range of a firm's functional and operational activities.

A rejection of the trade-off between low cost and differentiation implies a fundamental change in strategic mind-set—we cannot emphasize enough how fundamental a shift it is. The red ocean assumption that industry structural conditions are a given and firms are forced to compete within them is based on an intellectual worldview that academics call the *structuralist* view, or *environmental determinism*. According to this view, companies and managers are largely at the mercy of economic forces greater than themselves. Blue ocean strategies, by contrast, are based on a worldview in which market boundaries and industries can be reconstructed by the actions and beliefs of industry players. We call this the *reconstructionist* view.

The founders of Cirque du Soleil clearly did not feel constrained to act within the confines of their industry. Indeed, is Cirque really a circus with all that it has eliminated, reduced, raised, and created? Or is it theater? If it is theater, then what genre—Broadway show, opera, ballet? The magic of Cirque was created through a reconstruction of elements drawn from all of these alternatives. In the end, Cirque is none of them and a little of all of them. From within the red oceans of theater and circus, Cirque has created a blue ocean of uncontested market space that has, as yet, no name.

Barriers to Imitation

Companies that create blue oceans usually reap the benefits without credible challenges for ten to 15 years, as was the case with Cirque du Soleil, Home Depot, Federal Express, Southwest Airlines, and CNN, to name just a few. The reason is that blue ocean strategy creates considerable economic and cognitive barriers to imitation.

For a start, adopting a blue ocean creator's business model is easier to imagine than to do. Because blue ocean creators immediately attract customers in large volumes, they are able to generate scale

The simultaneous pursuit of differentiation and low cost

A blue ocean is created in the region where a company's actions favorably affect both its cost structure and its value proposition to buyers. Cost savings are made from eliminating and reducing the factors an industry competes on. Buyer value is lifted by raising and creating elements the industry has never offered. Over time, costs are reduced further as scale economies kick in, due to the high sales volumes that superior value generates.

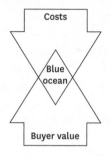

economies very rapidly, putting would-be imitators at an immediate and continuing cost disadvantage. The huge economies of scale in purchasing that Wal-Mart enjoys, for example, have significantly discouraged other companies from imitating its business model. The immediate attraction of large numbers of customers can also create network externalities. The more customers eBay has online, the more attractive the auction site becomes for both sellers and buyers of wares, giving users few incentives to go elsewhere.

When imitation requires companies to make changes to their whole system of activities, organizational politics may impede a would-be competitor's ability to switch to the divergent business model of a blue ocean strategy. For instance, airlines trying to follow Southwest's example of offering the speed of air travel with the flexibility and cost of driving would have faced major revisions in routing, training, marketing, and pricing, not to mention culture. Few established airlines had the flexibility to make such extensive organizational and operating changes overnight. Imitating a whole-system approach is not an easy feat.

The cognitive barriers can be just as effective. When a company offers a leap in value, it rapidly earns brand buzz and a loyal following in the marketplace. Experience shows that even the most expensive marketing campaigns struggle to unseat a blue ocean creator. Microsoft, for example, has been trying for more than ten years to occupy the center of the blue ocean that Intuit created with its financial software product Quicken. Despite all of its efforts and all of its investment, Microsoft has not been able to unseat Intuit as the industry leader.

In other situations, attempts to imitate a blue ocean creator conflict with the imitator's existing brand image. The Body Shop, for example, shuns top models and makes no promises of eternal youth and beauty. For the established cosmetic brands like Estée Lauder and L'Oréal, imitation was very difficult, because it would have signaled a complete invalidation of their current images, which are based on promises of eternal youth and beauty.

A Consistent Pattern

While our conceptual articulation of the pattern may be new, blue ocean strategy has always existed, whether or not companies have been conscious of the fact. Just consider the striking parallels between the Cirque du Soleil theater-circus experience and Ford's creation of the Model T.

At the end of the nineteenth century, the automobile industry was small and unattractive. More than 500 automakers in America competed in turning out handmade luxury cars that cost around $1,500 and were enormously *un*popular with all but the very rich. Anticar activists tore up roads, ringed parked cars with barbed wire, and organized boycotts of car-driving businessmen and politicians. Woodrow Wilson caught the spirit of the times when he said in 1906 that "nothing has spread socialistic feeling more than the automobile." He called it "a picture of the arrogance of wealth."

Instead of trying to beat the competition and steal a share of existing demand from other automakers, Ford reconstructed the industry boundaries of cars and horse-drawn carriages to create a blue ocean. At the time, horse-drawn carriages were the primary means of local transportation across America. The carriage had two distinct advantages over cars. Horses could easily negotiate the bumps and mud that stymied cars—especially in rain and snow—on the nation's ubiquitous dirt roads. And horses and carriages were much easier to maintain than the luxurious autos of the time, which frequently broke down, requiring expert repairmen who were expensive and in short supply. It was Henry Ford's understanding of these advantages that showed him how he could break away from the competition and unlock enormous untapped demand.

Ford called the Model T the car "for the great multitude, constructed of the best materials." Like Cirque, the Ford Motor Company made the competition irrelevant. Instead of creating fashionable, customized cars for weekends in the countryside, a luxury few could justify, Ford built a car that, like the horse-drawn carriage, was for everyday use. The Model T came in just one color, black, and there were few optional extras. It was reliable and durable, designed to travel effortlessly over dirt roads in rain, snow, or sunshine. It was easy to use and fix. People could learn to drive it in a day. And like Cirque, Ford went outside the industry for a price point, looking at horse-drawn carriages ($400), not other autos. In 1908, the first Model T cost $850; in 1909, the price dropped to $609, and by 1924 it was down to $290. In this way, Ford converted buyers of horse-drawn carriages into car buyers—just as Cirque turned theatergoers into circusgoers. Sales of the Model T boomed. Ford's market share surged from 9% in 1908 to 61% in 1921, and by 1923, a majority of American households had a car.

Even as Ford offered the mass of buyers a leap in value, the company also achieved the lowest cost structure in the industry, much as Cirque did later. By keeping the cars highly standardized with limited options and interchangeable parts, Ford was able to scrap the prevailing manufacturing system in which cars were constructed by skilled craftsmen who swarmed around one workstation and built a car piece by piece from start to finish. Ford's revolutionary assembly line replaced craftsmen with unskilled laborers, each of whom worked quickly and efficiently on one small task. This allowed Ford to make a car in just four days—21 days was the industry norm—creating huge cost savings.

———————

Blue and red oceans have always coexisted and always will. Practical reality, therefore, demands that companies understand the strategic logic of both types of oceans. At present, competing in red oceans dominates the field of strategy in theory and in practice, even as businesses' need to create blue oceans intensifies. It is time to even the scales in the field of strategy with a better balance of efforts across both oceans. For although blue ocean strategists have always existed, for the most part their strategies have been largely unconscious. But once corporations realize that the strategies for creating and capturing blue oceans have a different underlying logic from red ocean strategies, they will be able to create many more blue oceans in the future.

Originally published in October 2004. Reprint R0401D

Rediscovering Market Segmentation

by Daniel Yankelovich and David Meer

THERE ARE MANY DIFFERENT KINDS of people, and they display about as many different buying patterns. That simple truth is well understood by those responsible for market research, product development, pricing, sales, and strategy. But they haven't been getting much help from a venerable technique—market segmentation—which, if properly applied, would guide companies in tailoring their product and service offerings to the groups most likely to purchase them. Instead, market segmentation has become narrowly focused on the needs of advertising, which it serves mainly by populating commercials with characters that viewers can identify with—the marketing equivalent of central casting.

This is hardly the state of affairs we anticipated 40 years ago when one of us introduced the concept of nondemographic segmentation in HBR as a corrective to the narrow reliance on purely demographic ways of grouping consumers. In 1964, in "New Criteria for Market Segmentation," Daniel Yankelovich asserted that:

- Traditional demographic traits such as age, sex, education levels, and income no longer said enough to serve as a basis for marketing strategy.

- Nondemographic traits such as values, tastes, and preferences were more likely to influence consumers' purchases than their demographic traits were.

A Bit of Context

Although this article is most directly about marketing, segmenting patients into groups has critical strategic significance. If health care organizations are going to thrive in a value-oriented, competition-driven marketplace, they must identify the segments of customer-patients for which they want to compete and to whom they offer a uniquely compelling value proposition. (Corollary: they should also identify the segments for which they are *not* going to compete.) As this article reminds us, segmentation will change what your organization does.

I have argued that the path to a health care organization's competitive differentiation must include the following steps (see the last chapter in this book): Segment patients into groups with similar needs, often defined by their medical condition; measure the outcomes that matter to those patients and the costs required to achieve those outcomes; organize teams with the right skill mix to meet those needs well and efficiently; and then give those teams financial and nonfinancial incentives to improve value. This process cannot begin without the first step—segmenting the customers.

Segmentation is critical to strategy because the organization must understand how and for whom it creates value. Health care organizations each serve a population of patients so heterogeneous that it is tough to measure either outcomes that matter to patients or costs that have meaning to anyone. Without segmenting, the outcomes that can be measured are too blunt to have much meaning. For example, consider mortality, a very relevant measure of quality of care for some conditions (such as heart attacks) but less so for others (such as knee replacement). Similarly, the cost data are hard to attribute to any particular activities when the patient population is mixed, so many health care providers don't even bother to try to measure them.

This article provides useful guidance on how to go about doing that segmentation. Some of the most compelling advice to health care readers comes in the section toward the end of the article, "The Gravity of Decision Spectrum," which advises strategists what kind of segmentation is appropriate for what kind of consumer decisions. It is no accident that the example used for a consumer's deepest concerns and decisions is "Choosing a course of medical treatment" and that the patient's "core values and beliefs" should feature in the segmentation. That is yet another way of saying that health care organizations must focus on the outcomes that really matter to patients.

—Thomas H. Lee

Idea in Brief

Fifty-nine percent of recently surveyed companies executed a major market-segmentation initiative in the previous two years. Yet only 14% derived real value from the exercise. What's wrong with market segmentation?

Segmentation typically focuses on consumer "types" (High-Tech Harry, Joe Six-Pack). This categorization may help advertisers strengthen brand identity by developing messages that speak to different consumer groups. But it doesn't tell companies which products or services consumers might actually buy, so it can't help firms decide which new offerings to develop.

To get more from segmentation, Yankelovich and Meer suggest several tactics. For example, tailor your segmentation to a strategic decision. (Do you want to reduce customer defections? Extend a brand?) Define segments based on consumers' *actual* purchasing behavior (heaviness of use, brand switching) and their *likely* behavior. And redefine segments as market conditions change.

Apply such tactics, and you respond promptly to rapidly shifting market realities. You gain insight into how to compete. And you extract maximum value from scarce marketing resources.

- Sound marketing strategy depended on identifying segments that were potentially receptive to a particular brand and product category.

The idea was to broaden the use of segmentation so that it could inform not just advertising but also product innovation, pricing, choice of distribution channels, and the like. Yet today's segmentations do very little of this, even though markets and media are, if anything, even more fragmented today than they were in 1964 and consumers even more diverse and accustomed to following their own tastes and impulses.

Segmentation can do vastly more than serve as a source of human types, which individually go by such colorful monikers as High-Tech Harry and Joe Six-Pack and are known collectively by the term "psychographics." Psychographics may capture some truth about real people's lifestyles, attitudes, self-image, and aspirations, but it is very weak at predicting what any of these people is likely to

Idea in Practice

To segment markets effectively, apply these tactics:

- **Identify a strategic decision that would benefit from information about different customer segments.** For instance, a fast-food company is considering developing healthier menu alternatives. A personal-care company wants to extend a soap brand into deodorants.

- **Determine which customers drive profits.** Understand what makes your best customers so profitable, then identify segments that share at least some of those characteristics.

  Example: A luggage company finds that many people who buy its highest-margin carry-on bags are international flyers. It thus identifies international travelers as a promising target segment.

- **Analyze actual and potential purchasing behavior.** Current behaviors (including heaviness of use, brand switching, and channel selection) can help you predict future behaviors using a statistical technique called conjoint analysis. Through such analysis, you present consumers with combinations of product features and ask them how willing they'd be to purchase the product in question if particular attributes were added or removed, or if the price changed. You then segment based on your findings.

  Example: A pet food manufacturer used conjoint analysis to determine which features to include on food packaging (such as a resealable opening and a handle on 25-pound bags). It segmented

purchase in any given product category. It thus happens to be very poor at giving corporate decision makers any idea of how to keep the customers they have or gain new ones.

The failings of psychographics, however, and the disappointments it has produced in its users, should not cast doubt on the validity of careful segmentation overall. Indeed, marketers continue to rely on it, and line executives increasingly demand segmentations that the whole enterprise can put into action. Because of the technique's underlying validity, and managers' continuing need for what it can do, there's good reason to think that segmentation's drift from its original purpose and potency can be halted. Good segmentations consumers according to their degree of price sensitivity and desire for convenience. It then redesigned its packaging with added features that would maintain existing customers *and* attract new ones. And it jettisoned features whose cost would have required charging too high an overall price.

- **Segment in ways that make sense to senior management.** Resist any urge to flaunt your technical virtuosity by dissecting segments into ever finer slices containing improbable combinations of traits. Instead, define segments in ways that make intuitive sense to senior managers. They'll be more likely to accept your research and to fund resulting initiatives.

- **Revise your segmentation as market conditions change.** Unlike personality traits, which usually endure throughout life, consumers' attitudes, needs, and behavior can change quickly with new market conditions, so be willing to redraw your segments to reflect new realities.

Example: At the dawn of the Web, many companies segmented according to consumers' degree of online experience. "Early Adopters" felt comfortable exploring the Web on their own; "Newbies" sought extensive support. As newcomers became scarcer, companies segmented using other criteria, such as consumers' concerns about online security and interest in games or parental control devices.

identify the groups most worth pursuing—the underserved, the dissatisfied, and those likely to make a first-time purchase, for example. They are dynamic—they recognize that the first-time purchaser may become underserved or dissatisfied if his or her situation changes. And they tell companies what products to place before the most susceptible consumers.

In this article, we'll describe the elements of a smart segmentation strategy. We'll explain how segmentations meant to strengthen brand identity and make an emotional connection with consumers differ from those capable of telling a company which markets it should enter and what goods to make. And we'll introduce a tool we call the "gravity of decision spectrum," which focuses on the form of consumer behavior that should be of greatest interest to marketers—the relationship of consumers to a product or product category, not to their jobs, their friends, their family, or their community, all of which lay in the realm of psychographics.

The Drift into Nebulousness

The years after World War II were marked by extraordinary innovations in consumer products—transistor radios, disposable diapers, razor cartridges, pleasant-tasting sugarless colas, among them. For products so groundbreaking and widely desired, advertising did not have to do much more than announce their existence and describe their dazzling features.

By the early 1960s, however, consumers were becoming less predictable in their buying habits: Many people without much education had become affluent; others with sophisticated tastes had become very price conscious. As a result, tastes and purchasing patterns no longer neatly aligned with age and income, and purely demographic segmentations lost their ability to guide companies' decisions.

As time went on, product introductions remained frequent, but they increasingly amounted to refinements of existing offerings that had originally answered real consumer needs but now merely catered to mild preferences. With ever more trivial improvements to report on, and few ways to distinguish a client's product from the competition's, advertising grew boring and bored with itself. Gradually, the focus of creative departments shifted from the product to the consumer: If, by the 1970s, products had become less distinctive, people seemed to be bursting with unprecedented variety.

One way companies found to convince particular groups of consumers that a product was perfect for them was to place in the advertising message a person whom they resembled or wished they did. Another way, which followed from the consumer orientation of the first, was to emphasize the emotional rather than the functional benefits products offered—pride of ownership, increased status, sex appeal. Cake mixes to which a fresh egg had to be added, for example, may have tasted no better than earlier versions containing powdered egg. But they sold well because the extra step allowed the preparer to feel she was fulfilling a wife's traditional domestic role. In contrast to breakthrough products—such as an effective over-the-counter dandruff shampoo—that addressed intense unmet needs, ordinary third-generation products had to find customers who were already and especially susceptible to their allure. Since the attraction was based on things like status, it made sense to fashion segments reflecting the personal characteristics and lifestyles of the target consumers. As competitors increased the speed and skill with which they could copy or reengineer products, the functional dimension of existing offerings became less compelling. Ironically, by the mid-1970s, belief in the power of imagery to stimulate sales of dull items may have begun to take pressure off product developers to come up with products and services displaying genuinely innovative technology and fresh design, thus aggravating the problem.

Two concurrent developments gave this new emphasis on the consumer's self-conception, emotions, and personality an extra measure of rigor. Social scientists began to apply their modes of analysis to business problems, and business executives, confused by the fragmentation of the mass audience and the speed with which tastes were changing, welcomed their insights. Using attitudinal indicators similar to those elicited by personality tests, psychologists carved out marketing segments based on their members' shared worldview. Those early segments were populated with the Inner-Directed, Traditionalists, Hedonists, and the like.

In 1978, Arnold Mitchell and his colleagues at the Stanford Research Institute launched the Values and Lifestyles (VALS) program, a commercial research service, which was soon retained by scores of consumer product companies and advertising agencies. VALS drew heavily on frameworks developed by Harvard sociologist David Riesman, coauthor of *The Lonely Crowd,* and Brandeis psychologist Abraham Maslow, who posited the now well-known hierarchy of needs. VALS classified individuals according to nine enduring psychological types. An individual consumer's behavior, the theory went, could in turn be explained by his or her correspondence to one

Different segmentations for different purposes

Psychographic segmentations can be used to create advertising that will influence consumers to think warmly about a particular brand. But they're not as well suited for other purposes. You would need a different kind of nonde-mographic segmentation to investigate, for instance, what kinds of products to make. Here we set out the different characteristics of these two types of segmentation exercises.

	Segmentations to develop advertising	Segmentations to develop new products
Populations studied	Users of the product or service to be advertised	Users of related products or services that already meet similar needs; partners such as distributors and retailers
Data sources tapped	Attitude surveys	Purchase and usage data on consumers, supplemented by surveys; analyses of consumers' finances and channel preferences
Analytical tools used	Statistical analysis of survey results	Analysis of customers (both in the field and in the laboratory) who remain loyal and those who switch to competing offerings
Outputs	Segments that differ in their responses to a given message	Segments that differ in their purchasing power, goals, aspirations, and behavior

of those types. VALS and similar models soon turned psychographics into the most accepted mode of segmentation. Not surprisingly, it was embraced by advertising departments and agencies, which appreciated a certifiably scientific technique whose stock-in-trade was inventing characters, just as they themselves had been doing for some time.

Psychographics, it should be said, proved to be effective at brand reinforcement and positioning. The Pepsi Generation campaign of decades ago, for example, did coalesce a wide assortment of consumers into a group that identified with the youth culture emerging at the time. But even though campaigns built on psychographics are good at moving viewers emotionally, the characteristics and attitudes that such ads invoke are simply not the drivers of commercial activity. Those tend to be things like purchasing history, product loyalty, and a propensity to trade up, all of which are informed by attitudes and values that lead consumers to view particular offerings differently. What's more, psychographic segmentations have done little to enlighten the companies that commission them about which markets to enter or what kinds of offers to make, how products should be taken to market, and how they should be priced.

Despite its disappointing performance, market segmentation is still widely used. In 2004, for example, when Marakon Associates and the Economist Intelligence Unit surveyed 200 senior executives of large companies, 59% of them reported that they had conducted a major segmentation exercise during the previous two years. Yet the evidence suggests it's not a very effective tool: Only 14% of the executives said they derived real value from the exercise.

What happens when a company attempts to apply a segmentation appropriate for developing ad campaigns to product development or pricing decisions? Consider the experience of a company we'll call HomeAirCo, a leading manufacturer and installer of home heating and cooling systems. The chief marketing officer, after less than a year in that position, commissioned a respected consumer research company skilled in statistical analysis to conduct an expensive segmentation study with input from HomeAirCo's advertising agency. The agency was able to create an entertaining campaign featuring characters based on five typologies faithfully reflecting the interests and viewing habits of the members of each segment. One, for example, portrayed a Traditionalist male trying to work on his own heating system and botching it while his wife nagged him to call HomeAirCo; another showed a woman doing yoga in an ideal environment because she had a HomeAirCo system. But every segment had the same number of HomeAirCo customers in it, leaving the firm at a loss to know which groups would be most likely to want to upgrade their temperature control systems. The segmentation's many oversights included a failure to identify buyers of older homes in affluent neighborhoods who, the firm's own anecdotal experience suggested, would probably be the most likely purchasers of such a system.

The fact is that even the most memorable advertising, if based on a crudely drawn segmentation, will do little to spur sales or garner market share. The recent "Catfight" campaign for Miller Lite, for example, featuring mud-wrestling supermodels, certainly made an impression on the young, male segment it was intended to reach, but sales of that brand of beer did not increase. As it happens, there is a segment of light-beer drinkers that would gravitate to Miller Lite if only its members knew it had fewer carbohydrates than Bud Light. How do we know? A Miller campaign that told them so did indeed increase sales.

The Way Back

If meaningful segmentations depend on finding patterns in your customers' actual buying behavior, then to construct one properly, you need to gather the relevant data. Depending on the question your exercise is ultimately aimed at answering, you would want information about, say, which benefits and features matter to your customers. Or which customers are willing to pay higher prices or demand lower ones. Or the relative advantages and disadvantages customers identify in your existing offerings. You'll also need data on emerging social, economic, and technological trends that may alter purchasing and usage patterns.

Many companies capture this information routinely. If yours does not, you can use qualitative research to explore underlying motives and needs propelling current purchases and use quantitative research to understand competitive strengths and vulnerabilities. You can reexamine the sales data you already have to reveal the hidden patterns in customers' behavior. And you can retain trend-tracking services.

Armed with such data, you can then fashion segments that are both revealing and applicable. Such segments will:

- Reflect the company's strategy;

- Indicate where sources of revenue or profit may lie;

- Identify consumers' values, attitudes, and beliefs as they relate specifically to product or service offerings;

- Focus on actual customer behavior;

- Make sense to top executives;

- Accommodate or anticipate changes in markets or consumer behavior.

Let's consider each aspect in turn.

What are we trying to do?

When companies change marketing chiefs, a new segmentation is rarely far behind. The new CMO often uses a segmentation exercise as a way to put his or her stamp on the business. Unfortunately, few marketing chiefs know or have thought about which of their company's strategic decisions would benefit from the guidance of a segmentation. For a traditional brokerage house, for instance, the main strategic challenge might be how to reduce customer defections to discount brokers. For a personal-care products company, it might be how to extend a strong soap brand into deodorants. And for a fast-food chain, it might be whether to come up with healthier menu alternatives. Segmentations designed to shed light on these questions won't try to explore the personalities of customers; they will try to identify groups of potentially interested or susceptible customers sufficiently numerous and lucrative to justify pursuit. Subsequent strategic moves will, of course, call for new and different segmentations.

Which customers drive profits?

To be valid, a segmentation must identify groups that matter to a company's financial performance. To start, companies can rank their own customers by profitability so as to concentrate the right amount of attention on them. But to grow revenues, a company should understand what makes its best customers as profitable as they are and then seek new customers who share at least a couple of those characteristics. For instance, a luggage company whose soft but durable carry-on bags earn its highest margins might notice that the majority of the people who buy the bags are international flyers. It would therefore pursue other international travelers as potential customers.

To understand how important this question is, consider the experience of one leading bank with a large wealth management business. The bank had become concerned that its overall business was suffering from low rates of growth and a stagnant market share. Its existing segmentation sorted customers according to the level of employee that served them—relationship manager, senior branch personnel, or junior branch personnel—which mostly depended on customer assets and income. Relationship managers had the most profitable customers, and so forth. However, the bank knew next to nothing about what might distinguish one relationship-manager customer from another.

The bank decided to go beyond what it knew about its existing customer base and acquire market research on the lifetime value of wealthy prospects. The research was of three types:

- Demographic (age, occupation, assets, and so on);

- Behavioral (which services customers already used, how many institutions they did business with, how many transactions they made in a month);

- Attitudinal (financial sophistication, time spent on investments, risk tolerance).

The segmentation that resulted differed markedly from its predecessor. Every component of the three broad drivers of profitability contributed to an understanding of lifetime value. For instance, the new segments identified, such as Young Families, revealed high variations in profitability even in the existing high-profit segment. Equipped with this information, the bank was more willing to embark on the expensive task of tailoring offerings to potential clients, since it had greater confidence that the effort would turn out to be economically worthwhile. Three segments it discovered— On Their Way, Established Families, and Retirement Planners— contributed almost no profit, even though they accounted for half the customer base. Yet many of the individuals who fell into those segments had been assigned to relationship managers. The bank acted quickly to reduce the cost of servicing those people by reassigning them to more junior branch personnel, to call centers, or to the Web.

Which attitudes matter to the buying decision?

Even though segmenting customers according to immutable personality traits rarely bears much fruit, there is a place for examining people's lifestyles, attitudes, self-image, and aspirations. They should be explored, as the bank did, in a context that is directly related to the product or service under study. Unlike purely psychographic segments, these characteristics can be expected to change along with the customers' values and environment.

What are my customers actually doing?

While relevant attitudes, values, and expressed preferences can bring color and insight to a segmentation, they lack the predictive power of actual purchase behavior, such as heaviness of use, brand switching, and retail-format or channel selection. If you want to understand how a consumer would respond to products or features that have not yet been introduced, you can elicit the next best thing to actual behavior by creating laboratory simulations to which special analytic techniques can be applied. One of them, called "conjoint analysis," involves presenting consumers with combinations of features. It then asks the consumers how willing they would be to purchase the product in question if particular attributes were added or removed, or if the price changed.

Here's an example of how it works: A pet food manufacturer gave consumers an opportunity to design their ideal pet food container. The consumers in the test saw on their computer screens a generic package to which they could drag and drop features they valued, such as a resealable opening and a handle attached to the 25-pound size. They were next asked how much more they would pay for products containing different combinations of such features. The consumers were then segmented according to their degree of price sensitivity and desire for convenience. On this basis, the company could redesign its packaging with added features that would maintain existing customers and attract new ones. It could also jettison features whose cost would have required charging too high an overall price.

Will this segmentation make sense to senior management?

Modern marketing practitioners view their field as outward facing—that is, focused on listening and communicating to consumers and markets. In fact, marketing may do itself harm by failing to make itself understood by its internal constituency: senior management. As marketing has become more scientific and specialized, its practitioners have increasingly turned to advanced statistical techniques for dissecting segments into ever finer slices containing improbable combinations of traits. The masters of these techniques are often tempted to flaunt their technical virtuosity instead of defining segments that make intuitive sense to senior managers. If the segments seem inconsistent with managers' long experience, and managers cannot grasp how they were derived, the research they yield is unlikely to be accepted and applied.

One financial services company found this out the hard way. The firm, which develops investment products sold by third-party investment advisers, wanted a bigger role for itself in asset management, a service usually confined to wealthy investors. So it created a full-service offering designed to accommodate smaller investors. The challenge the company faced was to find out which kinds of advisers would be most likely to recommend the service to this new category of clients. Unfortunately, the advisers' existing classifications—national broker/dealer, regional broker/dealer, bank officer, and independent—revealed differences in recommendation patterns too minor to be meaningful.

The company therefore decided to segment its investment advisers in a more meaningful way—according to the kinds of recommendations they made to their clients. At first, the firm took an approach that was statistically powerful but highly complex. It developed profiles of typical investors based on their age, assets, risk tolerance, and the like. Then in a survey it asked the advisers to select a mix of investments suited to each customer profile. The statistical analysis teased out the underlying investment style of each adviser and then grouped together those with like patterns. Some advisers, for example, rarely recommended individually traded stocks, while others made stocks the foundation of their clients' portfolios.

Although the segmentation was mathematically sound, management did not trust its findings. For one thing, the segmentation relied heavily on whether advisers received fees or commissions, a distinction the statistical analysis determined was important. Since the new product was to be fee based, however, the commission-based segments would be largely irrelevant. So the senior managers could not understand why a segmentation along those lines had been made. Perhaps they would have accepted the study if they had been able to understand how its conclusions had been reached. But the study's reliance on esoteric statistical procedures foreclosed that possibility. If nothing else, the managers charged with applying the study's findings worried that they would lack answers for top management in the event the segmentation failed.

The in-house marketing science team and the consulting firm assisting it decided to recast the segmentation using simple criteria, not statistics. First, the advisers were grouped on the basis of the average net worth of their clients. And then they were grouped according to whether their clients' investments were actively managed. The result was four segments rated on two dimensions. We list them here by internal title in descending order of client wealth and portfolio activity.

- Active Investors (high-net-worth clients, strong reliance on actively managed investments such as stocks and bonds);

- Upscale Coaches (high-net-worth clients, little reliance on actively managed investments);

- Mass-Market Coaches (low-net-worth clients, strong reliance on actively managed investments);

- Product-Oriented (low-net-worth clients, little reliance on actively managed investments).

The Upscale Coaches, it turned out, were the most liable to consider the new asset-management product. The Mass-Market Coaches also showed some potential. The segments bracketing those two had almost no potential. In subsequent interviews, the Active Investors confessed they viewed the company developing the new product as a competitor offering a service uncomfortably close to their own. The Product-Oriented segment had the opposite objection: Their clients were not interested in having anyone actively manage their assets. But the new product could complement the service that the two middle groups provided without threatening to replace it. In other words, the more passive managers of high-net-worth clients and the more active managers of low-net-worth clients were found to be the two groups worth targeting, a conclusion management understood and unhesitatingly accepted.

Can our segmentation register change?

Segmentations are viewed by too many of their sponsors as onetime, go-for-broke efforts to provide a comprehensive portrait of customers that can inform all subsequent marketing decisions. In our view, segmentations should be part of an ongoing search for answers to important business questions as they arise. Consequently, effective segmentations are dynamic—in two senses. First, they concentrate on consumers' needs, attitudes, and behavior, which can change quickly, rather than on personality traits, which usually endure throughout a person's life. Second, they are reshaped by market conditions, such as fluctuating economics, emerging consumer niches, and new technologies, which in today's world are evolving more rapidly than ever. In short, effective segmentations focus on just one or two issues, and they need to be redrawn as soon as they have lost their relevance.

At the dawn of the World Wide Web, for example, a common segmentation criterion was the extent of a person's online experience. Early Adopters felt comfortable exploring the Web on their own; Newbies, or recent adopters, sought high levels of support. As newcomers became scarcer, the focus shifted to an emerging group of users, Transactors, for whom concern about sharing personal information, including credit card numbers, was no obstacle to transacting business online. Now that few people are worried about such things, many of today's segmentations tend to orient themselves around intrinsically Net-based services and functions such as games, parental control devices, and file sharing, each involving a set of separately measurable interests and concerns.

The Gravity of Decision Spectrum

The most common error marketers commit is applying segmentations designed to shed light on one kind of issue to some other purpose for which they were not designed. But which kinds of segmentations are best for which purposes? We suggest marketers begin by evaluating the expectations consumers bring to a particular kind of transaction. These can be located on our gravity of decision spectrum, which will tell you how deeply you need to probe consumers' motives, concerns, and even psyches.

Some decisions people make, such as trying a new brand of toilet paper or applying for a credit card, are relatively inconsequential. If the product is unsatisfactory, at worst a small amount of money has been wasted and a bit of inconvenience incurred. But decisions such as buying a home or choosing a cancer treatment have momentous significance given their potential for benefit or harm and the expense associated with them.

At the shallow end of the spectrum, consumers are seeking products and services they think will save them time, effort, and money. So segmentations for items such as toiletries and snacks try to measure things like the price sensitivity, habits, and impulsiveness of the target consumer. Segmentations for big-ticket purchases like cars and electronic devices, in the middle of the spectrum, test how concerned consumers are about quality, design, complexity, and the status a product might confer. At the deepest end, consumers' emotional investment is great, and their core values are engaged. Those values are often in conflict with market values, and segmentations need to expose these tensions. Health care is the archetypal high-gravity issue. The exhibit, "What is at stake?" maps out

What is at stake?

Knowing how important a product or service is to your customers will help you decide which of their expectations are most likely to reveal their willingness to purchase your product. If your products are purely functional, you will probably want to investigate such garden-variety factors as the price sensitivity and brand loyalty of potential purchasers. But if such purchasers are facing life-altering choices, you will want to inquire into their most deeply held beliefs.

	Issues the business wants to address	Consumers' concerns	What the segmentation should try to find out
Shallowest decisions	• Whether to make small improvements to existing products • How to select targets of a media campaign • Whether to change prices	• How relevant and believable new-product claims are • How to evaluate a given product • Whether to switch products	• Buying and usage behavior • Willingness to pay a small premium for higher quality • Degree of brand loyalty
Middle-of-the-spectrum decisions	• How to position the brand • Which segments to pursue • Whether to change the product fundamentally • Whether to develop an entirely new product	• Whether to visit a clinic about a medical condition • Whether to switch one's brand of car • Whether to replace an enterprise software system	• Whether the consumers being studied are do-it-yourself or do-it-for-me types • Consumers' needs (better service, convenience, functionality) • Their social status, self-image, and lifestyle
Deepest decisions	• Whether to revise the business model in response to powerful social forces changing how people live their lives	• Choosing a course of medical treatment • Deciding where to live	• Core values and beliefs related to the buying decision

the differences in business decisions, consumer decisions, and approaches to segmentation that emerge as the gravity of a consumer's buying decision increases.

What follows are three illustrations representing three points along the spectrum. Of course, many gradations exist between them.

The shallow end

A manufacturer of men's shaving products faced a dilemma: how to spur fast growth when the firm already dominated the most profitable subcategory—shaving systems (a razor handle plus replaceable blades). Fearing it would cannibalize sales of its own shaving systems, the company shied away from disposable shavers, an obvious area to enter. But under pressure from senior management, the razor-and-blade business unit commissioned a new segmentation to find out whether there really was any basis for its fears.

Shavers are a small-ticket item. Though men naturally want to look neat and clean, most do not agonize over which technology or brand to choose, since all produce more or less the same result. Men's main concerns traditionally have been the comfort and closeness of the shave, how easy the razor is to use (which often determines whether people favor a system or a disposable), and the price.

Accordingly, to determine whether a new product would cannibalize existing ones, a first segmentation used detailed household purchase records to put customers into one of three classifications: those who buy systems exclusively, those who buy disposables exclusively, and those who switch between the two. To management's surprise, the switching segment was very small, suggesting that the company could introduce a more expensive disposable razor without taking business away from its systems.

The next question was whether enough disposables users, who are thought of as looking for a low-cost way to shave, would buy a higher-quality but more expensive device. A second segmentation, therefore, sought to judge price sensitivity in order to reveal customers' propensity to trade up. As suspected, many men were not interested in a better disposable that cost more. However, the research did expose a modest level of emotional investment in the product on the part of young men who had girlfriends or were on the dating scene. For them, how their skin felt to the touch was almost as important as how they looked. Consequently, they would be willing to pay more for that smooth feel. Equipped with that insight, the company launched a very high-margin disposable, which garnered a solid and sustained market share without hurting its sister brands.

In the middle

In 1997, Toyota introduced a quirky internal combustion–electric hybrid vehicle to great success in its home market. But Americans were wary of the new technology. They sought greater power and faster acceleration at the Prius's price point. Moreover, in the late 1990s, U.S. drivers were mostly unconcerned about fuel consumption, an economic issue for some but not an environmental one.

Because even relatively inexpensive cars are large expenditures for most households and the cars people drive strongly influence their image in their own and others' eyes, some exploration of consumers' emotions and values was warranted. Accordingly, when Toyota did so, the carmaker discovered that about 10% of car buyers not only liked the car's design and accepted its performance but also were pleased that it was less harmful to the environment than other cars. Although a Prius would be an adventurous purchase, in certain communities it might even be an admired one because of the values it represented. If the small group of potential purchasers could be reached efficiently rather than through an expensive media campaign, Toyota could make money on the car. As it turned out, the best prospects were contacted via the Internet, and the Prius easily met its first-year sales and profit targets.

The deep end

Continuing care retirement communities (CCRCs) are residential facilities for healthy and affluent retirees. Such a community typically includes single-family houses, duplexes, or flats where residents live before graduating into assisted-living or nursing care, both of which are available on the same campus. Sponsored by both nonprofit and for-profit institutions such as Hyatt, CCRCs have quintupled in number in the past 15 years.

CCRCs are expensive. Seniors pay a hefty entry fee—from $125,000 to over $400,000 (depending on the size and geographical location of the dwelling they choose) usually after selling the family home. Still, residents do not own their unit and thus do not build equity. A major component of the fee is an insurance policy that covers the cost of assisted living and skilled nursing care if the resident's health declines. Residents also pay a monthly fee covering meals, housekeeping, utilities, and other amenities. Even though a typical continuing care retirement community returns 90% of the initial fee when a resident moves out or dies, the individual or estate suffers a significant financial sacrifice, given the rate of appreciation of today's real estate market.

What, then, explains the demand for CCRCs? The answer was revealed by a segmentation oriented around changing family values. Published comments of CCRC residents and industry experts indicate that the segment of seniors attracted to this option is seeking to avoid dependence on family and longtime friends, who in earlier decades would have looked after them. Two key values characterize this segment:

- The desire for autonomy—to avoid being a burden on their loved ones;

- The willingness to embrace, in lieu of the security and warmth of having family and friends nearby, life in a quasi-institutional setting among strangers.

This segmentation obviously operates at the deepest level of the gravity of decision framework. It tells the retirement industry that adding Alzheimer's care to the package offered would appeal to the large numbers of the elderly who worry about becoming a burden and that proximity to or affiliation with a university would add to the sense of community valued in CCRCs.

Segmentation initiatives have generally been disappointing to the companies launching them. Their failures have mostly taken three forms. The first is excessive interest in consumers' identities, which has distracted marketers from the product features that matter most to current and potential customers of particular brands and categories. The second is too little emphasis on actual consumer behavior, which definitively reveals their attitudes and helps predict business outcomes. And the third is undue absorption in the technical details of devising segmentations, which estranges marketers from the decision makers on whose support their initiatives depend.

We believe that organizations able to overcome these three weaknesses will be able to respond more quickly and effectively to rapidly changing market conditions, develop insights into where and how to compete, and gain maximum benefit from scarce marketing resources. Nondemographic segmentation began more than 40 years ago as a way to focus on the differences among customers that matter the most strategically. Since for more than half of that span, it has not managed to do so, we hope that the rediscovery we are proposing here can make up for lost time and, over the next 40 years, at last fulfill segmentation's original purpose.

Originally published in February 2006. Reprint R0602G

The Office of Strategy Management

by Robert S. Kaplan and David P. Norton

MOST COMPANIES HAVE AMBITIOUS PLANS for growth. Few ever realize them. In their book *Profit from the Core,* Chris Zook and James Allen report that between 1988 and 1998, seven out of eight companies in a global sample of 1,854 large corporations failed to achieve profitable growth. That is, these companies were unable to deliver 5.5% annual real growth in revenues and earnings while earning their cost of capital (a rather modest hurdle). Yet 90% of the companies in the study had developed detailed strategic plans with much higher targets.

Why is there such a persistent gap between ambition and performance? The gap arises, we believe, from a disconnect in most companies between strategy formulation and strategy execution. Our research reveals that, on average, 95% of a company's employees are unaware of, or do not understand, its strategy. If the employees who are closest to customers and who operate processes that create value are unaware of the strategy, they surely cannot help the organization implement it effectively.

It doesn't have to be like this. For the past 15 years, we have studied companies that have achieved performance breakthroughs by adopting the Balanced Scorecard and its associated tools to help them better communicate strategy to their employees and to guide and monitor the execution of that strategy. (For background on the

Balanced Scorecard, see our book *The Strategy-Focused Organization,* Harvard Business School Press, 2000.)

Some companies, of course, have achieved better and longer-lasting improvements than others. The organizations that have managed to sustain their strategy focus have typically established a new unit at the corporate level to oversee all strategy related activities, an *office of strategy management* (OSM), as we call it.

This might appear to be nothing more than a new name for the familiar strategic planning unit. But the two are quite different. The typical planning function facilitates the annual strategic planning process but takes little or no leadership role in seeing that the strategy gets executed. The companies we studied, however, recognize that effective strategy execution requires communicating corporate strategy; ensuring that enterprise-level plans are translated into the plans of the various units and departments; executing strategic initiatives to deliver on the grand plan; and aligning employees' competency development plans, and their personal goals and incentives, with strategic objectives. What's more, they recognize that the company's strategy must be tested and adapted to stay abreast of the changing competition. The OSM becomes the central point for coordinating all these tasks. It does not do all the work, but it facilitates the processes so that strategy execution gets accomplished in an integrated fashion across the enterprise.

In the following pages, we will describe how the concept of the office of strategy management came into being and how it has helped companies align key management processes to strategy. Although the companies we have studied use the Balanced Scorecard as the framework for their strategy management systems, we believe that the lessons we draw are also applicable to companies that do not use the Balanced Scorecard.

Strategy Management: The New Support Function

The exhibit "The Old Strategy Calendar" depicts the strategy management schedule at a typical large company. The process starts about midway through the fiscal year, when the CEO and the

Idea in Brief

Most large organizations fail to achieve profitable growth—despite ambitious plans. Why the gap between intended and actual performance? There's an alarming disconnect between the parts of the organization that formulate corporate strategy and the functions, processes, and people required to execute it.

67% of HR and IT departments' strategies don't reflect corporate strategy. 60% of organizations don't link their financial budgets to strategic priorities. Compensation packages of 90% of frontline employees show no connection to the success or failure of strategy execution. 95% of the typical company's workers are unaware of, or don't understand, its strategy.

How to close the breach between strategy formulation and execution? Create an **office of strategy management (OSM)**. Your OSM couples the units responsible for strategic planning with those performing the activities required to implement strategy—such as establishing budgets, communicating strategy to the workforce, and designing compensation systems that reward strategic performance.

The payoff for designing an effective OSM? A corporate strategy that delivers on its promises. Thanks in part to its OSM, the Chrysler Group generated $1.2 billion in earnings and launched a series of exciting new cars in 2004—while the rest of the U.S. domestic auto market languished.

executive team get together to clarify their strategic vision and update the strategy. Sometime afterward, similar processes take place at the business and functional units, led by unit heads and other senior executives. Toward the end of the third quarter, the finance function takes the baton, finalizing corporate and unit budgets. At the end of the year, the HR function conducts employees' annual performance reviews and orchestrates the setting of professional goals and development programs. Throughout the year, meanwhile, different teams and units have engaged in performance reviews, corporate communication, and knowledge sharing.

The problem with this approach is that the activities are carried out largely in isolation and without guidance from the enterprise strategy. This partition of responsibilities creates the gulf between an organization's strategy and its processes, systems, and people.

The old strategy calendar

Strategy management at most companies consists of processes carried out in isolation by different groups with different reporting lines. That's why strategy becomes disconnected from the units responsible for executing it.

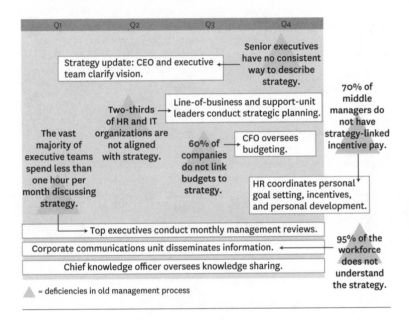

Surveys that we conducted of HR and IT managers reveal that the strategies of fully 67% of those organizations are not aligned with business unit and corporate strategies; nor do HR and IT departmental plans support corporate or business-unit strategic initiatives. Budgeting is similarly disconnected: Some 60% of organizations do not link their financial budgets to strategic priorities. Incentives aren't aligned, either: The compensation packages of 70% of middle managers and more than 90% of frontline employees have no link to the success or failure of strategy implementation. Periodic management meetings, corporate communication, and knowledge management are similarly not focused on strategy execution.

What can companies do to change this state of affairs? The experience of the Chrysler Group first suggested to us that the answer lies in bringing all strategy-related activities into a single functional unit. After a string of innovative successes in the early 1990s, Chrysler had hit a dry spell. Performance problems were exacerbated by an economic downturn, rising costs, and encroaching imports, and by 2000, the company was staring at a projected deficit of more than $5 billion for the coming year. At this point, the parent company, DaimlerChrysler, appointed a new CEO, Dieter Zetsche, who introduced the Balanced Scorecard as part of a major change in strategy. The project was spearheaded by Bill Russo, vice president of business strategy, whose unit worked with Chrysler's executive team to translate the company's new strategy into a Balanced Scorecard. Russo's unit also served as trainer and consultant to help Chrysler's business and support units create local scorecards that were aligned with corporate objectives and customized to local operations. Once the design phase had been completed and scorecards had been cascaded throughout the company, the strategy group maintained responsibility for the data collection and reporting processes for the scorecards.

Up to this point, Chrysler's Balanced Scorecard project had followed a traditional course. Where Chrysler broke new ground was in the roles assumed by the strategy group. The group took the lead in preparing scorecard-related materials to communicate the strategy to the more than 90,000 employees. Russo began to brief Zetsche before each management meeting about issues that had been revealed through the scorecard reporting and that required management attention and action. In his capacity as a member of the executive team, Russo followed up after each meeting to make sure that the required items were communicated and acted upon. As a result of this proactive involvement in agenda setting and follow-up, the responsibilities of the business strategy function expanded to incorporate many new cross-enterprise strategy execution processes. Thus was born Chrysler's Office of Strategy Management—a unit currently employing some 13 full-time people who not only manage the company's strategy but also assist the business units

Idea in Practice

Design your office of strategy management to perform these functions:

Create and Oversee Your Strategy Management System

Help the executive team select performance targets and identify required strategic initiatives. Initiate and administer your company's strategic performance reporting system. To maintain integrity of performance data, create and enforce uniform organization-wide metrics.

Incorporate changes in corporate strategy into all documents and tools that the company uses to track strategic performance—such as strategy maps and the Balanced Scorecard.

Align the Organization

Actively manage organizational alignment with corporate strategy.

Institutionalize the use of a common strategic performance reporting system by all units. Ensure that business unit and support unit strategies are linked to one another and to the company's strategy.

Communicate Strategy

Through newsletters, CEO speeches, and other channels, communicate corporate strategy, targets, and initiatives to the workforce. Coordinate with HR to ensure that education about the strategy management process is included in training programs.

Review Strategy

Organize and lead monthly strategy-review meetings, briefing the CEO about strategic concerns in advance. Document needed adjustments to strategy and execution identified during

in developing new products. Chrysler's new approach to strategy execution appears to have paid off handsomely. In 2004, despite a weak domestic automobile market, Chrysler successfully launched a series of exciting new cars and generated $1.2 billion in earnings.

The U.S. Army's Balanced Scorecard project produced an office of strategy management in much the same way. A central project team at the Pentagon headquarters, under the leadership of the Army chief of staff, developed the initial scorecard, which the Army called the Strategic Readiness System (SRS). The project team also selected the software to be used for scorecard reporting and established systems and processes so that the scorecard would be regularly populated with valid, timely data. In the next phase, the team helped meetings and follow up to ensure that changes are implemented. Help the chief financial officer prepare strategy updates for board meetings.

Refine Strategy

Evaluate new strategic ideas coming from within the organization and convey promising ones to senior management.

Manage Strategic Initiatives

Manage strategy-related initiatives that cross unit and functional lines, to ensure they receive sufficient resources and attention. Monitor progress of all strategic initiatives and report on them to top management.

Consult with Key Strategy Support Functions

- **Planning and budgeting.** Work with the finance department to ensure that corporate and unit budgets reflect those established during the strategic planning process and that each unit's budget includes resources needed for the unit's contribution to cross-functional strategic initiatives.

- **Human resource alignment.** See that the HR function manages employee incentives, competency development programs, and annual performance reviews in a manner consistent with corporate and business unit strategic objectives.

- **Knowledge management.** Coordinate with the chief learning officer to ensure that the best practices and ideas most critical to the corporate strategy are shared throughout the organization.

to cascade scorecards to 13 major subcommands and subsequently to more than 300 subsidiary commands throughout the world. The centralized project team provided training, consulting, software, and online support for the dispersed project teams. The central team also reviewed the scorecards produced by local project teams to ensure that their goals were aligned with those articulated on the chief of staff's scorecard.

The Army's project team, like its counterpart at Chrysler, soon took on more than the traditional roles of scorecard custodian and consultant. It established and took ownership of a strategy communication program. The Army team created a Web site that was accessible from around the world in both classified and unclassified versions, developed an online portal and library containing information about the SRS, wrote articles about the initiative, published a bimonthly newsletter, conducted an annual conference, led periodic conference calls with SRS leaders at each command level, and conducted scorecard training, both in person and on the Web. This extensive communication process was critical for educating soldiers and civilian employees and gaining their support for the new strategy. And the Army project team, much as Chrysler's did, began to facilitate the monthly discussions at headquarters about the readiness status of units around the world. Once again, an ad hoc project team had turned into a sustainable part of the organization's structure (the team and the SRS survived the appointment of a new chief of staff in June 2004).

The creation of a central office for strategy execution may appear to risk reinforcing top-down decision making and inhibiting local initiative, but it does just the opposite. A unit with responsibility for the implementation of strategy becomes a convenient focal point for ideas that percolate up through the organization. These emerging ideas can then be put on the agendas of quarterly and annual strategy reviews, with the best concepts being adopted and embedded in enterprise and business unit strategies. The OSM is a facilitating organization, not a dictating one.

What Good OSMs Do

Most of the organizations we have studied follow the path Chrysler and the Army took: The Balanced Scorecard project team incrementally and organically assumes more and more responsibilities on its own initiative. But that's not the only way to institute an OSM. From these cases, we have learned what functions an effective OSM must perform and how an OSM must relate to other functions within the organization. As a consequence, a few organizations we advise have recently opted to make the creation of an OSM an early and integral part of their scorecard initiatives. Canadian Blood Services, the main provider of blood services in Canada with an annual budget of Can$900 million, more than 4,000 employees, and 17,000 volunteers, is an excellent example of an organization that created an OSM at the *beginning* of its journey to becoming more strategy focused. (See the sidebar "How to Wield Influence and Stay Informed," by CEO Graham Sher.)

What should people designing an OSM bear in mind as they embark on the project? Through research into Balanced Scorecard best practices, we've identified the activities that should be directly managed by or coordinated with an OSM. Some of these activities—specifically those involved in creating and managing the scorecard, aligning the organization, and setting the agenda for monthly strategy reviews—are the natural turf of an OSM. They did not exist prior to the introduction of the Balanced Scorecard, so they can be given to a new unit without infringing on the current responsibilities of any other department. But many other activities—strategic planning, budget supervision, or HR training, for instance—are already the territory of other units. In these cases, the company needs to be explicit about the allocation of responsibilities between the OSM and other functional units. We have identified the following basic OSM tasks:

Create and manage the scorecard

As the owner of the scorecard process, the OSM must ensure that any changes made at the annual strategy-planning meeting get translated into the company's strategy map and Balanced Scorecard. Once the executive team has approved the objectives and measures for the subsequent year, the OSM coaches the team in selecting performance targets on the scorecard measures and identifying the strategic initiatives required to achieve them. As guardian of the scorecard, the OSM also standardizes the terminology and measurement definitions across the organization, selects and manages the scorecard reporting system, and ensures the integrity of the scorecard data. The OSM need not be the primary data collector for the scorecard, but it should oversee the processes by which data are collected, reported, and validated. Finally, the OSM serves as the central scorecard resource, consulting with units on their scorecard development projects and conducting training and education.

How to Wield Influence and Stay Informed

by Graham Sher

AS THE CHIEF EXECUTIVE OF THE NONPROFIT that manages the supply of blood products for all of Canada except the province of Quebec, I instituted an office of strategy management to help me cope with three big challenges in implementing a strategic agenda. First, I spend a great deal of time dealing with external demands and constituents. In addition to reporting to the board of directors of my organization, Canadian Blood Services (CBS), I must also focus on the 12 Canadian provincial and territorial governments that provide its funding. So I have limited time and information with which to manage internal issues.

Also, while many people believe that chief executives wield direct and easy influence, the reality is that any CEO has a difficult time influencing his or her organization. A CEO's attempts to command and control undermine the authority of senior executives. I want to exert my influence indirectly and in a way that empowers my executives and creates an environment in which they can lead and manage their parts of the organization. I set the tone, and I define the strategic agenda, communicate it, and ensure that it gets undertaken, but I don't command any parts of the organization.

My third challenge is staying informed. Information, particularly bad news, is filtered before it gets to me. I typically do not see the most timely, valid information about CBS's current performance. Before our OSM was implemented, we were spending way too much time debating the quality of our information—obviously an unwieldy way of executing strategy and a very time-intensive way of conducting management meetings.

I see the Balanced Scorecard, managed by an office of strategy management, as a way of overcoming these three barriers to success. The Balanced Scorecard empowers executives, as opposed to invading their territory and undermining their authority. It gives me performance management information that is aligned at all executive levels and appropriately validated before it comes to my attention. Much of management is a search for the truth. The Balanced Scorecard provides me with easy access to timely, unfiltered information about our strategy implementation.

Because of my urgent need to accomplish change, I followed the unconventional route of establishing an office of strategy management at the outset of our Balanced Scorecard project. I also wanted the OSM to report directly to me—that was a way to highlight the importance of this office to my strategic agenda. But the OSM needed other clearly defined linkages or relationships, too; I want change at CBS to come from within, not to be imposed from above. To that end, I created a dotted-line reporting relationship between the OSM and two other key executives at CBS, the CFO and the COO, who ultimately are going to help execute the change agenda. I did not create the new corporate-level OSM unit lightly. Its positioning in the organization enables me to fulfill my internal duties as a change leader but doesn't affect my ability to meet the many external obligations I have as the CEO of a rapidly evolving public-sector organization emerging from crisis—Canada's blood-supply system was completely revamped after thousands of people received contaminated blood in the 1980s and 1990s.

As for the OSM's responsibilities, I see strategy management as being made up of three high-level processes: *strategy formulation,* leading to *strategy execution,* leading in turn to *strategy learning,* which then cycles back to strategy formulation. The exhibit "The processes of strategy" shows the activities within the categories. The OSM has primary responsibility for most of these processes, but not all. For example, in 2004, the OSM led the project team that developed the strategy maps and scorecards for the enterprise, our three operating divisions, and two support units—human resources and information technology. For some

The processes of strategy

The Canadian Blood Services' Office of Strategy Management has direct or indirect (shaded items) responsibility for strategic processes, which fall into three categories.

Strategy formulation	Strategy execution	Strategy learning
Environmental assessments	Balanced Scorecard performance reporting	Benchmarking
Strategic planning	Initiative management	Best-practice sharing
Budgeting	Communicating strategy	Internal coaching and change management
	Personal scorecards	

(continued)

processes, however, the OSM's role is more integrative and facilitative than direct. For example, the chief financial officer has primary responsibility for budgeting, with the OSM playing a coordinating role.

We launched the OSM with three full-time individuals. The OSM leader is a vice president and a member of the executive management team; her position in the organization is consistent with the importance we give this function. She leads and facilitates the integration of strategy into all our core processes. In addition, we have two individuals reporting to the OSM leader to provide day-to-day management of the office; to manage the multiple work streams and cross-functional teams; to lead and facilitate meetings; to educate people on the Balanced Scorecard and other strategy-focused practices and tools; and to perform analyses of problems, performance, and metrics. This should be the right complement of individuals to help support the leader of the OSM, and ultimately the rest of the executive team, in undertaking our ambitious change agenda for this year.

Graham Sher is the CEO of Canadian Blood Services, based in Ottawa.

Align the organization

A company can execute its strategy well only if it aligns the strategies of its business units, support functions, and external partners with its broad enterprise strategy. Alignment creates focus and coordination across even the most complex organizations, making it easier to identify and realize synergies. At present, few companies actively manage the process of alignment; in many cases, unit strategies have only rhetorical links with corporate strategy. The OSMs we've studied help the entire enterprise to have a consistent view of strategy and to systematically manage organizational alignment. The OSM oversees the process of developing scorecards and cascading them through the levels of the organization. It defines the synergies to be created through cross-business behavior at lower organization levels and ensures that individual business unit and support unit strategies and scorecards are linked to each other and to the corporate strategy.

Review strategy

For all their professed commitment to strategy, senior managers spend remarkably little time reviewing it. Our research suggests that 85% of executive leadership teams spend less than one hour per month discussing their unit's strategy, with 50% spending no time at all. Companies that manage strategy well behave differently. Top managers usually meet once a month for four to eight hours. This meeting provides the opportunity to review performance and to make adjustments to the strategy and its execution. The underlying hypotheses of the company's strategy can be tested and new actions initiated. Managing this meeting is a core function of the OSM. It briefs the CEO in advance about the strategic issues identified in the most recent scorecard so that the agenda can focus on strategy review and learning, rather than just a short-term financial performance review and crisis management. The OSM then monitors the meeting to determine action plans and follows up to ensure that the plans are carried out. Since the board of directors also plays an important role in reviewing and guiding strategy, the OSM helps the chief financial officer prepare the board packet and agenda for board meetings.

Develop strategy

Typically, strategy formulation is the responsibility of the existing strategic planning unit. The unit performs external and internal competitive analysis, conducts scenario planning, organizes and runs an annual strategy meeting, and coaches the executive team on strategic options. But developing strategy should not be a onetime annual event. After all, performance measures, such as those supplied by the Balanced Scorecard, provide continual evidence about the validity of the assumptions underlying a company's strategy. Those assumptions can be discussed periodically by the executive team, which can update the strategy if appropriate. And strategy development should not be done only by senior managers. The OSM or strategic planning unit can act as a filter for new ideas that come from within the organization. We've found that most planning units adapt fairly quickly to the continual strategy development process we observe at scorecard-driven companies. The additional processes represent a natural extension of, and complement to, their traditional work. Problems arise when a scorecard project is managed by a group from outside planning (such as HR, quality, or an ad hoc team). As the scorecard acquires strategic importance, conflicts over strategy development can arise between the planning unit and the scorecard team. If this occurs, top management should quickly merge the two groups.

Communicate strategy

Effective communication to employees about strategy, targets, and initiatives is vital if employees are to contribute to the strategy. Canon U.S.A., a scorecard user, describes its internal communication process as "democratizing strategy," and it actively promotes understanding of the company's strategy and the scorecard in all business units and support functions. Strategy communication, therefore, is a natural turf for an OSM. But as with strategy planning, internal communication is sometimes another unit's existing responsibility. In these situations, the OSM has tended to take an editorial role, reviewing the messages to see that they communicate the strategy correctly. In cases where the corporate communications group has little knowledge of or focus on strategy, such as at Chrysler and the U.S. Army, the OSM takes on primary responsibility for communicating both the scorecard and strategy to employees. In either situation, the OSM should always take the lead in crafting strategy messages delivered by the CEO, because one of the most effective communication channels is having each employee hear about strategy directly from the CEO. Finally, as part of its communication responsibilities, the OSM must cooperate with HR to ensure that education about the scorecard and its role is included in employee training programs.

Manage strategic initiatives

Strategic initiatives—such as a TQM program or the implementation of CRM software—are discretionary programs that help companies accomplish strategic objectives. The executive team typically identifies these initiatives as part of its annual planning process, although new initiatives may arise throughout the year. Ideally, the entire portfolio of such initiatives should be assessed and reprioritized several times annually. The screening, selection, and management of strategic initiatives are what drive change in the company and produce results. Our experience suggests that such initiatives should be managed separately from routine operations. Typically, they are managed by the units most closely associated with them (a CRM project, for instance, is best managed by customer service) or by an ad hoc team drawn from the functions or units affected. Responsibility for managing initiatives that already have a natural home should remain with the associated unit or function. The OSM intervenes only when an initiative falls behind schedule, is over budget, or is not delivering expected results. But the OSM should manage initiatives that cross unit and functional lines—it can thus make sure that they get the resources and attention they need. In all cases, the OSM retains responsibility for monitoring the progress of strategic initiatives and reporting on them to top management.

Integrate strategic priorities with other support functions

Existing functional departments retain prime responsibility for three other key processes necessary for successful strategy implementation: planning and budgeting, human resource alignment, and knowledge management. These processes are critical for effective strategy execution, and the OSM should play a consultative and integrative role with the respective functional departments.

Planning and budgeting. At most corporations, the various functional departments are responsible for planning how the corporation will allocate resources over the year. The finance department oversees budgeting and the allocation of cash to the units and cross-functional initiatives; IT makes recommendations about investments in databases, infrastructure, and application programs; and HR makes plans for hiring, training, and leadership development. For a strategy to be effective, all the functional plans must be aligned with the strategy. The budgets prepared by the finance department, for example, should reflect those established in the strategic planning process and should incorporate funding and personnel resources for cross-functional strategic initiatives.

To ensure this alignment, the OSM must work closely with all these functional units.

Human resource alignment. No strategy can be effective unless the people who have to carry it out are motivated and trained to do so. Motivation and training is, of course, the natural domain of HR, which typically carries out annual performance reviews and personal goal setting and manages employee incentive and competency development programs. It is the responsibility of the OSM to ensure that HR performs these activities in a manner consistent with corporate and business unit strategic objectives. The goal is to make strategy everyone's job.

Knowledge management. Finally, the OSM needs to ensure that knowledge management focuses on sharing the best practices most critical for the strategy. If managers use the wrong benchmarks, the company's strategy will fall short of its potential. At some companies, learning and knowledge sharing are already the responsibility of a chief knowledge or learning officer; in those cases, the OSM needs to coordinate with that person's office. But if such a function does not already exist, the OSM must take the lead in transferring ideas and best practices throughout the organization.

The exhibit "The new strategy calendar" illustrates the activities that a properly constituted OSM will be engaged in during the year. The strategy cycle launches at the beginning of the second quarter, when the OSM starts to plan strategy and update the enterprise scorecard. After the enterprise strategy meeting, the OSM starts the process of aligning the organization with the enterprise goals. Before the end of the third quarter, it will be coordinating with finance to bring unit-level plans and budgets in line with strategy, and by the beginning of the fourth quarter, it will be working with HR on aligning the competency development and incentives of employees with scorecard objectives. While these calendar-driven processes are going on, the unit continually engages in control and learning: reviewing and communicating strategy, managing initiatives, and sharing best practices.

The new strategy calendar

At scorecard-driven companies, the strategic processes are carried out or supervised by the office of strategy management in coordination with the appropriate management teams or executives. This ensures that the strategy is fully reflected in all strategy-related activities at all levels of the company.

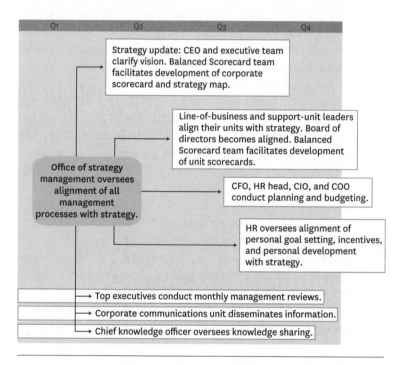

Positioning and Staffing the OSM

Executing strategy usually involves making changes that only a CEO can empower, and the OSM will be most effective when it has direct access to the CEO. Barbara Possin, the director of strategic alignment at St. Mary's Duluth Clinic, told us she was able to overcome resistance to her initiatives because managers knew she had a direct reporting line to the company's chief operating and chief executive officers. An OSM buried deep in the finance or planning department may find it difficult to command similar respect and attention from senior executives for strategy management priorities.

The simplest solution, therefore, is to place the OSM on a par with major functions, such as finance and marketing, that report directly to the CEO. The OSM serves, in effect, as the CEO's chief of staff. But if the OSM has originated within a powerful function, such a positioning may not be feasible. In that case, the OSM will usually report to the chief of the function in which it is nested—such as the CFO or vice president of strategic planning—but with occasional direct access to the CEO. At the Mexican insurance company Grupo Nacional Provincial (GNP), for example, the OSM reports both to the chief executive and to the chief financial officer. The OSM sets the agenda for a weekly meeting with the CEO and CFO and for a broader weekly meeting with the six top company executives. The office of strategy management at GNP also has a matrixed relationship with 20 Balanced Scorecard managers in the two major business units and nine support units and with the owners of the major strategic initiatives. The relationship enables the OSM to coordinate the strategic planning done in the business and support units.

The OSM may be an important functional unit, but it doesn't have to be large; it is certainly not our goal to encourage companies to build a new bureaucracy. Although Chrysler employs 13 full-time people in its OSM, reflecting the unit's involvement in product development, our experience suggests that firms with sales of $500 million to $5 billion and 1,000 to 10,000 employees can get by with fewer than ten people. In principle, as the next exhibit shows, a fully functioning OSM should not need more than six to eight full-time-equivalent positions to cope with its activities.

We have observed that establishing an OSM does not usually involve hiring expensive new talent. The OSM is typically staffed with people who led the Balanced Scorecard project—they often come from the planning and finance functions, but some come from other staff groups such as quality, HR, and IT. Several organizations we studied have reported that the people assigned to their OSMs do not constitute a net increase in the organization's head count. In

To fulfill its responsibilities successfully, an office of strategy management at a large company typically needs only six to eight full-time people.

Strategy management process	Typical # of FTE
Scorecard management	1.0
Organization alignment	1.0 – 1.5
Strategy reviews	0.5 – 1.0
Strategic planning	0.5
Strategy communication	0.5 – 1.0
Initiative management	1.0 – 1.5
Planning and budgeting	0.5
Workforce alignment	0.5
Best-practice sharing	0.5 – 1.0
TOTAL FTE POSITIONS	6.0 – 8.5

many cases, the evolution of a well-functioning OSM actually helps reduce overall head count, thanks to the OSM's role in streamlining and focusing management processes and helping managers eliminate layers of staff engaged in data gathering and reporting. The OSM, however, should be assessed by the value it creates through successful strategy execution, not by whether it can reduce head count.

Many organizations have achieved dramatic performance improvements by sustaining a focus on implementation of strategy. We have captured and codified a body of knowledge from these successful organizations that provides the foundation for an emerging professional function focusing on the management of strategy. An office of strategy management that is positioned at the level of other senior corporate staff offices and has responsibility for managing and coordinating all the key strategy management processes can help companies realize the benefits from this body of knowledge.

Originally published in October 2005. Reprint R0510D

The Strategy That Will Fix Health Care

by Michael E. Porter and Thomas H. Lee

IN HEALTH CARE, THE DAYS OF business as usual are over. Around the world, every health care system is struggling with rising costs and uneven quality despite the hard work of well-intentioned, well-trained clinicians. Health care leaders and policy makers have tried countless incremental fixes—attacking fraud, reducing errors, enforcing practice guidelines, making patients better "consumers," implementing electronic medical records—but none have had much impact.

It's time for a fundamentally new strategy.

At its core is maximizing value for patients: that is, achieving the best outcomes at the lowest cost. We must move away from a supply-driven health care system organized around what physicians do and toward a patient-centered system organized around what patients need. We must shift the focus from the volume and profitability of services provided—physician visits, hospitalizations, procedures, and tests—to the patient outcomes achieved. And we must replace today's fragmented system, in which every local provider offers a full range of services, with a system in which services for particular medical conditions are concentrated in health-delivery organizations and in the right locations to deliver high-value care.

Making this transformation is not a single step but an overarching strategy. We call it the "value agenda." It will require restructuring how health care delivery is organized, measured, and reimbursed.

In 2006, Michael Porter and Elizabeth Teisberg introduced the value agenda in their book *Redefining Health Care*. Since then, through our research and the work of thousands of health care leaders and academic researchers around the world, the tools to implement the agenda have been developed, and their deployment by providers and other organizations is rapidly spreading.

The transformation to value-based health care is well under way. Some organizations are still at the stage of pilots and initiatives in individual practice areas. Other organizations, such as the Cleveland Clinic and Germany's Schön Klinik, have undertaken large-scale changes involving multiple components of the value agenda. The result has been striking improvements in outcomes and efficiency, and growth in market share.

There is no longer any doubt about how to increase the value of care. The question is, which organizations will lead the way and how quickly can others follow? The challenge of becoming a value-based organization should not be underestimated, given the entrenched interests and practices of many decades. This transformation must come from within. Only physicians and provider organizations can put in place the set of interdependent steps needed to improve value, because ultimately value is determined by how medicine is practiced. Yet every other stakeholder in the health care system has a role to play. Patients, health plans, employers, and suppliers can hasten the transformation—and all will benefit greatly from doing so.

Defining the Goal

The first step in solving any problem is to define the proper goal. Efforts to reform health care have been hobbled by lack of clarity about the goal, or even by the pursuit of the wrong goal. Narrow goals such as improving access to care, containing costs, and boosting profits have been a distraction. Access to poor care is not the objective, nor is reducing cost at the expense of quality. Increasing profits is today misaligned with the interests of patients, because profits depend on increasing the volume of services, not delivering good results.

Idea in Brief

The Problem

Health care worldwide is struggling with rising costs and unsatisfactory quality. No "silver bullet" approaches or incremental fixes address those problems. Without a true solution, physicians will face lower incomes, patients will pay more, and services will be restricted.

The Approach

If we can agree on the overarching goal of value for health care systems—improving outcomes that matter to patients relative to the cost of achieving those outcomes—then we can begin to make progress.

A Model for Change

The strategic agenda for moving to a high-value health care delivery system comprises six interdependent components: organizing around patients' medical condition rather than physicians' medical specialty, measuring costs and outcomes for each patient, developing bundled prices for the full care cycle, integrating care across separate facilities, expanding geographic reach, and building an enabling IT platform.

In health care, the overarching goal for providers, as well as for every other stakeholder, must be improving value for patients, where value is defined as the health outcomes achieved that matter to patients relative to the cost of achieving those outcomes. Improving value requires either improving one or more outcomes without raising costs or lowering costs without compromising outcomes, or both. Failure to improve value means, well, failure.

Embracing the goal of value at the senior management and board levels is essential, because the value agenda requires a fundamental departure from the past. While health care organizations have never been *against* improving outcomes, their central focus has been on growing volumes and maintaining margins. Despite noble mission statements, the real work of improving value is left undone. Legacy delivery approaches and payment structures, which have remained largely unchanged for decades, have reinforced the problem and produced a system with erratic quality and unsustainable costs.

All this is now changing. Facing severe pressure to contain costs, payors are aggressively reducing reimbursements and finally

Why Change Now?

MOST HOSPITALS AND PHYSICIAN GROUPS still have positive margins, but the pressure to consider a new strategic framework has increased dramatically.

Market forces are driving increasing numbers of hospital mergers and acquisitions, and the number of hospital beds has declined in the U.S. from 3 beds per 1,000 people in 1999 to 2.6 in 2010. Reimbursement rates are under pressure. Physician income has remained static over the past decade, and physicians know that simply working harder, faster, or longer can't compensate for their steadily increasing expenses. Meanwhile, national retailers like Walmart, CVS, and Walgreens are going after the primary care market on a large scale, by offering in-store clinics that provide basic services at prices as much as 40% below what physicians' offices charge.

These developments are not unique to the United States: A similar story is playing out in virtually every national health care system across the globe.

The economics of health care are changing, too. A provider's ability to increase fee-for-service revenue is threatened from every direction. U.S. government payors (Medicare and Medicaid) raise payment levels each year minimally, if at all. Yet most providers have been losing money on Medicare and Medicaid patients for a decade or more, and the magnitude of those losses only increases each year. Exacerbating the problem, the proportion of patients covered by government programs is growing: Medicaid will expand substantially in many states in 2014, as the Affordable Care Act is implemented, and the aging of the population will increase the percentage of Medicare patients for years beyond that. Reimbursement for these patients will continue to be pressured by tight federal and state government budgets. National Institutes of Health research cuts will make matters even worse for academic medical centers.

In the past, providers would cover losses from Medicare and Medicaid and from uninsured populations by demanding higher payment rates from commercial insurance plans—often winning increases of 8% to 10% per year.

moving away from fee-for-service and toward performance-based reimbursement. In the U.S., an increasing percentage of patients are being covered by Medicare and Medicaid, which reimburse at a fraction of private-plan levels. These pressures are leading more independent hospitals to join health systems and more physicians to move out of private practice and become salaried employees of hospitals. (For more, see the sidebar "Why Change Now?") The

Those days are over. Employers are looking for decreases in their health care costs, and they're getting them by engaging in price negotiations, reducing benefits, raising deductibles, and expanding "narrowed network" products that direct patients to providers that accept lower rates or prove better outcomes. A program recently introduced by the California Public Employees' Retirement System (CalPERS) and Anthem Blue Cross, for example, requires many employees seeking a hip or knee replacement to use only hospitals that have agreed to a bundled fee for the procedure—or to pay the difference if they choose a higher-priced provider outside the network.

The intensifying pressure from employers and insurers for transparent pricing is already beginning to force providers to explain—or eliminate—hard-to-justify price variations. In our state, Massachusetts, the price for a brain MRI ranges from $625 to $1,650. And prices can vary by more than 50% for the same procedure in the same hospital, depending on the patient's insurer and the insurance product.

Patients will be asked to pay more and more. The percentage of the population in high-deductible health plans is now well into double digits, and it is rising. Many employees in these plans are increasingly unwilling or are simply unable to pay historical charges, and providers incur losses or bad publicity, or both, as they try to collect on the debts.

Provider organizations understand that, without a change in their model of doing business, they can only hope to be the last iceberg to melt. Facing lower payment rates and potential loss of market share if they charge higher prices, they have no choice but to improve value and be able to "prove it." As one senior executive recently told us, "We've been able to hide our prices for years inside insurance products, but that's going to end as more and more people move into new, high-deductible products. We are going to have to be able to communicate exactly what we are giving patients, employers, and insurers for their money." He's right.

transition will be neither linear nor swift, and we are entering a prolonged period during which providers will work under multiple payment models with varying exposure to risk.

In this environment, providers need a strategy that transcends traditional cost reduction and responds to new payment models. If providers can improve patient outcomes, they can sustain or grow their market share. If they can improve the efficiency of providing excellent care, they will enter any contracting discussion from a position of strength. Those providers that increase value will be the most competitive. Organizations that fail to improve value, no matter how prestigious and powerful they seem today, are likely to encounter growing pressure. Similarly, health insurers that are slow to embrace and support the value agenda—by failing, for example, to favor high-value providers—will lose subscribers to those that do.

The Strategy for Value Transformation

The strategic agenda for moving to a high-value health care delivery system has six components. They are interdependent and mutually reinforcing; as we will see, progress will be easiest and fastest if they are advanced together. (See the exhibit "The Value Agenda.")

The current structure of health care delivery has been sustained for decades because it has rested on its own set of mutually rein-forcing elements: organization by specialty with independent private- practice physicians; measurement of "quality" defined as process compliance; cost accounting driven not by costs but by charges; fee-for-service payments by specialty with rampant cross-subsidies; delivery systems with duplicative service lines and little integration; fragmentation of patient populations such that most providers do not have critical masses of patients with a given medical condition; siloed IT systems around medical specialties; and others. This interlocking structure explains why the current system has been so resistant to change, why incremental steps have had little impact (see the sidebar "No Magic Bullets"), and why simultaneous progress on multiple components of the strategic agenda is so beneficial.

The components of the strategic agenda are not theoretical or radical. All are already being implemented to varying degrees in organizations ranging from leading academic medical centers to community safety-net hospitals. No organization, however, has yet put in place the full value agenda across its entire practice. Every organization has room for improvement in value for patients—and always will.

The value agenda

The strategic agenda for moving to a high-value health care delivery system has six components. They are interdependent and mutually reinforcing. Progress will be greatest if multiple components are advanced together.

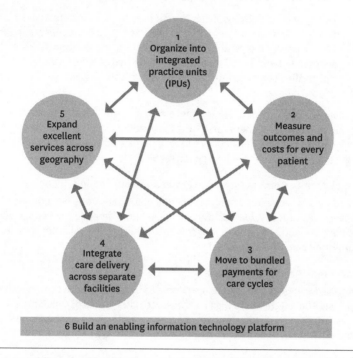

1. Organize into Integrated Practice Units (IPUs)

At the core of the value transformation is changing the way clinicians are organized to deliver care. The first principle in structuring any organization or business is to organize around the customer and the need. In health care, that requires a shift from today's siloed organization by specialty department and discrete service to organizing around the patient's medical condition. We call such a structure an integrated practice unit. In an IPU, a dedicated team made up

No Magic Bullets

THE HISTORY OF HEALTH CARE reform has featured a succession of narrow "solutions," many imposed on provider organizations by external stakeholders and introduced with great fanfare. For the most part, the solutions have focused on the levers that particular stakeholders can push and have been designed to preserve existing roles. None of them tackle the underlying strategic and structural problems that work against value for patients.

Individually and collectively, these "magic bullets" have inspired false hope and distracted attention from the real work at hand. Disappointment with their limited impact has created skepticism that value improvement in health care is possible and has led many to conclude that the only solution to our financial challenges in health care is to ration services and shift costs to patients or taxpayers.

A realistic assessment of these piecemeal reforms reveals that none of them—or even all of them taken together—address the root causes of low value. While many of the steps are useful, there is no substitute for the strategic transformation the value agenda requires.

Regulation to Combat Physician Fraud and Self-Dealing

Fraud and self-dealing occur, but enforcement here does not address the root causes of low-value health care. Regulations intended to reduce self-dealing can actually impede progress toward improving value, by inhibiting integrated care across specialties.

Consumer-Driven Health Care

To date, incentives that encourage people to be better health care "consumers" have done little more than shift costs to patients. Also, consumer shopping can have only limited impact in a fragmented system where information about outcomes and price is lacking.

Evidence-Based Medicine (Requiring Providers to Report Compliance with Guidelines)

Research-based practice guidelines are of course desirable, but compliance with them does not necessarily lead to improved outcomes or efficiency. Guidelines cover only a small slice of the overall care cycle and fail to reflect many individual patient circumstances. Rapid advances in medical knowledge constantly improve the state of the art, which means that providers are measured on compliance with guidelines that are often outdated.

New, More Convenient Models of Primary Care

New models of delivering routine primary care in lower-cost settings (such as retail clinics) have a role, but they will do little to address the bulk of health care costs, most of which are generated by care for more-complex diseases. Also, retail clinics and other adjuncts to primary care practices are not equipped to provide holistic and continuous care for healthy patients or acute and preventive care for patients with complex, chronic, or acute conditions.

Global Capitation to Control Spending

Capitation—a payment model in which providers receive a flat fee for taking care of an individual enrolled in a health care plan, covering any and all needed services—provides a strong incentive to reduce spending but not necessarily to improve value. Patients and providers alike worry about the lack of alignment of a single global payment with patients' interests. This payment model also exposes providers to risks over which they have little control. Capitation motivates providers to offer every service line in an attempt to keep spending internal, instead of providing only services where they can offer excellent value.

Reduction of Medical Errors

Reducing errors is essential, but errors are just one of the outcomes that matter to patients. Reducing errors does not itself lead to a redesign of overall care that improves value.

Care Coordination, Especially for Expensive Patients

If care coordinators are simply layered on top of a fragmented and dysfunctional delivery system, savings are modest (4% to 7% at best). When coordination takes place organically in IPUs, savings can reach 30% or more.

Electronic Medical Records (EMR)

Information technology is a powerful tool for enabling value-based care. But introducing EMR without restructuring care delivery measurement, and payment yields limited benefits. And siloed IT systems make cost and outcomes measurement virtually impossible, greatly impeding value improvement efforts.

of both clinical and nonclinical personnel provides the full care cycle for the patient's condition.

IPUs treat not only a disease but also the related conditions, complications, and circumstances that commonly occur along with it—such as kidney and eye disorders for patients with diabetes, or palliative care for those with metastatic cancer. IPUs not only provide treatment but also assume responsibility for engaging patients and their families in care—for instance, by providing education and counseling, encouraging adherence to treatment and prevention protocols, and supporting needed behavioral changes such as smoking cessation or weight loss.

In an IPU, personnel work together regularly as a team toward a common goal: maximizing the patient's overall outcomes as efficiently as possible. They are expert in the condition, know and trust one another, and coordinate easily to minimize wasted time and resources. They meet frequently, formally and informally, and review data on their own performance. Armed with those data, they work to improve care—by establishing new protocols and devising better or more efficient ways to engage patients, including group visits and virtual interactions. Ideally, IPU members are co-located, to facilitate communication, collaboration, and efficiency for patients, but they work as a team even if they're based at different locations. (See the sidebar "What Is an Integrated Practice Unit?")

Take, for example, care for patients with low back pain—one of the most common and expensive causes of disability. In the prevailing approach, patients receive portions of their care from a variety of types of clinicians, usually in several different locations, who function more like a spontaneously assembled "pickup team" than an integrated unit. One patient might begin care with a primary care physician, while others might start with an orthopedist, a neurologist, or a rheumatologist. What happens next is unpredictable. Patients might be referred to yet another physician or to a physical therapist. They might undergo radiology testing (this could happen at any point—even before seeing a physician). Each encounter is separate from the others, and no one coordinates the care. Duplication of effort, delays, and inefficiency is almost inevitable. Since no one

What Is an Integrated Practice Unit?

1. An IPU is organized around a medical condition or a set of closely related conditions (or around defined patient segments for primary care).

2. Care is delivered by a dedicated, multidisciplinary team of clinicians who devote a significant portion of their time to the medical condition.

3. Providers see themselves as part of a common organizational unit.

4. The team takes responsibility for the full cycle of care for the condition, encompassing outpatient, inpatient, and rehabilitative care, and supporting services (such as nutrition, social work, and behavioral health).

5. Patient education, engagement, and follow-up are integrated into care.

6. The unit has a single administrative and scheduling structure.

7. To a large extent, care is co-located in dedicated facilities.

8. A physician team captain or a clinical care manager (or both) oversees each patient's care process.

9. The team measures outcomes, costs, and processes for each patient using a common measurement platform.

10. The providers on the team meet formally and informally on a regular basis to discuss patients, processes, and results.

11. Joint accountability is accepted for outcomes and costs.

measures patient outcomes, how long the process takes, or how much the care costs, the value of care never improves.

Contrast that with the approach taken by the IPU at Virginia Mason Medical Center, in Seattle. Patients with low back pain call one central phone number (206-41-SPINE), and most can be seen the same day. The "spine team" pairs a physical therapist with a physician who is board-certified in physical medicine and rehabilitation, and patients usually see both on their first visit. Those with serious causes of back pain (such as a malignancy or an infection) are quickly identified and enter a process designed to address the specific diagnosis. Other patients will require surgery and will enter a process for that. For most patients, however, physical therapy is the most effective next intervention, and their treatment often begins the same day.

Virginia Mason did not address the problem of chaotic care by hiring coordinators to help patients navigate the existing system—a "solution" that does not work. Rather, it eliminated the chaos by creating a new system in which caregivers work together in an integrated way. The impact on value has been striking. Compared with regional averages, patients at Virginia Mason's Spine Clinic miss fewer days of work (4.3 versus 9 per episode) and need fewer physical therapy visits (4.4 versus 8.8). In addition, the use of MRI scans to evaluate low back pain has decreased by 23% since the clinic's launch, in 2005, even as outcomes have improved. Better care has actually lowered costs, a point we will return to later. Virginia Mason has also increased revenue through increased productivity, rather than depending on more fee-for-service visits to drive revenue from unneeded or duplicative tests and care. The clinic sees about 2,300 new patients per year compared with 1,404 under the old system, and it does so in the same space and with the same number of staff members.

Wherever IPUs exist, we find similar results—faster treatment, better outcomes, lower costs, and, usually, improving market share in the condition. But those results can be achieved only through a restructuring of work. Simply co-locating staff in the same building, or putting up a sign announcing a Center of Excellence or an Institute, will have little impact.

IPUs emerged initially in the care for particular medical conditions, such as breast cancer and joint replacement. Today, condition-based IPUs are proliferating rapidly across many areas of acute and chronic care, from organ transplantation to shoulder care to mental health conditions such as eating disorders.

Recently, we have applied the IPU model to primary care (see Michael E. Porter, Erika A. Pabo, and Thomas H. Lee, "Redesigning Primary Care," *Health Affairs*, March 2013). By its very nature, primary care is holistic, concerned with all the health circumstances and needs of a patient. Today's primary care practice applies a common organizational structure to the management of a very wide range of patients, from healthy adults to the frail elderly. The complexity of meeting their heterogeneous needs has made value improvement very difficult in primary care—for example, heterogeneous needs make outcomes measurement next to impossible.

In primary care, IPUs are multidisciplinary teams organized to serve groups of patients with similar primary and preventive care needs—for example, patients with complex chronic conditions such as diabetes, or disabled elderly patients. Different patient groups require different teams, different types of services, and even different locations of care. They also require services to address head-on the crucial role of lifestyle change and preventive care in outcomes and costs, and those services must be tailored to patients' overall circumstances. Within each patient group, the appropriate clinical team, preventive services, and education can be put in place to improve value, and results become measureable.

This approach is already starting to be applied to high-risk, high-cost patients through so-called Patient-Centered Medical Homes. But the opportunity to substantially enhance value in primary care is far broader. At Geisinger Health System, in Pennsylvania, for example, the care for patients with chronic conditions such as diabetes and heart disease involves not only physicians and other clinicians but also pharmacists, who have major responsibility for following and adjusting medications. The inclusion of pharmacists on teams has resulted in fewer strokes, amputations, emergency department visits, and hospitalizations, and in better performance on other outcomes that matter to patients.

2. Measure Outcomes and Costs for Every Patient

Rapid improvement in any field requires measuring results—a familiar principle in management. Teams improve and excel by tracking progress over time and comparing their performance to that of peers inside and outside their organization. Indeed, rigorous measurement of value (outcomes and costs) is perhaps the single most important step in improving health care. Wherever we see systematic measurement of results in health care—no matter what the country—we see those results improve.

Yet the reality is that the great majority of health care providers (and insurers) fail to track either outcomes or costs by medical condition for individual patients. For example, although many institutions have "back pain centers," few can tell you about their patients' outcomes (such as their time to return to work) or the actual resources used in treating those patients over the full care cycle. That surprising truth goes a long way toward explaining why decades of health care reform have not changed the trajectory of value in the system.

When outcomes measurement *is* done, it rarely goes beyond tracking a few areas, such as mortality and safety. Instead, "quality measurement" has gravitated to the most easily measured and least controversial indicators. Most "quality" metrics do not gauge quality; rather, they are process measures that capture compliance with practice guidelines. HEDIS (the Healthcare Effectiveness Data and Information Set) scores consist entirely of process measures as well as easy-to-measure clinical indicators that fall well short of actual outcomes. For diabetes, for example, providers measure the reliability of their LDL cholesterol checks and hemoglobin A1c levels, even though what really matters to patients is whether they are likely to lose their vision, need dialysis, have a heart attack or stroke, or undergo an amputation. Few health care organizations yet measure how their diabetic patients fare on all the outcomes that matter.

It is not surprising that the public remains indifferent to quality measures that may gauge a provider's reliability and reputation but say little about how its patients actually do. The only true measures of quality are the outcomes that matter to patients. And when those outcomes are collected and reported publicly, providers face tremendous pressure—and strong incentives—to improve and to adopt best practices, with resulting improvements in outcomes. Take, for example, the Fertility Clinic Success Rate and Certification Act of 1992, which mandated that all clinics performing assisted reproductive technology procedures, notably in vitro fertilization, provide their live birth rates and other metrics to the Centers for Disease

Outcomes measurement and reporting drive improvement

Since public reporting of clinic performance began, in 1997, in vitro fertilization success rates have climbed steadily across all clinics as process improvements have spread.

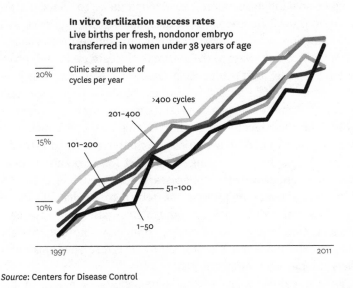

In vitro fertilization success rates
Live births per fresh, nondonor embryo transferred in women under 38 years of age

Clinic size number of cycles per year

>400 cycles

201–400

101–200

51–100

1–50

20%

15%

10%

1997 ———— 2011

Source: Centers for Disease Control

Control. After the CDC began publicly reporting those data, in 1997, improvements in the field were rapidly adopted, and success rates for all clinics, large and small, have steadily improved. (See the exhibit "Outcomes measurement and reporting drive improvement.")

Measuring outcomes that matter to patients

Outcomes should be measured by medical condition (such as diabetes), not by specialty (podiatry) or intervention (eye examination). Outcomes should cover the full cycle of care for the condition, and track the patient's health status after care is completed. The outcomes that matter to patients for a particular medical condition fall into three tiers. (For more, see Michael Porter's article "Measuring

Health Outcomes: The Outcome Hierarchy," *New England Journal of Medicine,* December 2010.) Tier 1 involves the health status achieved. Patients care about mortality rates, of course, but they're also concerned about their functional status. In the case of prostate cancer treatment, for example, five-year survival rates are typically 90% or higher, so patients are more interested in their providers' performance on crucial functional outcomes, such as incontinence and sexual function, where variability among providers is much greater.

Tier 2 outcomes relate to the nature of the care cycle and recovery. For example, high readmission rates and frequent emergency-department "bounce backs" may not actually worsen long-term survival, but they are expensive and frustrating for both providers and patients. The level of discomfort during care and how long it takes to return to normal activities also matter greatly to patients. Significant delays before seeing a specialist for a potentially ominous complaint can cause unnecessary anxiety, while delays in commencing treatment prolong the return to normal life. Even when functional outcomes are equivalent, patients whose care process is timely and free of chaos, confusion, and unnecessary setbacks experience much better care than those who encounter delays and problems along the way.

Tier 3 outcomes relate to the sustainability of health. A hip replacement that lasts two years is inferior to one that lasts 15 years, from both the patient's perspective and the provider's.

Measuring the full set of outcomes that matter is indispensable to better meeting patients' needs. It is also one of the most powerful vehicles for lowering health care costs. If Tier 1 functional outcomes improve, costs invariably go down. If any Tier 2 or 3 outcomes improve, costs invariably go down. A 2011 German study, for example, found that one-year follow-up costs after total hip replacement were 15% lower in hospitals with above-average outcomes than in hospitals with below-average outcomes, and 24% lower than in very-low-volume hospitals, where providers have relatively little experience with hip replacements. By failing to consistently measure the outcomes that matter, we lose perhaps our most powerful lever for cost reduction.

Outcomes That Matter to Patients:
A Hierarchy

IN MEASURING QUALITY OF CARE, providers tend to focus on only what they directly control or easily measured clinical indicators. However, measuring the full set of outcomes that matter to patients by condition is essential in meeting their needs. And when outcomes are measured comprehensively, results invariably improve.

Tier 1: Health status achieved or retained

Survival	***Example: hip replacement*** • Mortality rate (inpatient)
Degree of health or recovery	• Functional level achieved • Pain level achieved • Extent of return to physical activities • Ability to return to work

Tier 2: Process of recovery

Time to recovery	• Time to begin treatment • Time to return to physical activities • Time to return to work
Disutility of care or treatment process (for instance, diagnostic errors, ineffective care, treatment-related discomfort, complications, adverse effects)	• Delays and anxiety • Pain during treatment • Length of hospital stay • Infection • Pulmonary embolism • Deep-vein thrombosis • Myocardial infarction • Need for re-operation • Delirium

Tier 3: Sustainability of health

Sustainability of health or recovery Nature of recurrences	• Maintained functional level • Ability to live independently • Need for revision or replacement
Long-term consequences of therapy (for instance, care-induced illnesses)	• Loss of mobility due to inadequate rehabilitation • Risk of complex fracture • Susceptibility to infection • Stiff knee due to unrecognized complications • Regional pain syndrome

Source: "Measuring Health Outcomes," Michael E. Porter, *New England Journal of Medicine,* December 2010

Over the past half dozen years, a growing array of providers have begun to embrace true outcome measurement. Many of the leaders have seen their reputations—and market share—improve as a result. A welcomed competition is emerging to be the most comprehensive and transparent provider in measuring outcomes.

The Cleveland Clinic is one such pioneer, first publishing its mortality data on cardiac surgery and subsequently mandating outcomes measurement across the entire organization. Today, the Clinic publishes 14 different "outcomes books" reporting performance in managing a growing number of conditions (cancer, neurological conditions, and cardiac diseases, for example). The range of outcomes measured remains limited, but the Clinic is expanding its efforts, and other organizations are following suit. At the individual IPU level, numerous providers are beginning efforts. At Dartmouth-Hitchcock's Spine Center, for instance, patient scores for pain, physical function, and disability for surgical and nonsurgical treatment at three, six, 12, and 24 months are now published for each type of low back disorder.

Providers are improving their understanding of what outcomes to measure and how to collect, analyze, and report outcomes data. For example, some of our colleagues at Partners HealthCare in Boston are testing innovative technologies such as tablet computers, web portals, and telephonic interactive systems for collecting outcomes data from patients after cardiac surgery or as they live with chronic conditions such as diabetes. Outcomes are also starting to be incorporated in real time into the process of care, allowing providers to track progress as they interact with patients.

To accelerate comprehensive and standardized outcome measurement on a global basis, we recently cofounded the International Consortium for Health Outcomes Measurement. ICHOM develops minimum outcome sets by medical condition, drawing on international registries and provider best practices. It brings together clinical leaders from around the world to develop standard outcome sets, while also gathering and disseminating best practices in outcomes data collection, verification, and reporting. Just as railroads converged on standard track widths and the telecommunications industry on standards to allow data exchange, health care providers globally should consistently measure outcomes by condition to enable universal comparison and stimulate rapid improvement.

Measuring the cost of care

For a field in which high cost is an overarching problem, the absence of accurate cost information in health care is nothing short of astounding. Few clinicians have any knowledge of what each component of care costs, much less how costs relate to the outcomes achieved. In most health care organizations there is virtually no accurate information on the cost of the full cycle of care for a patient with a particular medical condition. Instead, most hospital cost-accounting systems are department-based, not patient-based, and designed for billing of transactions reimbursed under fee-for-service contracts. In a world where fees just keep going up, that makes sense. Existing systems are also fine for overall department budgeting, but they provide only crude and misleading estimates of actual costs of service for individual patients and conditions. For example, cost allocations are often based on charges, not actual costs. As health care providers come under increasing pressure to lower costs and report outcomes, the existing systems are wholly inadequate.

To determine value, providers must measure costs at the medical condition level, tracking the expenses involved in treating the condition over the full cycle of care. This requires understanding the resources used in a patient's care, including personnel, equipment, and facilities; the capacity cost of supplying each resource; and the support costs associated with care, such as IT and administration. Then the cost of caring for a condition can be compared with the outcomes achieved.

The best method for understanding these costs is time-driven activity-based costing, TDABC. While rarely used in health care to date, it is beginning to spread. Where TDABC is being applied, it is helping providers find numerous ways to substantially reduce costs without negatively affecting outcomes (and sometimes even improving them). Providers are achieving savings of 25% or more by tapping opportunities such as better capacity utilization, more-standardized processes, better matching of personnel skills to tasks, locating care in the most cost-effective type of facility, and many others.

For example, Virginia Mason found that it costs $4 per minute for an orthopedic surgeon or other procedural specialist to perform a service, $2 for a general internist, and $1 or less for a nurse practitioner or physical therapist. In light of those cost differences, focusing the time of the most expensive staff members on work that utilizes their full skill set is hugely important. (For more, see Robert Kaplan and Michael Porter's article "How to Solve the Cost Crisis in Health Care," HBR, September 2011.)

Without understanding the true costs of care for patient conditions, much less how costs are related to outcomes, health care organizations are flying blind in deciding how to improve processes and redesign care. Clinicians and administrators battle over arbitrary cuts, rather than working together to improve the value of care. Because proper cost data are so critical to overcoming the many barriers associated with legacy processes and systems, we often tell skeptical clinical leaders: "Cost accounting is your friend." Understanding true costs will finally allow clinicians to work with administrators to improve the value of care—the fundamental goal of health care organizations.

3. Move to Bundled Payments for Care Cycles

Neither of the dominant payment models in health care—global capitation and fee-for-service—directly rewards improving the value of care. Global capitation, a single payment to cover all of a patient's needs, rewards providers for spending less but not specifically for improving outcomes or value. It also decouples payment from what providers can directly control. Fee-for-service couples payment to something providers can control—how many of their services, such as MRI scans, they provide—but not to the overall cost or the outcomes. Providers are rewarded for increasing volume, but that does not necessarily increase value.

The payment approach best aligned with value is a bundled payment that covers the full care cycle for acute medical conditions, the overall care for chronic conditions for a defined period (usually a year), or primary and preventive care for a defined patient population (healthy children, for instance). Well-designed bundled payments directly encourage teamwork and high-value care. Payment is tied to overall care for a patient with a particular medical condition, aligning payment with what the team can control. Providers benefit from improving efficiency while maintaining or improving outcomes.

Sound bundled payment models should include: severity adjustments or eligibility only for qualifying patients; care guarantees that hold the provider responsible for avoidable complications, such as infections after surgery; stop-loss provisions that mitigate the risk of unusually high-cost events; and mandatory outcomes reporting.

Governments, insurers, and health systems in multiple countries are moving to adopt bundled payment approaches. For example, the Stockholm County Council initiated such a program in 2009 for all total hip and knee replacements for relatively healthy patients. The result was lower costs, higher patient satisfaction, and improvement in some outcomes. In Germany, bundled payments for hospital inpatient care—combining all physician fees and other costs, unlike payment models in the U.S.—have helped keep the average payment for a hospitalization below $5,000 (compared with more than $19,000 in the U.S., even though hospital stays are, on average, 50% longer in Germany). Among the features of the German system are care guarantees under which the hospital bears responsibility for the cost of rehospitalization related to the original care.

In the U.S., bundled payments have become the norm for organ transplant care. Here, mandatory outcomes reporting has combined with bundles to reinforce team care, speed diffusion of innovation, and rapidly improve outcomes. Providers that adopted bundle approaches early benefitted. UCLA's kidney transplant program, for example, has grown dramatically since pioneering a bundled price arrangement with Kaiser Permanente, in 1986, and offering the payment approach to all its payors shortly thereafter. Its outcomes are among the best nationally, and UCLA's market share in organ transplantation has expanded substantially.

Employers are also embracing bundled payments. This year, Walmart introduced a program in which it encourages employees who need cardiac, spine, and selected other surgery to obtain care at one of just six providers nationally, all of which have high volume and track records of excellent outcomes: the Cleveland Clinic, Geisinger, the Mayo Clinic, Mercy Hospital (in Springfield, Missouri), Scott & White, and Virginia Mason. The hospitals are reimbursed for the care with a single bundled payment that includes all physician and hospital costs associated with both inpatient and outpatient pre- and post-operative care. Employees bear no out-of-pocket costs for their care—travel, lodging, and meals for the patient and a care-giver are provided—as long as the surgery is performed at one of the centers of excellence. The program is in its infancy, but expectations are that Walmart and other large employers will expand such programs to improve value for their employees, and will step up the incentives for employees to use them. Sophisticated employers have learned that they must move beyond cost containment and health promotion measures, such as co-pays and on-site health and wellness facilities, and become a greater force in rewarding high-value providers with more patients.

As bundled payment models proliferate, the way in which care is delivered will be transformed. Consider how providers participating in Walmart's program are changing the way they provide care. As clinical leaders map the processes involved in caring for patients who live outside their immediate area, they are learning how to better coordinate care with all of patients' local physicians. They're also questioning existing practices. For example, many hospitals routinely have patients return to see the cardiac surgeon six to eight weeks after surgery, but out-of-town visits seem difficult to justify for patients with no obvious complications. In deciding to drop those visits, clinicians realized that maybe local patients do not need routine postoperative visits either.

Providers remain nervous about bundled payments, citing concerns that patient heterogeneity might not be fully reflected in reimbursements, and that the lack of accurate cost data at the condition level could create financial exposure. Those concerns are legitimate, but they are present in any reimbursement model. We believe that concerns will fall away over time, as sophistication grows and the evidence mounts that embracing payments aligned with delivering value is in providers' economic interest. Providers will adopt bundles as a tool to grow volume and improve value.

4. Integrate Care Delivery Systems

A large and growing proportion of health care is provided by multisite health care delivery organizations. In 2011, 60% of all U.S. hospitals were part of such systems, up from 51% in 1999. Multisite health organizations accounted for 69% of total admissions in 2011. Those proportions are even higher today. Unfortunately, most multisite organizations are not true delivery systems, at least thus far, but loose confederations of largely stand-alone units that often duplicate services. There are huge opportunities for improving value as providers integrate systems to eliminate the fragmentation and duplication of care and to optimize the types of care delivered in each location.

To achieve true system integration, organizations must grapple with four related sets of choices: defining the scope of services, concentrating volume in fewer locations, choosing the right location for each service line, and integrating care for patients across locations. The politics of redistributing care remain daunting, given most providers' instinct to preserve the status quo and protect their turf. Some acid-test questions to gauge board members' and health system leaders' appetite for transformation include: Are you ready to give up service lines to improve the value of care for patients? Is relocating service lines on the table?

Define the scope of services
A starting point for system integration is determining the overall scope of services a provider can effectively deliver—and reducing or eliminating service lines where they cannot realistically achieve high value. For community providers, this may mean exiting or establishing partnerships in complex service lines, such as cardiac

surgery or care for rare cancers. For academic medical centers, which have more heavily resourced facilities and staff, this may mean minimizing routine service lines and creating partnerships or affiliations with lower-cost community providers in those fields. Although limiting the range of service lines offered has traditionally been an unnatural act in health care—where organizations strive to do everything for everyone—the move to a value-based delivery system will require those kinds of choices.

Concentrate volume in fewer locations

Second, providers should concentrate the care for each of the conditions they do treat in fewer locations. The stated promise of consumer-oriented health care—"We do everything you need close to your home or workplace"—has been a good marketing pitch but a poor strategy for creating value. Concentrating volume is essential if integrated practice units are to form and measurement is to improve.

Numerous studies confirm that volume in a particular medical condition matters for value. Providers with significant experience in treating a given condition have better outcomes, and costs improve as well. A recent study of the relationship between hospital volume and operative mortality for high-risk types of cancer surgery, for example, found that as hospital volumes rose, the chances of a patient's dying as a result of the surgery fell by as much as 67%. Patients, then, are often much better off traveling longer distance to obtain care at locations where there are teams with deep experience in their condition. That often means driving past the closest hospitals.

Concentrating volume is among the most difficult steps for many organizations, because it can threaten both prestige and physician turf. Yet the benefits of concentration can be game-changing. In 2009, the city of London set out to improve survival and prospects for stroke patients by ensuring that patients were cared for by true IPUs—dedicated, state-of-the-art teams and facilities including neurologists who were expert in the care of stroke. These were called hyper-acute stroke units, or HASUs. At the time, there were too many hospitals providing acute stroke care in London (32 of them) to allow any to amass a high volume. UCL Partners, a delivery system comprising six well-known teaching hospitals that serve North Central London, had two hospitals providing stroke care—University College London Hospital and the Royal Free Hospital— located less than three miles apart. University College was selected to house the new stroke unit. Neurologists at Royal Free began practicing at University College, and a Royal Free neurologist was appointed as the overall leader of the stroke program. UCL Partners later moved all emergency vascular surgery and complex aortic surgery to Royal Free.

These steps sent a strong message that UCL Partners was ready to concentrate volume to improve value. The number of stroke cases treated at University College climbed from about 200 in 2008 to more than 1,400 in 2011. All stroke patients can now undergo rapid evaluation by highly experienced neurologists and begin their recovery under the care of nurses who are expert in preventing stroke-related complications. Since the shift, mortality associated with strokes at University College has fallen by about 25% and costs per patient have dropped by 6%.

Choose the right location for each service

The third component of system integration is delivering particular services at the locations at which value is highest. Less complex conditions and routine services should be moved out of teaching hospitals into lower-cost facilities, with charges set accordingly. There are huge value improvement opportunities in matching the complexity and skills needed with the resource intensity of the location, which will not only optimize cost but also increase staff utilization and productivity. Children's Hospital of Philadelphia, for instance, decided to stop performing routine tympanostomies (placing tubes into children's eardrums to reduce fluid collection and risk of infection) at its main facility and shifted those services to suburban ambulatory surgery facilities. More recently, the hospital applied the same approach to simple hypospadias repairs, a urological procedure. Relocating such services cut costs and freed up operating rooms and staff at the teaching hospital for more-complex procedures. Management estimated the total cost reduction resulting from the shift at 30% to 40%.

In many cases, current reimbursement schemes still reward providers for performing services in a hospital setting, offering even higher payments if the hospital is an academic medical center—another example of how existing reimbursement models have worked against value. But the days of charging higher fees for routine services in high-cost settings are quickly coming to an end. (See again the sidebar "Why Change Now?")

Integrate care across locations

The final component of health system integration is to integrate care for individual patients across locations. As providers distribute services in the care cycle across locations, they must learn to tie together the patient's care across these sites. Care should be directed by IPUs, but recurring services need not take place in a single location. For example, patients with low back pain may receive an initial evaluation, and surgery if needed, from a centrally located spine IPU team but may continue physical therapy closer to home. Wherever the services are performed, however, the IPU manages the full care cycle. Integrating mechanisms, such as assigning a single physician team captain for each patient and adopting common scheduling and other protocols, help ensure that well-coordinated, multidisciplinary care is delivered in a cost-effective and convenient way.

5. Expand Geographic Reach

Health care delivery remains heavily local, and even academic medical centers primarily serve their immediate geographic areas. If value is to be substantially increased on a large scale, however, superior providers for particular medical conditions need to serve far more patients and extend their reach through the strategic expansion of excellent IPUs. Buying full-service hospitals or practices in new geographic areas is rarely the answer. Geographic expansion should focus on improving value, not just increasing volume.

Targeted geographic expansion by leading providers is rapidly increasing, with dozens of organizations such as Vanderbilt, Texas Children's, Children's Hospital of Philadelphia, MD Anderson Cancer

Center, and many others taking bold steps to serve patients over a wide geographic area.

Geographic expansion takes two principle forms. The first is a hub-and-spoke model. For each IPU, satellite facilities are established and staffed at least partly by clinicians and other personnel employed by the parent organization. In the most effective models, some clinicians rotate among locations, which helps staff members across all facilities feel they are part of the team. As expansion moves to an entirely new region, a new IPU hub is built or acquired.

Patients often get their initial evaluation and development of a treatment plan at the hub, but some or much care takes place at more-convenient (and cost-effective) locations. Satellites deliver less complicated care, with complex cases referred to the hub. If complications occur whose effective management is beyond the ability of the satellite facility, the patient's care is transferred to the hub. The net result is a substantial increase in the number of patients an excellent IPU can serve.

This model is becoming more common among leading cancer centers. MD Anderson, for example, has four satellite sites in the greater Houston region where patients receive chemotherapy, radiation therapy, and, more recently, low-complexity surgery, under the supervision of a hub IPU. The cost of care at the regional facilities is estimated to be about one-third less than comparable care at the main facility. By 2012, 22% of radiation treatment and 15% of all chemotherapy treatment were performed at regional sites, along with about 5% of surgery. Senior management estimates that 50% of comparable care currently still performed at the hub could move to satellite sites—a significant untapped value opportunity.

The second emerging geographic expansion model is clinical affiliation, in which an IPU partners with community providers or other local organizations, using their facilities rather than adding capacity. The IPU provides management oversight for clinical care, and some clinical staff members working at the affiliate may be employed by the parent IPU. MD Anderson uses this approach in its partnership with Banner Phoenix. Hybrid models include the approach taken by MD Anderson in its regional satellite program, which leases outpatient facilities located on community hospital campuses and utilizes those hospitals' operating rooms and other inpatient and ancillary services as needed.

Local affiliates benefit from the expertise, experience, and reputation of the parent IPU—benefits that often improve their market share locally. The IPU broadens its regional reach and brand, and benefits from management fees, shared revenue or joint venture income, and referrals of complex cases.

The Cleveland Clinic's Heart and Vascular Institute, a pioneering IPU in cardiac and vascular care, has 19 hospital affiliates spanning the Eastern seaboard. Successful clinical affiliations such as these are robust—not simply storefronts with new signage and marketing campaigns—and involve close oversight by physician and nurse leaders from the parent organization as well as strict adherence to its practice models and measurement systems. Over time, outcomes for standard cases at the Clinic's affiliates have risen to approach its own outcomes.

Vanderbilt's rapidly expanding affiliate network illustrates the numerous opportunities that arise from affiliations that recognize each partner's areas of strength. For example, Vanderbilt has encouraged affiliates to grow noncomplex obstetrics services that once might have taken place at the academic medical center, while affiliates have joint ventured with Vanderbilt in providing care for some complex conditions in their territories.

6. Build an Enabling Information Technology Platform

The preceding five components of the value agenda are powerfully enabled by a sixth: a supporting information technology platform. Historically, health care IT systems have been siloed by department, location, type of service, and type of data (for instance, images). Often IT systems complicate rather than support integrated, multidisciplinary care. That's because IT is just a tool; automating broken service-delivery processes only gets you more-efficient broken processes. But the right kind of IT system can help the parts of an IPU work with one another, enable measurement and new reimbursement approaches, and tie the parts of a well-structured delivery system together.

A value-enhancing IT platform has six essential elements:

It is centered on patients

The system follows patients across services, sites, and time for the full cycle of care, including hospitalization, outpatient visits, testing, physical therapy, and other interventions. Data are aggregated around patients, not departments, units, or locations.

It uses common data definitions

Terminology and data fields related to diagnoses, lab values, treatments, and other aspects of care are standardized so that everyone is speaking the same language, enabling data to be understood, exchanged, and queried across the whole system.

It encompasses all types of patient data

Physician notes, images, chemotherapy orders, lab tests, and other data are stored in a single place so that everyone participating in a patient's care has a comprehensive view.

The medical record is accessible to all parties involved in care

That includes referring physicians and patients themselves. A simple "stress test" question to gauge the accessibility of the data in an IT system is: Can visiting nurses see physicians' notes, and vice versa? The answer today at almost all delivery systems is "no." As different types of clinicians become true team members—working together in IPUs, for example—sharing information needs to become routine. The right kind of medical record also should mean that patients have to provide only one set of patient information, and that they have a centralized way to schedule appointments, refill prescriptions, and communicate with clinicians. And it should make it easy to survey patients about certain types of information relevant to their care, such as their functional status and their pain levels.

The system includes templates and expert systems for each medical condition

Templates make it easier and more efficient for the IPU teams to enter and find data, execute procedures, use standard order sets, and measure outcomes and costs. Expert systems help clinicians identify needed steps (for example, follow-up for an abnormal test) and possible risks (drug interactions that may be overlooked if data are simply recorded in free text, for example).

The system architecture makes it easy to extract information

In value-enhancing systems, the data needed to measure outcomes, track patient-centered costs, and control for patient risk factors can be readily extracted using natural language processing. Such systems also give patients the ability to report outcomes on their care, not only after their care is completed but also during care, to enable better clinical decisions. Even in today's most advanced systems, the critical capability to create and extract such data remains poorly developed. As a result, the cost of measuring outcomes and costs is unnecessarily increased.

The Cleveland Clinic is a provider that has made its electronic record an important enabler of its strategy to put "Patients First" by pursuing virtually all these aims. It is now moving toward giving patients full access to clinician notes—another way to improve care for patients.

Getting Started

The six components of the value agenda are distinct but mutually reinforcing. Organizing into IPUs makes proper measurement of outcomes and costs easier. Better measurement of outcomes and costs makes bundled payments easier to set and agree upon. A common IT platform enables effective collaboration and coordination within IPU teams, while also making the extraction, comparison, and reporting of outcomes and cost data easier. With bundled prices in place, IPUs have stronger incentives to work as teams and to improve the value of care. And so on.

Implementing the value agenda is not a one-shot effort; it is an open-ended commitment. It is a journey that providers embark on, starting with the adoption of the goal of value, a culture of patients first, and the expectation of constant, measurable improvement. The journey requires strong leadership as well as a commitment to roll out all six value agenda components. For most providers, creating IPUs and measuring outcomes and costs should take the lead.

As should by now be clear, organizations that progress rapidly in adopting the value agenda will reap huge benefits, even if regulatory change is slow. As IPUs' outcomes improve, so will their reputations and, therefore, their patient volumes. With the tools to manage and reduce costs, providers will be able to maintain economic viability even as reimbursements plateau and eventually decline. Providers that concentrate volume will drive a virtuous cycle, in which teams with more experience and better data improve value more rapidly—attracting still more volume. Superior IPUs will be sought out as partners of choice, enabling them to expand across their local regions and beyond.

Maintaining market share will be difficult for providers with nonemployed physicians if their inability to work together impedes progress in improving value. Hospitals with private-practice physicians will have to learn to function as a team to remain viable. Measuring outcomes is likely to be the first step in focusing everyone's attention on what matters most.

All stakeholders in health care have essential roles to play. (See the sidebar "Next Steps: Other Stakeholder Roles.") Yet providers must take center stage. Their boards and senior leadership teams must have the vision and the courage to commit to the value agenda, and the discipline to progress through the inevitable resistance and disruptions that will result. Clinicians must prioritize patients' needs and patient value over the desire to maintain their traditional autonomy and practice patterns.

Providers that cling to today's broken system will become dinosaurs. Reputations that are based on perception, not actual

Next Steps: Other Stakeholder Roles

THE TRANSFORMATION TO A HIGH-VALUE health care delivery system must come from within, with physicians and provider organizations taking the lead. But every stakeholder in the health care system has a role to play in

Strategic agenda	Board members
Organize into integrated practice units	• Lead the reorganization of care away from departments and toward IPUs
Measure outcomes and costs for every patient	• Commit to comprehensive measurement and reporting of outcomes as a basic strategy • Ensure that the organization adopts costing practices that accurately measure costs by patient condition
Develop bundled prices for care cycles	• Charge management with leading the development of bundled payments for common conditions and working proactively with payors to roll them out
Integrate care delivery systems	• Make an organizational commitment to full health system integration through consolidating service lines, siting care in the most cost-effective locations, and charging according to value
Grow excellent services across geography	• Expand areas of excellence across geography through satellite facilities or affiliations
Build an enabling information technology platform	• Make a long-term investment in an IT platform that supports high-value, patient-centric care

improving the value of care. Patients, health plans, employers, and suppliers can hasten the transformation by taking the following steps—and all will benefit greatly from doing so.

Patients	Health plans and employers
• Seek care only from experienced, multidisciplinary teams that provide integrated care for your condition	• Offer strong incentives and information to enable patients to seek care from high-value IPUs for their condition
• Expect data on the full set of outcomes that matter • Seek care from organizations with demonstrated high-value care • Participate in patient-reported outcomes measurement	• Require measurement and reporting of outcomes as a condition of network membership • Make sure that understandable outcomes information by condition is easily accessible to patients and their families
• Pursue care from providers that offer bundled payments and who offer good value compared with those of peers	• Accelerate the shift to bundled payments for medical conditions and primary care • Redesign billing systems to enable bundles
• Obtain care at the appropriate site within your health system • Expect care that is coordinated across sites with a clear leader	• Reimburse for care on the basis of the type of facility that is appropriate for the condition and complexity of services, irrespective of where care is actually delivered
• Seek care for complex conditions from the highest-value provider, even if the provider or care site is not local	• Focus networks on high-value providers for each condition regionally and nationally • Guide patients toward high-value providers and reward them for using those providers, reimbursing for travel where appropriate
• Expect providers to have a single repository of your patient information and to offer you full access to your electronic medical record, tools for easy scheduling and prescription renewal, and the ability to communicate with clinicians	• Offer incentives and support for providers to develop value- and patient-centric IT systems

outcomes, will fade. Maintaining current cost structures and prices in the face of greater transparency and falling reimbursement levels will be untenable. Those organizations—large and small, community and academic—that can master the value agenda will be rewarded with financial viability and the only kind of reputation that should matter in health care—excellence in outcomes and pride in the value they deliver.

Originally published in October 2013. Reprint R1310B

About the Contributors

RICHARD BOHMER is a physician and also a senior lecturer at Harvard Business School.

CLAYTON M. CHRISTENSEN is the Robert and Jane Cizik Professor of Business Administration at Harvard Business School.

JIM COLLINS operates a management research laboratory in Boulder, Colorado.

LEEMORE S. DAFNY is the MBA Class of 1960 Professor of Business Administration at Harvard Business School and the former Deputy Director for Health Care and Antitrust at the Federal Trade Commission.

MARK W. JOHNSON is the chairman and a cofounder of Innosight, a strategic innovation and investing company based in Boston.

HENNING KAGERMANN is a former CEO of SAP AG, a software corporation based in Germany.

ROBERT S. KAPLAN is the Baker Foundation Professor at Harvard Business School in Boston.

JOHN KENAGY is a physician, a visiting scholar at Harvard Business School, and a clinical associate professor of surgery at the University of Washington in Seattle.

W. CHAN KIM is the Boston Consulting Group Bruce D. Henderson Chaired Professor of Strategy and International Management at INSEAD in France.

THOMAS H. LEE, MD, is Chief Medical Officer of Press Ganey, and a professor at Harvard Medical School and Harvard School for Public Health. He is the former Network President for Partners Healthcare System.

RENÉE MAUBORGNE is the INSEAD Distinguished Fellow and a professor of strategy at INSEAD in France.

DAVID MEER is a partner in the New York office of Marakon Associates, an international strategy consulting firm.

DAVID P. NORTON is the founder and president of the Balanced Scorecard Collaborative (www.bscol.com), based in Lincoln, Massachusetts.

JERRY I. PORRAS is the Lane Professor, Emeritus, at Stanford University's Graduate School of Business.

MICHAEL E. PORTER is the Bishop William Lawrence University Professor at Harvard Business School.

DANIEL YANKELOVICH is chairman of Viewpoint Learning, a firm that promotes problem solving through dialogue, and DYG, a market research firm that tracks social trends. He is based in San Diego.

Index

The most important management ideas all in one place.

We hope you enjoyed this book from *Harvard Business Review*. Now you can get even more with HBR's 10 Must Reads Boxed Set. From books on leadership and strategy to managing yourself and others, this 6-book collection delivers articles on the most essential business topics to help you succeed.

HBR's 10 Must Reads Series

The definitive collection of ideas and best practices on our most sought-after topics from the best minds in business.

- Change Management
- Collaboration
- Communication
- Emotional Intelligence
- Innovation
- Leadership
- Making Smart Decisions

- Managing Across Cultures
- Managing People
- Managing Yourself
- Strategic Marketing
- Strategy
- Teams
- The Essentials

hbr.org/mustreads

Buy for your team, clients, or event.
Visit hbr.org/bulksales for quantity discount rates.

Harvard
Business
Review
Press